THE FOR

GW01388318

MAURICE HEWLETT

CHAPTER I

PROSPER LE GAI RIDES OUT

My story will take you into times and spaces alike rude and uncivil. Blood will be spilt, virgins suffer distresses; the horn will sound through woodland glades; dogs, wolves, deer, and men, Beauty and the Beasts, will tumble each other, seeking life or death with their proper tools. There should be mad work, not devoid of entertainment. When you read the word *Explicit*, if you have laboured so far, you will know something of Morgraunt Forest and the Countess Isabel; the Abbot of Holy Thorn will have postured and schemed (with you behind the arras); you will have wandered with Isoult and will know why she was called La Desirous, with Prosper le Gai, and will understand how a man may fall in love with his own wife. Finally, of Galors and his affairs, of the great difference there may be between a Christian and the brutes, of love and hate, grudging and open humour, faith and works, cloisters and thoughts uncloistered—all in the green wood—you will know as much as I do if you have cared to follow the argument. I hope you will not ask me what it all means, or what the moral of it is. I rank myself with the historian in this business of tale-telling, and consider that my sole affair is to hunt the argument dispassionately. Your romancer must be neither a lover of his heroine nor (as the fashion now sets) of his chief rascal. He must affect a genial height, that of a jigger of strings; and his attitude should be that of the Pulpiteer:—Heaven help you, gentlemen, but I know what is best for you! Leave everything to me.

It is related of Prosper le Gai, that when his brother Malise, Baron of Starning and Parrox, showed him the door of their father's house, and showed it with a meaning not to be mistaken, he stuck a sprig of green holly in his cap. He put on his armour; his horse and sword also he took: he was for the wilds. Baron Jocelyn's soul, the priests reported, was with God; his body lay indubitably under a black effigy in Starning Church. Baron Malise was lord of the fee, with a twisted face for Prosper whenever they met in the hall: had there been scores no deeper this was enough. Prosper was a youth to whom life was a very pretty thing; he could not afford to have tarnish on the glass; he must have pleasant looks about him and a sweet air, or at least scope for the making of them. Baron Malise blew like a miasma and cramped him like a church-pew: then Adventure beaconed from far off, and his heart leapt to greet the light. He left at dawn, and alone. Roy, his page, had begged as hard as he dared for pillion or a donkey. He was his master's only friend, but Prosper's temper needed no props. "Roy," said he, "what I do I will do alone, nor will I imperil any man's bread. The bread of my brother Malise may be a trifle over-salt to my taste, but to you it is better than none at all. Season your tongue, Roy, enure it. Drink water, dry your eyes, and forget me not."

He kissed him twice and went his way without any more farewells than the boy's snivelling. He never looked behind at Starning demesne, where he had been born and bred and might have followed his father to church, nor sideways at the broad oaks, nor over to the well-tilled fields on either side his road; but rather pricked forward at a nimble pace which tuned to the running of his blood. The blood of a lad sings sharpest in the early morning; the air tingles, the light thrills, all the great day is to come. This lad therefore rode with a song towards the West, following his own shadow, down the deep Starning lanes, through the woods and pastures of Parrox, over the grassy spaces of the Downs, topping the larks in thought, and shining beam for beam against the new-risen sun. The time of his going-out was September of the harvest: a fresh wet air was abroad. He looked at the thin blue of the sky, he saw dew and gossamer lie heavy on the hedge-rows. All his heart laughed. Prosper was merry.

Whither he should go, what find, how fare, he knew not at all. Morgraunt was before him, and of Morgraunt all the country spoke in a whisper. It as far, it was deep, it was dark as night, haunted with the waving of perpetual woods; it lay between the mountains and the sea, a mystery as inviolate as either. In it outlaws, men desperate and hungry, ran wild. It was a den of thieves as well as of wolves. Men, young men too, had ridden in, high-hearted, proud of their trappings, horses, curls, and what not; none had ever seen them come out. They might be roaming there yet, grown old with roaming, and gaunt with the everlasting struggle to kill before they were killed: who could tell? Or they might have struck upon the vein of savage life; they might go roaring and loving and robbing with the beasts—why not? Morgraunt had swallowed them up; who could guess to what wild uses she turned her thralls? That was a place, pardieu! Prosper, very certain that at twenty-three it is a great thing to be hale and astride a horse, felt also that to grow old without having given Morgraunt a chance of killing you young would be an insipid performance. "As soon be a priest!" he would cry, "or, by the Rood, one of those flat-polled monks kept there by the Countess Isabel." Morgraunt then for Prosper, and the West; beyond that—"One thing at a time," thought he, for he was a wise youth in his way, and held to the legend round his arms. Seeing that south of him he could now smell the sea, and beyond him lay Morgraunt, he would look no further till Morgraunt lay below him appeased or subjugate.

A tall and lean youth was Prosper le Gai, fair-haired and sanguine, square-built and square-chinned. He smiled at you; you saw two capital rows of white teeth, two humorous blue eyes; you would think, what a sweet-tempered lad! So in the main he was; but you would find out that he could be dangerous, and that (curiously) the more dangerous he was, the sweeter his temper seemed to be. If you crossed him once, he would stare; twice, he would laugh; three times, you would swear he was your humble servant; but before you could cross him again he would have knocked you down. The next moment he would give you a hand up, and apologize; after that, so far as he was concerned, you might count him your friend for life. The fact is, that he was one of those men who, like kings, require a nominal fealty before they can love you with a whole heart: it is a mere nothing. But somebody, they think, must lead. Prosper always felt so desperately sure it must be he. That was apt to lend a frenzy to his stroke and a cool survey to his eye (as being able to take so much for granted), which made him a good friend and a nasty enemy.

It also made him, as you will have occasion to see, a born fighter. He went, indeed, through those years of his life on tiptoe, as it were, for a fight. He had a light and springing carriage of the head, enough to set his forelock nodding; his eye roved like a sea-bird's; his lips often parted company, for his breath was eager. He had a trick of laughing to himself softly as he went about his business; or else he sang, as he was now singing. These qualities, little habits, affectations, whatever you choose to call them, sound immaterial, but they really point to the one thing that made him remarkable—the curious blend of opposites in him. He blent benevolence with savagery, reflectiveness with activity. He could think best when thought and act might jump together, laugh most quietly when the din of swords and horses drowned the voice, love his neighbour most sincerely when about to cut his throat. The smell of blood, the sight of wounds, or the flicker of blades, made him drunk; but he was one of those who grow steady in their cups. You might count upon him at a pinch. Lastly, he was no fool, and was disposed to credit other people with a balance of wit.

He disliked frippery, yet withal made a brave show in the sun. His plain black mail was covered with a surcoat of white and green linen; over this a narrow baldrick of red bore in gold stitches his device of a hooded falcon, and his legend on a scroll, many times repeated and intercrossed—*I bide my time*. In his helmet were three red feathers, on his shield the blazon of his house of Gai—*On a field sable, a fesse dancettée or*, with a mullet for difference. He carried no spear; for a man of his light build the sword was the arm. Thus then, within and without, was Messire Prosper le Gai, youngest son of old Baron Jocelyn, deceased, riding into the heart of the noon, pleased with himself and the world, light-minded, singing of the movement and the road.

Labourers stayed their reaping to listen to him; but there was nothing for them. He sang of adventure. Girls leaned at cottage doorways to watch him down the way. There was nothing for them either, for all he sang of love.

"She who now hath my heart is so in every part;" etc., etc.

The words came tripping as a learnt lesson; but he had never loved a girl, and fancied he never would. Women? Petticoats! For him there was more than one adventure in life. Rather, my lady's chamber was the last place in which he would have looked for adventure.

On the second day of his journey—in a country barren and stony, yet with a hint of the leafy wildernesses to come in the ridges spiked with pines, the cropping of heather here and there, and the ever-increasing solitude of his way—he was set upon by four foot-pads, who thought to beat the life out of his body as easily as boys that of a dog. He asked nothing better than that they should begin; and he asked so civilly that they very soon did. The fancy of glorious youth transformed them into knights-at-arms, and their ashen cudgels into blades. The only pity was that the end came so soon.

His sword dug its first sod, and might have carved four cowards instead of one; but he was no vampire, so thereafter laid about him with the flat of the tool. The three survivors claimed quarter. "Quarter, you rogues!" cried he. "Kindly lend me one of your staves for the purpose." He gave them a drubbing as one horsed his brother in turn, and dropped them, a chapfallen trio, beside their dead. "Now," said he, "take that languid gentleman with you, and be so good for the rest of your journey as to imitate his indifference to strangers. Thus you will have a prosperous passage. Good day to you."

He slept on the scene of his exploit, rose early, rode fast, and by noon was plainly in the selvage of the great woods. The country was split into bleak ravines, a pell-mell of rocks and boulders, and a sturdy crop of black pines between them. An overgrowth of brambles and briony ran riot over all. Prosper rode up a dry river-bed, keeping steadily west, so far as it would serve him; found himself quagged ere a dozen painful miles, floundered out as best he might, and by evening was making good pace over a rolling bit of moorland through which ran a sandy road. It was the highway from Wanmouth to Market Basing and the north, if he had known. Ahead of him a solitary wayfarer, a brown bunch of a friar, from whose hood rose a thin neck and a shag of black hair round his tonsure—like storm-clouds gathering about a full moon—struck manfully forward on a pair of bare feet.

"God be with you, brother gentleman," cried the friar, turning a crab-apple face upwards.

"And with you, my brother, who carry your slippers," Prosper replied.

"Eh, eh, brother! They go softer than steel for a gouty toe."

"Poor gout, Master Friar, I hope, for Saint Francis' peace of mind."

"My gentleman," said the friar, "let me tell you the truth. I am a poor devil out of Lucca, built for matrimony and the chimney corner, as Grandfather Adam was before me. Brother Bonaccord of Outremer they call me in religion, but ill-accord I am in temper, by reason of the air of this accursed land, and a most tempestuous blood of my own. For why! I go to the Dominicans of Wanmouth, supplicating that I am new landed, and have no convent to my name and establishment in the Church. They take me in. Ha! they do that. Look now. 'A sop of bread and wine,' I cry, 'for the love of God.' It is a Catholic food, very comfortable for the stomach. Ha! they give me beer. Beer? Wet death! I am by now as gouty as a cardinal, and my eye is inflamed. I think of the Lucchese—those shafts of joy miscalled women—when I should be thinking of my profession. I am ready as ever to admit two vows, but Saint Paul himself cannot reconcile me to the third. Beer, my friend, beer."

"You will do well enough, friar, if you are going the forest road. You will find no Lucchesan ladies thereabouts."

"I am none so sure, gentleman. There were tales told at the Wanmouth hostel. Do you know anything of a very holy place in these parts, the Abbey of Saint Giles of the Thorn? Black monks, my brother; black as your stallion."

"I think they are white monks," said Prosper, "Bernardines."

"I spoke of the colour of their deeds, young sir," answered Brother Bonaccord.

"I know as little of them as of any monks in Christendom, friar," Prosper said. "But I have seen the Abbot and spoken with him. Richard Dieudonné is his name, well friended by the Countess."

"He is well friended by many ladies, some of account, and some of none at all, by what I hear," said the friar, rather dryly for such a twinkling spirit.

"Ah, with ladies," Prosper put in, "you have me again; for I know less of them than of monks, save that both have petticoats. Your pardon, brother."

"Not a bit, not a bit, brother again," replied the friar. "I admit the hindrance; and could tell you of the advantages if I had the mind. But as to the ladies, suffer me to predict that you will know more of them before you have done."

"I think not," said Prosper. Brother Bonaccord began to laugh.

"They will give you no peace yet awhile," said he. "And let me tell you this, from a man who knows what he is talking about, that if you think to escape them by neglecting them, you are going the devil's way to work. If you wish them to let you alone, speak them fair, drop easily to your knee, be a hand-kisser, a cushion-disposer, a goer on your toes. They will think you a lover and shrug you away. Never do a woman a service as if to oblige her; do it as if to oblige yourself. Then she will believe you her slave. Then you are safe. That is your game, brother."

"You have studied ladies, friar?"

"Ah, ah! I have indeed. They are a wondrous fair book. I know no other. Why should I?"

"Oh, why indeed?" Prosper assented. "For my part, I find other studies more engrossing."

With such talk they went until they reached a little wood, and then disposed of themselves for the night. When Prosper woke next morning the good man had gone. He had left a written message to the effect that, petticoats or none, he had stolen a march on steel, and might be looked for at Malbank.

"I wonder how much stuff for his mind that student of ladies will win at Malbank," laughed Prosper to himself, little knowing, indeed.

CHAPTER II

MORGRAUNT, AND A DEAD KNIGHT

Leaving the high road on his right hand, Prosper struck over the heath towards a solemn beech-wood, which he took to be the very threshold of Morgraunt. As a fact it was no more than an outstretched finger of its hand, by name Cadnam Thicket. He skirted this place, seeking an entry, but found nothing to suit him for an hour or more. Then at last he came to a gap in the sandy bank, and saw that a little mossy ride ran straight in among the trees. He put his horse at the gap, and was soon cantering happily through the wood. Thus he came short upon an adventure. The path ran ahead of him in a tapering vista, but just where it should meet in a point it broadened out suddenly so as to make a double bay. The light fell splashing upon this cleared space, and he saw what he saw.

This was a tall lady, richly dressed in some gauzy purple stuff, dragging a dead man by the heels, and making a very bad business of it. She was dainty to view, her hands and arms shone like white marble; but apart from all this it was clear to Prosper that she lacked the mere strength for the office she had proposed herself. The dead man was not very tall, but he was too tall for the lady. The roughness of the ground, the resistance of the underwood, the incapacity of the performers, made the procession unseemly.

Prosper, forgetting Brother Bonaccord, quickened his horse to a gallop, and was soon up with the toiling lady. She stopped when she heard him coming, stood up to wait for him, quick-breathing and a little flushed, and never took her eyes off him.

It was clearly a time for discretion: so much she signalled from her brown eyes, which were watchful, but by no means timid. He remembered afterwards that they had been apt to fall easily into set stares, and thus to give her a bold look which seemed to invite you to be bold also. But though he could not see this now, and though he had no taste for women, it was certain she was handsome in a profuse way. She had a broad full bust; her skin, dazzling white at the neck, ran into golden russet before it reached the burnt splendour of her cheeks; her mouth, rather long and curved up at the corners, had lips rich and crimson; of which, however, the upper was short to a fault, and so curled back as to give her, a pettish or fretful look. Her dark hair, which was plentiful and drawn low over her ears into a heavy knot at the nape of her neck, was dressed within a fine gold net. Her arms were bare to the elbow, large and snowy white; from her fingers gems and gold flashed at him. Prosper, who knew nothing whatever about it, judged her midway between thirty and forty. Such was the lady; the man he had no chance of overlooking, for the other had dropped her handkerchief upon his face before she left him. "Sir," she now said, in a smooth and distinguishable voice, when Prosper had saluted her, "you may do me a great service if you will, which is to carry this dead man to his grave in the wood."

"By the faith I have," Prosper replied, "I will help you all I can. But when we have buried him you shall tell me how he came by his death, and how it is that his grave is waiting for him."

"I can tell you that at once," she said quickly; "I have but just dug it with a mattock I was so lucky as to find by a stopped earth on the bank yonder. The rest I will gladly acquaint you with by and by. But first let us be rid of him."

Prosper dismounted and went to take up his burden. First of all, however, he deliberately removed the handkerchief and looked it in the face. The dead man lay stiff and staring, with open eyes and a wry mouth. Hands and face were livid, a light froth had gathered on his lips. He looked to have suffered horribly —as much in mind as body: the agony must have bitten deep into him for the final peace of death never to have come. Now Prosper knew very little of death as yet, save that he had an idea that he himself would never come to endure it; but he knew enough to be sure that neither battle nor honour had had any part here. The man had been well-dressed in brown and tawny velvet, was probably handsome in a sharp, foreign sort. There was a ring upon his finger, a torn badge upon his left breast, with traces of a device in white threads which could not be well made out. Puzzling over it, Prosper thought to read three white forms on it —water-bougets, perhaps, or billets—he could not be sure. The whole affair seemed to him to hold some shameful secret behind: he thought of poison, or the just visitation of God; but then he thought of the handsome lady, and was ashamed to see that such a conclusion must involve her in the mess. Pitying, since he could not judge, he lifted the body in his arms and followed the lady's lead through the brushwood. At the end of some two hundred yards or more of battling with the boughs, she stopped, and pointed to a pit, with a mattock lying on the heaped earth close by. "There is the grave," she said.

"The grave is a shallow grave," said Prosper.

"It is deeper than he was," quoth the lady. There was a ring in this rather ugly to hear, as all scorn is out of tune with a dead presence. You might as well be contemptuous of a baby. But Prosper was no fool, to think at the wrong time. He laid the body down in the grave, and busied himself to compose it into some semblance of the rest there should be in that bed at least. This was hard to be done, since it was as stiff as a board, and took time. The lady grew impatient, fidgeted about, walked up and down, could not stand for a moment: but she said nothing. At last Prosper stood up by the side of the grave, having done his best.

"I am no priest," says he, "God knows; but I cannot put a man's body into the earth without in some sort commending his soul. I must do what I can, and you must pardon an indifferent advocate, as God will."

"If you are advised by me," said the lady, "you will leave that affair where it is. The man was worthless."

"We cannot measure his worth, madam: we have no tools for that. The utmost we can do is to bury part of him, and pray for the other part."

"You speak as a priest whom I had thought a soldier," said she with some asperity. "If you are what you now seem, I will remind you of a saying which should be familiar—Let the dead bury their dead."

"As I live by bread," Prosper cried out, "I will commend this man's soul whither it is going."

"Then I will not listen to you, sir," she answered in a pale fume. "I cannot listen to you."

Prosper grew extremely polite. "Madam, there is surely no need," he said. "If you cannot you will not. Moreover, I should in any case address myself elsewhere."

He had folded the dead man's arms over his breast, and shut his eyes. He had wiped his lips. The thing seemed more at peace. So he crossed himself and began, *In nomine patris*, etc., and then recited the *Paternoster*. This almost exhausted his stock, though it did not satisfy his aspirations. His words burst from him. "O thou pitiful dead!" he cried out, "go thou where Pity is, in the hope some morsels may be justly thine. Rest thou there, who wast not restful in thine end, and quitted not willingly thy tenement; rest thou there till thou art called. And when thou art called to give an account of thyself and thine own works, may that which men owe thee be remembered with that which thou dost owe! *Per Christum dominum*," etc.

He bowed his head, crossed himself very piously; then stood still, smiling gently upon the man he knew nothing of, save that he had been young and had lost his race. He did not see the lady; she was, however, near by, not looking at the man at the grave, but first at Prosper and then at the ground. Her fingers were twisting and tangling together, and her bosom, restless as the sea, rose and fell fitfully. She was pale, save at the lips; like Prosper she smiled, but the smile was stiff. Prosper set to work with the shovel and soon filled up the grave. Then he turned to the lady.

"And now, madam, we will talk a little, if you please." He had a cool and level voice; yet it came upon her as if it could have but one answer.

She looked at him for some seconds without reply. For his part, Prosper had kept his eyes fixed equally on her; hers fell first.

She coloured a little as she said-"Very willingly. You have done me a service for which I am very much in your debt. You shall command me as you will, and find me ready to recompense you with what I have." She stopped as if to judge the weight of her words, then went on slowly—"I know not, indeed, how could I deny you anything."

Prosper could have seen, if he would, the quickened play of her breath.

"Let us go into the open," said he, "and find my horse. Then you shall tell me whence you are, and whither I may speed you, and how safeliest—with other things proper to be known."

They went together. "My lord," said she then, "my lodging is far from here and ill to come by. Nevertheless, I know of a hermitage hard at hand where we could rest a little, and thereafter we could find the way to my house. Will you come with me thither?"

"Whither?" asked Prosper.

"Ah, the hermitage, or wheresoever you will."

Prosper looked steadily at her.

"Tell me the name and condition of the dead man," said he.

"Ranulf de Genlis, a knight of Brittany."

"The badge on his breast was of our blazonry," said Prosper, half to himself, "and he looked to have been of this side the Southern Sea."

"Do you doubt my word, Sir Knight?"

"Madam, I do not question it. Will you tell, me how he came by his death?"

"I was hunting very early in the morning with my esquires and ladies, and by ill-hap lost them and my way. After many wanderings in search of either, I encountered this man now dead, and inquired news of him. He held me some time in talk, delayed me with sham diligence, and at last and, suddenly professed an ardent love for me. I was frightened, for I was alone in the wood with him, in a glade not far from here. And it seemed that I had reason, since from words he went on to force and clamour and violence. I had almost succumbed—I know not how to hint at the fate which threatened me, or guess how long I could have struggled against it. He had closed with me, he held me in a vice; then all at once he loosed hold of me and shuddered. Some seizure or sudden stroke of judgment overtook him, I suppose, so that he fell and lay writhing, with a foam on his lips, as you saw. You may judge," she added, after waiting for some comment from Prosper, which did not come, "you may judge whether this is a pleasant tale for me to tell, and whether I should tell it willingly to any man. For what one attempted against me another might also try—and not fail."

She stopped and glanced at her companion. The manner in each of them was changed; the lady was not the scornful beauty she had seemed, while Prosper's youth was dry within him. She seemed a suppliant, he a judge, deliberate. Such a story from such an one would have set him on fire an hour ago; but now his words came sharply from him, whistling like a shrill wind.

"The grave was dug overnight," was what he said.

The lady started and paled. Then she drew a deep breath, and said—"Do you again doubt my word, sir?"

11

"I do not question it," he replied as before. It is a fact that he had noticed the turned earth by the pit. There was gossamer upon it, but that said little. Rabbits had been there also, and that said everything.

The lady said nothing more, and in silence they went on until they reached a fork in the path. Prosper stopped here. One path led north, the other west.

"Here is my road," said he, pointing to the west.

"The hermitage is close by, my lord," urged the lady in a low voice. "I pray my lord to rest him there."

"That I cannot do," says he.

She affected indignation. "Is it then in the honour of a knight to desert a lonely lady? I am learning strange doctrine, strange chivalry! Farewell, sir. You are young. Maybe you will learn with years that when a lady stoops to beg it is more courtly to forestall her."

Prosper stood leaning on his shield. "The knight's honour," he said, "is in divers holds—in his lady's, in God's, and in the king's. These three fly not always the same flag, but two at least of them should be in pact."

"Ah," said she slyly, "ah, Sir Discreet, I see that you have the lady first."

Prosper grew graver. "I said 'his lady,'" he repeated.

"And could not I, for such service as yours, be your lady, fair sir?" she asked in a very low and troubled voice. "At least I am here—alone—in the wood—and at your mercy."

Prosper looked straight in front of him, grave, working his mouth. Those who knew him would have gone by the set of his chin. He may have been thinking of Brother Bonaccord's prediction, or of the not very veiled provocation of the lady's remarkable candour. There grew to be a rather bleak look in his face, something blenched his blue eyes. He turned sharply upon the woman, and his voice was like a frost.

"Having slain one man this day," he said, "I should recommend you to be wary how you tread with another."

She stared open-mouthed at him for a full minute and a half. Then, seeing he never winked or budged, she grew frightened and piteous, threw her arms up, turned, and fled up the north path, squealing like a wounded rabbit.

Prosper clapped-to his spurs and made after her with his teeth grinding together. Very soon, however, he pulled up short. "The man is dead. Let her go for this present. And I am not quite sure. I will bide my time."

That was the motto of the Gais—"I bide my time." He was, nevertheless, perfectly sure in his private mind; but then he was always perfectly sure, and recognized that it was a weakness of his. So the woman went her way, and he his for that turn…

Riding forward carelessly, with a loose rein, he slept that night in the woods. Next day he rode fast and long without meeting a living soul, and so came at last into Morgraunt Forest, where the trees shut out the light of the day, and very few birds sing. He entered the east purlieus in the evening of his fifth day from Starning, and slept in a rocky valley. Tall black trees stood all round him, the vanguards of the forest host.

CHAPTER III

HOLY THORN AND HOLY CHURCH

In South Morgraunt stands Holy Thorn, more properly the Abbey of Saint Giles of Holy Thorn, a broad and fair foundation, one of the two set up in the forest by the Countess Isabel, Dowager of March and Bellesme, Countess of Hauterive and Lady of Morgraunt in her own right. Where the Wan river makes a great loop, running east for three miles, and west again for as many before it drives its final surge towards the Southern Sea, there stands Holy Thorn, Church and Convent, watching over the red roofs of Malbank hamlet huddled together across the flood. Here are green water-meadows and good corn-lands, the abbey demesne; here also are the strips of tillage which the tenants hold; here the sluices which head up the river for the Abbey mills, make thunderous music all day long. Over this cleared space and over some leagues of the virgin forest, the Abbot of Saint Thorn has sac and soc, tholl and theam, catch-a-thief-in, catch-a-thief-out, as well as other sovereign prerogatives, all of which he owes to the regret and remorse of the Countess Isabel over the death of her first husband and only lover, Fulk de Bréauté. Further north, in Mid-Morgraunt, is Gracedieu, her other foundation—equally endowed, but holding white nuns instead of white monks.

Now it so happened that as Prosper le Gai entered the purlieus of Morgraunt, the Countess Isabel sat in the Abbey parlour of Saint Thorn, knitting her fine brows over a business of the Abbot's, no less than the granting of a new charter of pit and gallows, pillory and tumbril to him and his house over the villeins of Malbank, and the whole fee and soke. The death of these unfortunates, or the manner of it, was of little moment; but the Countess, having much power, was jealous how she lent it. She sat now, therefore, in the Abbot's great chair, and before her stood the Abbot himself, holding in his hands the charter fairly written out on parchment, with the twisted silk of three colours ready to receive her seal. It was exactly this which she was not very ready to give, for though she knew nothing of his villeins, she knew much of the Abbot, and was of many minds concerning him. There was yet time; their colloquy was in secret; but now she tapped with her foot upon the stool, and the Abbot watched her narrowly. He was a tall and personable man, famous for his smile, stout and smooth, his skin soft as a woman's, his robe, his ring, his cross and mere slippers all in accord.

At length, says he, "Madam, for the love of the Saints, but chiefly for Mary's love; to the glory of God and of Saint Giles of Holy Thorn; to the ease of his monks and the honour of the Church, I beseech your Ladyship this small boon."

The clear-cold eyes of the Countess Isabel looked long at him before she said —"Do I then show love to the Saints and give God honour, Lord Abbot, by helping you swing your villeins? Pit and gallows, pillory and tumbril! You go too far."

"Dear lady," said he, "I go no further, if I have them, than my Sisters of Gracedieu. That hedged community of Christ's brides hath all these commodities and more, even the paramount privilege of Sanctuary, which is an appanage of the very highest in the Holy Fold. And I must consider it as scarcely decent, as (by the Mass) not seemly at all, that your Holy Thorn, this sainted sprig of your planting, should lack the power to prick. Our people, madam, do indeed expect it. It is not much. Nay!"—for he saw his Lady frown and heard her toe-taps again—"indeed, it is not much. A little pit for your female thief to swim at large, for your witch and bringer-in of hell's ordinances; a decent gallows a-top for your proper male rascal; a pillory for your tenderer blossom of sin while he qualify for an airy crown, or find space for repentance and the fruits of true contrition; lastly, a persuasive tumbril, a close lover for your incorrigible wanton girls—homely chastisement such as a father Abbot may bestow, and yet wear a comely face, and yet be loved by those he chasteneth. Madam, is this too much for so great a charge as ours? We of Holy Thorn nurture the good seed with scant fortune, being ridden down by evil livers, deer-stealers, notorious persons, scandalous persons. A little pit, therefore! a little limber gallows!"

But the Countess mused with her hand to her chin, by no means persuaded. She was still a young woman, and a very lonely one; her great prerogatives (which she took seriously) tired her to death, but the need of exercising them through other people was worst of all. Now she said doubtfully, "I have no reason in especial to trust you, Abbot."

The Abbot, who knew better than she how true this was, bit his lip and remained silent. He was a very comely man and leaned much to persuasion, particularly with women. He was always his own audience: the check, therefore, amounted to exposure, almost put him to open shame. The Countess went on to ask, who in particular of his villeins he had dread of, who was turbulent, who a deer-stealer, who notorious as a witch or wise woman, who wanton and a scandalous liver? And here the Abbot was apt with his names. There was Red Sweyn, half an outlaw already, and by far too handy with his hunting-knife; there was Pinwell, as merry a little rogue as ever spoiled for a cord. There were Rogerson and Cutlaw; there was Tom Sibby, the procuress. Mald also, a withered malignant old wife, who had once blighted a year's increase by her dealing with the devil. Here was stuff for gallows, pit and pillory, all dropping-ripe for the trick. For tumbril, he went on (watching his adversary like a cat), "who so proper as black-haired Isoult, witch, and daughter of a witch, called by men Isoult la Desirous—and a gaunt, half-starved, loose-legged baggage she is," he went on; "reputed of vile conversation for all the slimness of her years—witch, and a witch's brat."

He looked sideways at the great lady as he spoke of this creature, and saw that all was going exactly as he would wish it. He had not been the Countess' confessor for nothing, nor had he learnt in vain the story of her secret marriage with Fulk de Bréauté, and of the murder of this youth on Spurnt Heath one blowy Bartlemy Eve. And for this reason he had dared to bring the name of Isoult into his catalogue of rogues, that he knew his woman, and all woman-kind; how they hate most in their neighbours that which they are tenderest of in themselves. Let there be no mistake here. The Countess had been no luxurious liver, though a most unhappy one. The truth is that, beautiful woman as she still was, she had been a yet more beautiful girl, Countess of Hauterive in her own right, and as such betrothed to the great Earl Roger of March and Bellesme. Earl Roger, who was more than double her age, went out to fight; she stayed at home, in the nursery or near it, and Fulk de Bréauté came to make eyes. These he made with such efficacy that Isabel lost her heart first and her head afterwards, wedded Fulk in secret, bore him a child, and was the indirect means of his stabbing by the Earl's men as he was riding through the dark over Spurnt Heath. The child was given to the Abbot's keeping (whence it promptly and conveniently vanished), the Countess was married to the Earl; then the Earl died. Whereupon she, still young, childless so far as she could learn, and possessed of so much, founded her twin abbeys in Morgraunt to secure peace for the soul of Fulk and her own conscience. This will suffice to prove that the Abbot had some grounds for his manoeuvring. The breaking of her troth to the Earl she held to make her an adulteress; the stabbing of Fulk by the Earl to prove her a murderess. There was neither mercy nor discernment in these reproaches. She believed herself a wanton when she had been but a lover. For no sin, therefore, had she so little charity as for that which the Abbot had imputed to his candidate for the tumbril. Isoult la Desirous it was who won the charter, as the Abbot had intended she should, to serve his end and secure her own according to his liking.

For the charter was sealed and seisin delivered in the presence of Dom Galors, almoner of the Abbey, of Master Porges, seneschal of High March, and of one or two mesne lords of those parts. Then the Countess went to bed; and at this time Prosper le Gai was also lying in the fringes of Morgraunt, asleep on his shield with his red cloak over him, having learned from a hind whom he met on the hill that at Malbank Saint Thorn he would find hospitality, and that his course must lie in such and such a direction.

CHAPTER IV

DOM GALORS

Next day, as soon as the Countess had departed for High March, the Abbot Richard called Dom Galors, his almoner, into the parlour and treated him in a very friendly manner, making him sit down in his presence, and putting fruit and wine before him. This Galors, who I think merits some scrutiny, was a bullet-headed, low-browed fellow, too burly for his monkish frock (which gave him the look of a big boy in a pinafore), with the jowl of a master-butcher, and a sullen slack mouth. His look at you, when he raised his eyes from the ground, had the hint of brutality—as if he were naming a price—which women mistake for mastery, and adore. But he very rarely crossed eyes with any one; and with the Abbot he had gained a reputation for astuteness by seldom opening his lips and never shutting his ears. He was therefore a most valuable book of reference, which told nothing except to his owner. With all this he was a great rider and loved hunting. His *Sursum Corda* was like a view-holloa, and when he said, *Ite missa est*, you would have sworn he was crying a stag's death instead of his

Saviour's. In matters of gallantry his reputation was risky: it was certain that he had more than a monk, and suspected that he had less than a gentleman should have. The women of Malbank asseverated that venison was not his only game. That may or may not have been. The man loved power, and may have warred against women for lack of something more difficult of assault. He was hardly the man to squander himself at the bidding of mere appetite; he was certainly no glutton for anything but office. Still, he was not one to deny himself the flutter of the caught bird in the hand. He had, like most men who make themselves monks by calculation, a keen eye for a girl's shape, carriage, turn of the head, and other allies of the game she loves and always loses: such things tickled his fancy when they came over his path; he stooped to take them, and let them dangle for remembrances, as you string a coin on your chain to remind you at need of a fortunate voyage. At this particular moment he was tempted, for instance, to catch and let dangle. The chance light of some shy eye had touched and then eluded him. I believe he loved the chase more than the quarry. He knew he must go a-hunting from that moment in which the light began to play will-o'-the-wisp; for action was his meat and dominion what he breathed. If you wanted to make Galors dangerous you had to set him on a vanishing trail. The girl had been a fool to run, but how was she to know that?

To him now spoke the Abbot Richard after this fashion. "Galors," he said, "I will speak to you now as to my very self, for if you are not myself you may be where I sit some day. A young monk who is almoner already may go far, especially when he is young in religion, but in years ripe. If you prove to be my other self, you shall go as far as myself can push you, Galors. Rest assured that the road need not stop at a mitred abbey. In the hope, then, that you may go further, and I with you, it is time that I speak my full mind. We have our charter, as you have seen—and at what cost of sweat and urgency, who can tell so surely as I? But there, we have it: a great weapon, a lever whereby we may raise Holy Thorn to a height undreamed of by the abbots of this realm, and our two selves (perched on the top of Holy Thorn) yet higher. Yet this charter, gotten for God's greater glory (as He knoweth who readeth hearts!), may not work its appointed way without an application which poor and frail men might scarcely dare for any less object. There is abroad, Galors, dear brother, a most malignant viper, lurking, as I may say, in the very bosom of Holy Church; warmed there, nesting there, yet fouling the nest, and grinding her tooth that she may strike at the heart of us, and shiver what hath been so long a-building up. Of that viper you, Galors, are the chosen instrument—you and the charter—to draw the tooth."

The Abbot spoke in a low voice, and was breathless; it was not hard to see that he was uncommonly in earnest. Galors turned over in his mind all possible plots against an Abbey's peaceful being—tale-bearing to the Archbishop, a petition for a Papal Legate, a foreshore trouble, a riot among the fishermen of Wanmouth, some encroachment by the ragged brethren of Francis and Dominic —and dismissed them all as not serious enough to lose breath about.

"Who is your viper, father?" was what he said.

"It is the girl Isoult of Matt-o'-the-Moor; Isoult whom they call La Desirous," replied his spiritual father. The heart of Galors gave a hot jump; he knew the girl well enough—too well for her, not well enough yet for himself. It was precisely to win the woeful beauty of her that he had set his snares and unleashed his dogs. Did the Abbot know anything? Impossible; his reference forbad the fear. Was the girl something more than a dark woodland elf, a fairy, haggard and dishevelled, whose white shape shining through rags had made his blood stir? The mask of his face safeguarded him through this maze of surmise; nothing out of the depths of him was ever let to ruffle that dead surface. He commanded his voice to ask, How should he find such a girl? "For," said he, "in Malbank girls and boys swarm like dies on a sunny wall." The deceit implied was gross, yet the Abbot took it in his haste.

"Thus you shall know her, Galors," he said. "A slim girl, somewhat under the common size of the country, and overburdened with a curtain of black hair; and a sullen, brooding girl who says little, and that nakedly and askance; and in a pale face two grey eyes a-burning."

All this Galors knew better than his Abbot. Now he asked, "But what is her offence, father? For even with power of life and member the law of the land has force, that neither man nor maid, witch nor devil, may be put lightly away."

For this "put away" the Abbot thanked him with a look, and added, that she was suspected of witchcraft, seeing Mald her mother was a notorious witch, and the wench herself the byword and scorn of all the country-side. Sorcery, therefore, or incontinence—"whichever you will," said he. "Any stick will do to beat a dog with."

Galors had much to say, but said nothing. There was something behind all this, he was sure, knowing his man by heart. He judged the Abbot to be bursting with news, and watched him pace the parlour now struggling with it. Sure enough the murder was out before he had taken a dozen turns. "Now, Galors," he said, in a new and short vein, "listen to me. I intend to do what I should have done fourteen years ago, when I held this girl in my two hands. I let slip my chance, and blame myself for it; but having slipt it indeed, it was gone until this charter of ours brought it back fresh. You know how we stand here, you and I and the Convent-all of us at the disposition of her ladyship. A great lady, my friend, and a young one, childless, it is said, without heir of her own. Morgraunt may go to the Crown or Holy Thorn and Gracedieu may divide it."

"She may marry again," put in Galors.

"She is twice a widow," the Abbot snapped him up, and gave his first shock. "She is twice a widow, once against her will. She will never marry again."

"Then, my father," said Galors, "we should be safe as against the Crown, which the Countess probably loves as little as the rest of her kind."

"The Countess Isabel," said the Abbot, speaking like an oracle, "is not childless."

Galors understood.

"Do not misunderstand me in this, Brother Galors," said the Abbot. "We will do the girl no unnecessary harm. We will slip her out of the country if we can get any one to take her. Put it she shall be married or hanged." Galors again thought that he understood. The Abbot went on. "There shall be no burning, though that were deserved; not even tumbril, though that were little harm to so hot a piece. There shall be, indeed, that which the Countess believes to have been already-a sally at dawn and a flitting. There will then be no harm done. The tithing will be free of a sucking witch, and the heart of our benefactress turned from the child of her sin (for such it was to break troth to the earl, and sin she deems it) to the child of her spiritual adoption, to wit, our Holy Thorn." He added "You are in my obedience, Galors. I love you much, and will see to your advancement. You have a great future. But, my brother, remember this. Between a woman's heart and her conscience there can be no fight. There is, rather, a triumph, wherein the most glorious of the' victor's spoils is that same conscience, shackled and haled behind the car. That you should know, and on that you must act. Remember you are fighting for Saint Giles of Holy Thorn, and be speedy while the new tool still burns in your hand."

So with his blessing he dismissed Dom Galors for the day.

CHAPTER V

LA DESIROUS

Prosper le Gai—all Morgraunt before him—rose from his bed before the Countess had turned in hers; and long before the Abbot could get alone with Dom Galors he was sighing for his breakfast. He had, indeed, seen the dawn come in, caught the first shiver of the trees, the first tentative chirp of the birds, watched the slow filling of the shadowy pools and creeks with the grey tide of light. From brake to brake he struggled, out of the shade into the dark, thence into what seemed a broad lake of daylight. He met no living thing; or ever the sun kissed the tree-tops he was hungry. He was well within Morgraunt now, though only, as it might be, upon the hem of its green robe; the adventurous place opened slowly to him like some great epic whose majesty and force dawns upon you by degrees not to be marked. It was still twilight in the place where he was when he heard the battling of birds' wings, the screaming of one bird's grief, and the angry purr of another, or of others. He peered through the bush as the sound swelled. Presently he saw a white bird come fluttering with a dropt wing, two hen-harriers in close pursuit. They were over her, upon her, there was a wrangle of wings—brown and white—even while he watched; then the white got clear again, and he could see that she bled in the breast. The sound of her screaming, which was to him like a girl crying, moved him strangely. He jumped from his saddle, ran to the entangled birds and cuffed the two hawks off; but seeing that they came on again, hunger-bold no doubt, he strangled them and freed the white pigeon. He took her up in his hands to look at her; she was too far gone for fear; she bled freely, but he judged she would recover. So she did, after he had washed out the wound; sufficiently at least to hop and flutter into covert. Prosper took to his horse and journey with her voice still ringing in his head.

In another hour's travel he reached a clearing in the wood, hedged all about with yew-trees and holm oaks very old; and in the midst of it saw a little stone altar with the figure of a woman upon it. He was not too hungry to be curious, so he dismounted and went to examine. The saint was Saint Lucy the Martyr, he saw; the altar, hoary as it was with lichen and green moss, had a slab upon it well-polished, with crosses let into the four corners and into the middle of the stone; there were sockets for tapers, and marks of grease new and thick. Before he approached it a hind and her calf had been cropping the grass between the cracks of the altar-steps; all else was very still, yet had a feeling of habitancy and familiar use.

His instinct when he saw an altar being to say his prayers, he knelt down then and there, facing the image, yet a little remote from it. A very soft tread behind him broke in upon his exercises; some one was coming, whence or how he did not then know. The comer was a young girl clothed in a white woollen garment, which was bound about her waist with a green cord; she was bareheaded; on her feet were thick sandals, bound also with thongs of green. Prosper watched her spread a white cloth upon the altar-slab, and set a Mass-book upon a stand; he saw her go and return with two lighted tapers for the sockets, he saw a silver crucifix shine between them. The girl, when all this business was done, stepped backwards down the steps, and stood at the foot of the altar with hands clasped upon her bosom and head bent lowly. "By the Saints," thought Prosper, "Morgraunt is a holy place, it seems. There is to be a Mass."

So it was. An old priest came out of the thicket in a vestment of yellow and gold thread, bearing in his hands the Sacrament under a green silk veil. The girl knelt down as he passed up the steps; he began his Mass, but in so low a voice that it hardly touched the forest peace.

Rabbits came creeping out of bush and bracken, a wood-dove began her moan, two or three deer stood up. Then Prosper thought—"If the beasts come to prayers, it behoves me as a Christian man to hear Mass also. Moreover, it were fitting that adventure should begin in that manner, to be undertaken in the name of our Lord Jesus Christ." He went forward accordingly, flush with the girl, and knelt down by her. When it was the time of Communion, both drew nearer and received Christ's body. Prosper, for his part, did not forget the soul of the dead man, De Genlis or another, whose body he had buried in Cadnam Wood, but commended it to God together with the sacrifice of the altar. The woman came into his mind. "No, by God," thought he; "she is the devil, or of him; I will never pray for her," which was Prosper all over.

Mass done, he remembered that he had the honour to be uncommonly hungry. The priest had gone back into the wood, the girl was removing the altar furniture, and seemed unconscious of his presence; but Prosper could not afford that.

"My young gentlewoman," he said with a bow, "you will see before you, if you turn your head, a very hungry man."

"Are you hungry, sir?" she said, looking and smiling at him, "then in three minutes you shall be filled." Whereupon she went away with her load, and quickly returned with another more to Prosper's mind. She gave him bread and hot milk in a great bowl, she gave him a dishful of wild raspberries, and waited on him herself in the prettiest manner. Without word said she watered his horse for him; and all the while she talked to him, but of nothing in the world but the birds and beasts, the falling of the leaf, and the thousand little haps and chances of her quiet life. Prosper suited his conversation to her book. He told her of the white bird's rescue, and she opened her blue eyes in wonder.

"Why, I dreamed of it last night," she said very solemnly.

"You dreamed of it, Alice?" he echoed. She was called, she had told him, Alice of the Hermitage.

"Yes, yes. A white bird and two hen-harriers. Ah, and there was more. You have not yet done all. You have not yet begun!" She was full of the thing.

"By my faith, I have wrung the necks of the pair of them," said Prosper. "I know not how they can expect more of me than that."

"Listen," said Alice of the Hermitage, "the bird will be again chased, again wounded. Morgraunt is full of hawks. You will see her again. My dream was very precise. You will see her again; but this time the chase will be long, and achievement only at the peril of your own honour. But it seems that you shall win in the end what you have thought to have won already, and the wound in the breast will be staunched."

"Hum," said Prosper. "Now you shall tell me what I ought to do, how I ought to begin. For you know the saw—'The sooner begun, the sooner done.'"

"Oh, sir,". cries she, "you shall ride forward in the name of God, remembering your manhood and the vows you made when you took up your arms." She blushed as she spoke, kindling with her thoughts.

"I will do that," said Prosper, kindled in his turn. And so he left her, and travelled all day towards Malbank Saint Thorn. He lay at night in the open wood, not far, as he judged, from Spurnt Heath, upon whose westernmost border ran Wan; there, or near by, he looked to find the Abbey.

He spent the night at least better than did Dom Galors, whose thoughts turned equally to Spurnt Heath. That strenuous man had taken the Abbot's counsel to bed with him, a restless partner. An inordinate partner also it proved to be, not content to keep the monk awake. Turning every traffic of his mind to its own advantage, it shook out the bright pinions of adventure over the dim corridors of Holy Thorn, and with every pulse of the ordering bell came a reiteration of its urgency. All night long, through all the task work of the next morning, the thought was with him—"By means of this woman I may be free. Free!" he cried. "I may be set up on high through her. Lord of this land and patron of Holy Thorn; a maker and unmaker of abbots to whom now I must bow my knees. Is it nothing to be master of a lovely wife? Ha, is it nothing to rule a broad fee? A small thing to have abbots kiss my hands? Lord of the earth! is this not worth a broken vow, which in any case I have broken before? Oh, Isoult la Desirous, if I desired you before when you went torn and shamefaced through the mire, what shall I say to you going in silk, in a litter, with a crown, Isoult la Desirée!" He called her name over and over, Isoult la Desirée, la Moult-Desirée, and felt his head spinning.

Matins, Lauds, and Prime, he endured this obsession. The day's round was filled with the amazing image of a crowned, hollow-eyed, tattered little drab, the mock and wonder of throngs of witnesses, appreciable only by himself as a pearl of priceless value. The heiress of Morgraunt, the young Countess of Hauterive, La Desirous, La Desirée. Desirable she had been before, but dealing no smarter scald than could be drowned in the well of love which for him she might have been for an hour. But now his burn glowed; the Abbot had blown it red. Ambition was alight; he was the brazier. It danced in him like a leaping flame. Certainly Prosper slept better on his side of Spurnt Heath.

At dusk the monk could bear himself and his burden of knowledge no longer. He went to look for Isoult on the heath in a known haunt of hers. He found her without trouble, sitting below the Abbot's new gallows. She was a girl, childishly formed, thin as a haggard-hawk, with a white resentful face, and a pair of startled eyes which, really grey, had a look of black as the pupil swam over the iris. The rags which served her for raiment covered her but ill; her legs were bare, she was without head-covering; all about her face her black hair fell in shrouds. She sat quite still where she was, with her elbows on her knees, and chin between her two hands, gazing before her over the heath. Above her head two thieves, first-fruits of the famous charter, creaked as they swung in their chains. If Isoult saw Galors coming, she made no effort to escape him; when her eyes met his her brooding stare held its spell.

The monk drew near, stood before her, and said—"Isoult la Desirous, you shall come with me into the quarry, for I have much to say to you."

"Let it be said here," she replied, without moving. But he answered—"Nay, you shall come with me into the quarry."

"I am dead tired. Can you not let me be, Dom Galors?"

"I have what will freshen you, Isoult. Come with me."

"If I must, I must."

Then he led her away, and she went tamely enough to the quarry.

There he took her by both her hands, and so held her, waiting till she should be forced to look up at him. When at last, sick and sullen, she raised her eyes, he could hardly contain himself. But he did.

"What were you doing by the Abbot's new gallows, Isoult?"

"I would rather be there now than here. The company is more to my liking."

"You may be near enough by to-morrow, if what I have learned be true."

The girl's eyes grew larger and darker. "Are they going to hang me?" she asked.

"Are you not a witch?"

"It is said."

"Your mother Mald is a witch—eh?"

"Yes, she is a witch."

"And are not you? You know Deerleap—eh?"

"It is said that I do."

"And you know what must be done to witches."

"They will hang me, Dom Galors! Will they hang me by Cutlaw and Rogerson?"

"There is room for you there."

"What can they prove?"

"Pshaw! Is proof needed? Are you not a baggage?"

"I know not."

"A wanton?"

"Ah, you should know that!"

"If it depended upon me, Isoult, I could save you. But the Abbot means to make an example and set a terror up before the evil-doers in this walk of Morgraunt. What am I before the Abbot, or what is my love for you to be brought to his ears? It is doom more certain still, my dear."

"Then I shall be hanged."

"Listen to me now, Isoult. Listen close. No, leave your hands where they are; they are safer there than elsewhere. So leave them and listen close. No soul in Malbank but myself and the Lord Abbot knows of what I have told you now. Me he told this morning. Judge if that was good news for your lover's ear!"

Isoult shivered and hung her head. Galors went on—"At the risk of everything a monk should fear, and of everything, by God, that such a monk as I am should care to win, I contended with my spiritual father. Spare me the particulars; I got some shrewd knocks over it, but I did win this much. You are to be hanged to-morrow, Isoult, or noosed in another way. A ring is to play a part. You shall be bride of the tree or a man's bride. I won this, and left the Abbot chuckling, for much as he knows he has not guessed that the goose-girl, the tossed-out kitchen-girl, the scarecrow haunter of the heath, should be sought in marriage. But I knew more than he; and now," he said, stooping over the bent girl,—"and now, Isoult la Desirous, come with me!"

He tried to draw her towards him, but she trembled in his hands so much that he had to give over. He began his arguments again, reasoned, entreated, threatened, cajoled; he could not contain himself now, being so near fruition. The spell of the forest was upon him. "Let Love be the master," he said, "for there is no gainsaying him, nor can cloister walls bar his way; but his flamy wings top even these. Ah, Isoult!" he cried out in his passion; "ah, Isoult la Desirée, come, lest I die of love and you of the tree."

The girl, who feared him much more than the death he had declared, was white now and desperate. But she still held him off with her stiffened arms and face averted. She tried to cheapen herself. "I am Matt's bad daughter, I am Matt's bad daughter! All the tithing holds me in scorn. Never speak of love to such as I am, Galors." And when he tried to pull her she made herself rigid as a rod, and would not go.

So love made the man mad, and spread and possessed him. Contest goaded Galors: action was his meat and dominion what he breathed; by resisting she had made the end more sure. By her imprisoned wrists he drew her in, and when she was so close that her head was almost upon his breast, he breathed over her. "A mitred abbey have I trampled down for your love; yes, and to be bishop of a see. Therefore you must come."

She fell to whining and entreaty, white to the lips and dry with fear. All that she could say was, "I am bad. I am bad, but not so bad! Never ruin me, Dom Galors." Then it was that she heard the voice of Prosper singing afar off on the heath. Prosper sang—

"What   if   my   metal
Be   proved   as   high   as   a   hawk's   in   good   fettle!
Then   you   shall   see
The world my fee, And the hearts of men for my Seigniory."

And the girl thought to herself, "Help cometh!" and changed the voice of her grief and the beating of her heart. By this the guile a woman has always by her tongue had play: she could talk more gently to her gaoler, and beg a little time— a short hour or so—to plan and arrange their affairs. He thought her won and grew very tender; he kissed her hands many times, called her his dear heart, became, in a word, the clumsy gallant he claimed to be. All this too she endured: she began to gabble at random, sprightly as a minion, with all the shifts of a girl in a strait place ready at command. Her fear was double now: she must learn the trend of the singer and his horse, and prevent Galors from hearing either. This much she did. The sound came steadily on. She heard the horse's hoofs strike on a flint outside the quarry, she heard Prosper, singing softly to himself. Her time had come. She sprang at arm's-length from Galors and called out, "Help, for charity!" with all her might.

Prosper started, drew his sword, and headed his horse for the quarry. In the mouth of it he reined up to look about him. He was sure of his direction, but not of his way, "Help is here!" he cried with his sword on high and red plumes nodding. Air and the light of the sun seemed to follow him, as if he had cut a slit in a shroud and let in the day. Then it was that Isoult found strength to shake free from her enemy, to run to Prosper, to clasp his knee, to babble broken words, entreaties for salvation, and to stoop to his foot and kiss it.

"What is all this about, my child?" asked Prosper wondering.

"Oh" cried the girl, "my lord! the monk seeks to do me a wrong, and a shame greater than all!"

Prosper looked deeper into the quarry. There he saw Galors, the white monk, who stood fixed, biting his nails keenly there. Then he laughed, saying, "I cannot fight a monk," and sheathed his sword. He did not love monks, none of his house did. He had seen the new gallows, could measure the build of the fellow in the quarry; and though he could not plumb the girl's soul through her misty eyes, he could read her shaking lips and clinging hands; he could see, and be shocked to see, how young she was to be acquainted with grief, and with sin how likely familiar. The hint of the thing revolted him; he dared not leave her there.

"See here, child," said he, "I will set you before me, and we will ride together for a while. Perhaps the evening chills will temper the monk; but if not, I am to lodge at his abbey this night, and may prepare that for him which will cool him. Will you come up to me?"

The ghost of a smile hovered over her white drawn face for a minute. "I will go where you will take me, my lord," said she.

"Come up with you then," he replied. He stooped there and then, took her below the arms, and lightly swung her into the saddle before him. There she sat, modern fashion, with his sword arm for her stay. "I should like to read that hulk a lesson," said her protector wistfully, "but I doubt he will have it before night. Oh, let him hang!" So he turned and rode out of the quarry on to the heath.

Galors stood a long time in the place where they left him, drawing blood from his bitten fingers. Darkness gathered fast with a storm of wind and rain. Nevertheless he stayed on; and night came down to find him still there.

CHAPTER VI

THE VIRGIN MARRIAGE

He had to talk, and as the girl gave him no help, Prosper found himself asking questions and puzzling out the answers he got, trying to make them fit with the facts. He was amazed that one so delicately formed should go barefooted and bareheaded, clad in torn rags. To all his questions she replied in a voice low and tremulous, and very simply—that is to say, to such of them as she would answer at all. To many—to all which touched upon Galors and his business with her in the quarry—she was as dumb as a fish. Prosper was as patient as you could expect.

He asked her who she was, and how called. She told him—"I am Matt-of-the-Moors child, and men call me Isoult la Desirous."

"That is a strange name," said he. "How came you by such a name as that?"

"Sir," said Isoult, "I have never had any other; and I suppose that I have it because I am unhappy, and not at peace with those who seek me."

"Who seeks you, Isoult?"

To that she gave no reply. So Prosper went on.

"If many sought you, child," he said, "you were rightly called Isoult la Desirée, but if you, on the other hand, sought something or somebody, then you were Isoult la Desirous. Is it not so?"

"My lord," said Isoult, "the last is my name."

"Then it must be that you too seek something. What is it that you seek, that all the tithing knows of it?"

But she hung her head and had nothing to say. He went on to speak of Galors, to her visible disease. When he asked what the monk wanted with her, he felt her tremble on his arm. She began to cry, suddenly turned her face into his shoulder, and kept it there while her sobs shook through her.

"Well, child," said he, "dry your tears, and turn your face to such light as there is, being well assured of this, that whatever he asked of you he did not get, and that he will ask no more."

"I fear him, I fear him," she said very low—and again, "I fear him, I fear him."

"Drat the monk," said Prosper, laughing, "is he to cut me out of a compliment?"

Whereupon she turned a very woebegone and tearful face up to his. He looked smilingly down; a sudden wave of half-humbrous pity for a thing so frail and amazed swam about him; before he knew he had kissed her cheek. This set her blushing a little; but she seemed to take heart, smiled rather pitifully, and turned again with a sigh, like a baby's for sleep.

The night gathered apace with a chill wind; some fine rain began to fall, then heavy drops. Gradually the wind increased, and the rain with it. "Now we shall have it," said Prosper, sniffing for the storm. He covered Isoult with his cloak, folded it about her as best he could, and tucked it in; she lay in his arms snug enough, and slept while he urged his horse over the stubbed heath. The water hissed and ran over the baked earth; where had been dry channels, rents and scars, full of dust, were now singing torrents and broad pools fetlock deep. Prosper let his good beast go his own gait, which was a sober trot, and ever and again as he heard the ripple of running water and the swirl and suck of the eddies in it, he judged that he must soon or late touch the Wan river, whereon stood the Abbey and his bed. What to do with the girl when he got there? That puzzled him. "A well-ordered abbey," he thought, "has no place for a girl, and one ill-ordered has too many. In the first case, therefore, Holy Thorn would leave her at the gate, and in the second, that is where I myself would let her stay. So it seems that she must needs have a wet skin." He felt carefully about the sleeping child; the cloak kept her dry and warm as a toast. She was sound asleep. "Good Lord!" cried Prosper, "it's a pity to disturb this baby of mine. Saracen and I had better souse. Moreover, I make no nearer, by all that appears, to river Wan or Holy Thorn. Come up, horse; keep us moving."

The stream he had followed he now had lost. It was pitchy dark, with a most villainous storm of rain and wind. Saracen caught the infection of his master's doubts; he stopped short, and bowed his head to snuff the ground. Prosper laughed at the plight they were both in, and looked about him, considering what he should do. Very far off he could see a feeble light flickering; it was the only speck of brightness within his vision, and he judged it too steady for a fen-flame. Lodging of some sort should be there, for where there is a candle there is a candlestick. This was not firelight. To it he turned his tired beast, and found that he had been well advised. He was before a mud-walled hovel; there through the horn he saw the candle-flame. He drew his sword and beat upon the door. For answer the light was blown swiftly out, and the darkness swam about him like ink.

"Scared folk!" he laughed to himself, hammering at the door with a will.

Then Isoult stirred on his arm and awoke with a little whimper, half dreaming still, and not knowing where she was. She sat up in the saddle dazed with sleep.

"The night is wild," said Prosper, "and I have found us the shadow of a shade, but as yet we lack the substance." Then he set-to, pounding at the door again, and crying to those within to open for the sake of all the saints he could remember.

Isoult freed herself from the cloak, and slid down from her seat in the saddle. Putting her face close to the door she whistled a low note. The candle was re-lit, many bolts were withdrawn; finally the door opened a little way, and an old man put his head through the chink, staring out into the dark.

"God's life, you little rip," said the anxious rogue, "you gave us a turn!"

Isoult spoke eagerly and fast, but too low for Prosper to hear what she said. The man was in no mind to open further, and the more he speered at the horseman the less he seemed to like it. Nevertheless, after a time the girl was let into the hut, and the door slammed and bolted as before. Between the shocks of the storm Prosper could now hear a confusion of voices—Isoult's, low, even, clear and quick; the grating comments of the old rogue who kept the door, and another voice that trembled and wailed as if passion struggled with the age in it, to see which should be master. Once he thought to catch a fourth—a brisk man's voice, with laughter and some sort of authority in it, which seemed familiar; but he could not be sure about this. In the main three persons held the debate.

After a long wrangle it seemed that the women were to have their way. Again the door-bolts were drawn, again the door opened by the old man, and this time opened wide. With bows lower than the occasion demanded, Prosper was invited to be pleased to enter. He saw to his horse first, and made what provision he could for him in an outhouse. Then he stooped his head and entered the cottage.

He came directly into a bare room, which was, you may say, crouched under a pent of turves and ling, and stank very vilely. The floor was of beaten clay, like the walls; for furniture it had a table and bench. Sooty cobwebs dripped from the joists, and great spiders ran nimbly over them; there were no beds, but on a heap of rotting skins in one corner two rats were busy, and in another were some dry leaves and bracken. There was no chimney either, though there was a peat fire smouldering in what you must call the hearth. The place was dense with the fog of it; it was some time, therefore, before Prosper could leave blinking and fit his eyes to see the occupants of his lodging.... Isoult, he saw, stood in the middle of the room leaning on the table with both her hands; her bead was hanging, and her hair veiled all her face. Near her, also standing, was the old man—a sturdy knowing old villain, with a world of cunning and mischief in his pair of pig's eyes. His scanty hair, his beard, were white; his eyebrows were white and altogether monstrous. He blinked at Prosper, but said nothing. The third was a woman, infinitely old as it seemed, crouched over the fired peats with her back to the room. She never looked up at all, but muttered and sighed vainly to herself and warmed her hands. Lastly, in a round-backed chair, cross-legged, twirling his thumbs, twinkling with comfortable repletion, sat Prosper's friend of the road, Brother Bonaccord of Lucca.

"God save you, gentleman," he chirped. "I see we have the same taste in lodgings. None of your Holy Thorns for us—hey? But a shakedown under a snug thatch, with a tap of red wine such as I have not had out of my own country. What a port for what a night—hey?"

Prosper nodded back a greeting as he looked from one to another of these ill-assorted hosts of his, and whenever he chanced on the motionless girl he felt that he could not understand it. Look at her! how sweet and delicate she was, how small and well-set her head, her feet and hands how fine, her shape how tender. "How should a lily spring in so foul a bed?" thought he to himself. Morgraunt had already taught him an odd thing or two; no doubt it was Morgraunt's way.

The old man set bread and onions on the table, with some sour red wine in a jug. "Sit and eat, my lord, while you may," he said.

So Prosper and Isoult sat upon the bench and made the most of it, and he, being a cheerful soul, talked and joked with Brother Bonaccord. Isoult never raised her eyes once, nor spoke a word; as for the numbed old soul by the fire; she kept her back resolutely on the room, muttered her charms and despair, and warmed her dry hands as before.

When they had eaten what they could there came a change. The friar ceased talking; the old man faced Prosper with a queer look. "Sir, have you well-eaten and drunken?" he asked.

Prosper thanked him; he had done excellently.

"Well, now," said the man, "as I have heard, after the bride-feast comes the bridal. Will your worship rest with the bride brought home?"

Prosper got up in an awkward pause. He looked at the man as if he were possessed of the devil. Then he laughed, saying, "Are you merry, old rogue?"

"Nay, sir," said the ancient, "it is no jest. If she mate not this night—and it's marriage for choice with this holy man—come sunrise she'll be hanged on the Abbot's new gallows. For, she is suspected of witchcraft and many abominations."

"Is she your daughter, you dog, and do you speak thus of your daughter?" cried Prosper in a fury.

"Sir," said the man, "who would own himself father to a witch? Nevertheless she is my daughter indeed."

"What is the meaning of all this? Would you have me marry a witch, old fool?" Prosper shouted at him. The man shrugged.

"Nay, sir, but I said it was marriage for choice—seeing the friar was to hand. We know their way, to marry as soon as look at you. But it's as you will, so you get a title to her, to take her out of the country."

Prosper turned to look at Isoult. He saw her standing before the board, her head hung and her two hands clasped together. Her breathing was troubled—that also he saw. "God's grace!" thought he to himself, "is she so fair without and within so rotten? Who has been ill-ordering the world to this pass?" He watched her thoughtfully for some time; then he turned to her father.

"See now, old scamp," he said, "I have sworn an oath to high God to succour the weak, to right wrong, and to serve ladies. Nine times under the moon I sware it, watching my arms before the cross on Starning Waste. Judge you, therefore, whether I intend to keep it or not. As for your daughter, she can tell you whether some part of it I have not kept even now. But understand me, that I do not marry on compulsion or where love is not. For that were a sin done toward God, and me, and a maid."

The old rascal blinked his eyes, jerking his head many times at the shameful girl. Then he said, "Love is there fast and sure. She is all for loving. They call her Isoult la Desirous, you must know."

"Yes," said Prosper, "I do know it, for she has told me so already.'

"And to-morrow she will desire no more, since she will be hanged," said Matt-o'-the-Moor.

Prosper started and flushed, and—

"That is a true gospel, brother," put in the friar. "The Abbot means to air his gallows at her expense; but there is worse than a gallows to it. What did I tell you of the Black Monks when you called 'em White? There is a coal-black among them who'll have her if the gallows have her not. It is Galors or gallows, fast and sure."

Prosper rubbed his chin, looked at the friar, looked at Matt, looked at Isoult. She neither lifted her head nor eyes, though the others had met him sturdily enough. She stood like a saint on a church porch; he thought her a desperate Magdalen.

"Isoult, come here," said he. She came as obediently as you please, and stood before him; but she would not look up until he said again, "Isoult, look me in the face." Then she did as she was told, and her eyes were unwinking and very wide open, full of dark. She parted her lips and sighed a little, shivering somewhat. It seemed to him as if she had been with the dead already and seen their kingdom. Prosper said, "Isoult is this true that thou wilt be hanged to-morrow?"

"Yes, lord," said Isoult in a whisper.

"Or worse?"

"Yes, lord," she said again, quivering.

"Save only thy lot be a marriage this night?"

"Yes, lord," she said a third time. So he asked,

"Art thou verily what this old man thy father hath testified against thee—a witch, a worker of iniquity and black things, and of abominations with the devil?"

Isoult said in a very still voice—"Men say that I am all this, my lord."

But Prosper with a cry called out, "Isoult, Isoult, now tell me the truth. Dost thou deserve this death?"

She sighed, and smiled rather pitifully as she said—

"I cannot tell, lord; but I desire it."

"Dost thou desire death, child?" cried he, "and is this why thou art called La Desirous?"

"I desire to be what I am not, my lord, and to have that which I have never had," she answered, and her lip trembled.

"And what is that which you are not, Isoult?"

She answered him "Clean."

"And what is that which you have never had, my child?"

"Peace," said Isoult, and wept bitterly.

Then Prosper crossed himself very devoutly, and covered his face while he prayed to his saint. When he had done he said, "Cease crying, Isoult, and tell me the truth, by God and His Christ, and Saint Mary, and by the face of the sky. Art thou such a one as I would wed if love were to grow between me and thee, or art thou other?"

She ceased her crying at this and looked him full in the face, deadly pale. "What is the truth to you concerning me?" she said.

He answered her, "The truth is everything, for without it nothing can have good beginning or good ending."

This made her meek again and her eyes misty. She held out a hand to him, saying, "Come into the night, and I will tell my lord."

He took it. Hand-in-hand they went out of the cottage, and hand-in-hand stood together alone under the sky. It was still black and heavy weather, but without rain. Isoult dropped his hand and stood before him. She shut her arms over her breast so that her two wrists crossed at her throat. Looking full at him from under her brows she said—

"By God and His Christ, and Saint Mary, and by the face of the sky, I will tell you the truth, lord. If the witch's wax be not as abominable as the witch, or the vessel not foul that hath held a foul liquor, then thou couldst never point scorn at me."

"Speak openly to me, my child," said Prosper, "and fear nothing."

So she said, "I will speak openly. I am no witch, albeit I have seen witchcraft and the revelry of witches on Deerleap. And though I have seen evil also I am a maiden, my lord, and such as you would have your own sister to be before she were wed."

But Prosper put her from him at an arm's-length. He was not yet satisfied.

"What was thy meaning then," he asked, "to say that thou wouldst be that which thou wert not?" He could not bring himself to use the word which she had used; but she used it again.

"Ah, clean!" she said with a weary gesture. "Lord, how shall I be clean in this place? Or how shall I be clean when all say that I am unclean, and so use towards me?" She began to cry again, quite silently. Prosper could hear the drips fall from her cheeks to her breast, but no other sound. She began to moan in her trouble—"Ah, no, no, no!" she whispered, "I would not wed with thee, I dare not wed with thee."

"Why not?" said Prosper.

"I dare not, I dare not!" she answered through her teeth, and he felt her trembling under his hand. He thought before he spoke again. Then he said—

"I have vowed a vow to my saint that I will save you, soul and body; and if it can be done only by a wedding, then we will be married, you and I, Isoult. But if by battle I can serve your case as well, and rid the suspicion and save your neck, why, I will do battle."

"Nay, lord," said the girl, "I must be hanged, for so the Lord Abbot has decreed." And then she told him all that Galors had given her to understand when he had her in the quarry.

Prosper heard her to the end: it was clear that she spoke as she believed.

"Well, child," said he, "I see that all this is likely enough, though for the life of me I cannot bottom it. But how then," he cried, after a little more thinking, "shall I let you be hanged, and your neck so fine and smooth!"

"Lord," she said, "let be for that; for since I was born I have heard of my low condition, and if my neck be slim 'tis the sooner broke. Let me go then, but only grant me this grace, to stand beside me at the tree and not leave me till I am dead. For there may be a worse thing than death preparing for me." Again she cried out at her own thoughts "Ah, no, no, no, I dare not let thee wed me!" He heard the wringing of her hands, and guessed her beside herself.

He stood, therefore, reasoning it all out something after this fashion. "Look now, Prosper," thought he, "this child says truer than she knows. It is an ill thing to be hanged, but a worse to deserve a hanging, and worst of all for her, it seems, to escape a hanging. And it is good to find death sweet when he comes (since come he must), but better to prove life also a pleasant thing. And life is here urgent, though in fetters, in this child's breast; but death is not yet here. Yet if I leave her she gains death, or life (which is worse), and if I take her with me it can only be one way. What then! a man can lay down his life in many ways, giving it for the life that needeth, whether by jumping a red grave or by means slower but not less sure. And if by any deed of mine I pluck this child out of the mire, put clear light into her eyes (which now are all dark), and set the flush on her grey cheeks which she was assuredly designed to carry there; and if she breathe sweet air and grow in the grace of God and sight of men—why then I have done well, however else I do."

He thought no more, but took the girl's hand again in both of his. "Well, Isoult," he said cheerfully, "thou shalt not be hanged yet awhile, nor shall that worse thing befall thee. I will wed thee as soon as I may. At cock-crow we two will seek a priest."

"Lord," she said, "a priest is here in this place."

"Why, yes! Brother Bonaccord. Well," said Prosper, "let us go in."

But Isoult was troubled afresh, and put her hand against his chest to stay him; breathing very short.

"Lord," she said, "thou wilt wed me to save my soul from hell and my body from hanging; but thou hast no love for me in thy heart, as I know very well."

Here was a bother indeed. The girl was fair enough in her peaked elfin way; but the fact was that he did not love her—nor anybody. He had nothing to say therefore. She waited a little, and then, with her voice sunk to a low murmur, she said—

"We two will never come together except in love. Shall it not be so?"

Prosper bowed, saying—

"It shall be so."

The girl knelt suddenly down and kissed his foot. Then she rose and stood near him.

"Let us go in," she said.

Looking up, they saw the field of heaven strewn thick with stars, the clouds driven off, the wind dropt. And then they went into the hovel hand-in-hand, as they had gone out.

As soon as he saw them come in together the old man fell to chuckling and rubbing his hands.

"Wife Mald, wife Mald, look up!" cried he; "there will be a wedding this night. See, they are hand-fasted already."

Mald the witch rose up from the hearth at last and faced the betrothed. She was terrible to view in her witless old age; her face drawn into furrows and dull as lead, her bleared eyes empty of sight or conscience, and her thin hair scattered before them. It was despair, not sorrow, that Prosper read on such a face. Now she peered upon the hand-locked couple, now she parted the hair from her eyes, now slowly pointed a finger at them. Her hand shook with palsy, but she raised it up to bless them. To Prosper she said—

"Thou who art as pitiful as death, shalt have thy reward. And it shall be more than thou knowest."

To the girl she gave no promises, but with her crutch hobbled over the floor to where she stood. She put her hand into her daughter's bosom and felt there; she seemed contented, for she said to her very earnestly—

"Keep thou what thou hast there till the hour of thy greatest peril. Then it shall not fail thee to whomsoever thou shalt show it."

Then she withdrew her hand and crawled back to crouch over the ashes of the fire; nor did she open her lips again that night, nor take any part or lot in what followed.

"Call the priest, old man," said Prosper, "for the night is spending, and to-morrow we should be up before the sun."

The old thief went to a little door and opened it, whispering,

"Come, father;" and there came out Brother Bonaccord of Lucca, very solemn, vested in a frayed vestment.

"Young sir," he said, wagging a portentous finger, "you are of the simple folk our good Father Francis loved. No harm should come of this. And I pray our Lady that I never may play a worse trick on a maid than this which I shall play now."

"We have no ring," said Prosper to all this prelude.

"Content you, my master," replied Matt-o'-the-Moor; "here is what you need."

And he gave him a silver ring made of three thin wires curiously knotted in an endless plait.

"The ring will serve the purpose," Prosper said. "Now, brother, at your disposition."

Brother Bonaccord had no book, but seemed none the worse for that. He took the ring, blessed it, gave it to Prosper, and saw that he put it in its proper place; he said all the words, blessed the kneeling couple, and gave them a brisk little homily, which I spare the reader. There they were wedded.

Matt-o'-the-Moor at the end of the ceremony gave Prosper a nudge in the ribs. He pointed to a heap of leaves and litter.

"The marriage-bed," he said waggishly, and blew out the light.

Isoult lay down on the bed; Prosper took off his body-armour and lay beside her, and his naked sword lay between them.

CHAPTER VII

GALORS ABJURES

Dom Galors knew a woman in East Morgraunt whose name was Maulfry. She lived in Tortsentier, a lonely tower hidden deep in the woods, and had an unwholesome reputation. She was held to be a courtesan. Many gentlemen adventurous in the forest, it was said, had found dishonourable ease and shameful death at her hands. She would make them great cheer at first with hunting parties, dancing in the grass-rides, and love everywhere: so much had been seen, the rest was surmise. It was supposed that, being tired, or changing for caprice, she had them drugged, rifled them at leisure, slew them one way or another, and set her nets for the next newcomer. This, I say, was surmise, and so it remained. Tortsentier was hard to come at, Morgraunt wide, death as easy as lying. Men in it had other uses for their eyes than to spy at their neighbours, and found their weapons too often needed in their own quarrels to spare them for others. To see a man once did not set you looking for him to come again. You might wander for a month in Morgraunt before you got out. True, the odds were against your doing either; but whose business was that?

Galors probably knew the truth of it, for he was very often at Tortsentier. He knew, for instance, of Maulfry's taste for armour. The place was full of it, and had a frieze of shields, which Maulfry herself polished every day, as brave with blazonry as on the day they first went out before their masters. Maulfry was very fond of heraldry. It was a great delight of hers to go through her collection with such a man as Galors, who thoroughly understood the science, conning over the quarterings, the legends, the badges and differences, and capping each with its appropriate story, its little touch of romance, its personal reference to each owner in turn. There was no harm in all this, and for Galors' part he would be able to testify that there was no luxurious company there when he came, and no dark hints of violence, treachery, or mischief for the most suspicious eye to catch at. Tortsentier was not so far from the Abbey liberties that one might not fetch at it in a six hours' ride, provided one knew the road. Galors was a great rider and knew the road by heart. He was a frequent visitor of Maulfry's, therefore, and would have seen what there was to see. If the cavillers had known that it would have quieted many a whisper over the fire. They might have been told, further, that Maulfry and he were very old friends, and from a time long before his entry into religion at Holy Thorn. If there had been love between them, it had left no scar. Love with Galors was a pastime: he might make a woman his mistress, but he could never allow her to be his master. And whatever there had been in this sort, any love now left in Maulfry for the monk was largely tempered with respect. They were excellent friends.

It was to Tortsentier and to Maulfry that Dom Galors rode through the rain when he had finished biting his nails in the quarry. Very late that night he knocked at her door. Maulfry, who slept by day, opened at once, and when she saw who it was made him very welcome. She sent her page up with dry clothes, heaped logs on the fire, and set a table against his return, with venison, and white bread, and sweet wine. Galors, who was ravenous by now, needed no pressing: he sat down and ate without speaking, nor did she urge him for a message or for news, but kept her place by the fire, smiling into it until he had done. She was a tall, dark woman, very handsome and finely shaped, having the neck, arms, and bosom of Juno, or of that lady whom Nicholas the Pisan sculptor fashioned on her model to be Queen of Heaven and Earth. And Maulfry suffered no one to be in doubt as to the abundance and glory of her treasure.

When Galors was well fed she beckoned him with a nod to his place on the settle. He came and sat by the side of her, blinking into the fire for some minutes without a word.

"Well, friend," said Maulfry at last, "and what do you want with your servant at such an hour? For though I am not unused to have guests, it is seldom that you are of the party in these days."

Galors, who never made prefaces, told her everything, except the real rank and condition of Isoult. As to that, he said that the lady in question was undoubtedly an heiress, as she was undeniably a beauty, but he was careful to make it plain that her inheritance, and not her person, tempted him. This I believe to have been the truth by now. He then related what had passed in the quarry, and what he intended to do next. He added—

"Whether I succeed or not—and as to that much depends upon you—I am resolved to abjure my frock and my vows, and to aim henceforward for a temporal crown."

"I think the frock is all that need concern you," said Maulfry.

"You are right, pretty lady," he replied "and that shall concern me no more. You shall furnish me with a suit of mail out of your store, with a shield, a good spear and a sword. I have already a horse, which I owe to the vicarious bounty of the Lord Abbot, exercised through me, his right-hand man. This then will be all I shall ask of you on my account, so far as I can see at present. With what I know to back them they may win me an earldom and a pretty partner. At least they will enable me to pay Master Red-Feather my little score."

The pupils of Maulfry's eyes narrowed to a pair of pin points.

"What is this?" she said quickly. "Red feathers? A surcoat white and green? A gold baldrick? Did he bear a *fesse dancettée* upon his shield, a hooded falcon for his crest?" Her questions chimed with her panting.

"By baldrick and shield I know him for a Gai of Starning," said Galors. "So much is certain, but which of them in particular I cannot tell certainly. There were half-a-dozen at one time. Not Malise, I think. He is too thin-lipped for such work as that. He can do sums in his head, is a ready reckoner. This lad was quick enough to act, but not quick enough to refrain from acting. Malise would not have acted. He can see too far ahead. Nor is it Osric. He would have made speeches and let vapours. This lad was quiet."

"Quiet as God," said Maulfry with a stare.

"But," Galors went on, "you need not think for him, who or what he was. I shall meet him to-morrow, and if things go as they should you shall see me again very soon. You shall come to a wedding. A wedding in Tortsentier will not be amiss, dame. Moreover, it will be new. If I fail—well, then also you shall see me, and serve me other ways. Will you do this?"

Maulfry frowned a little as she thought. Then she laughed.

"You know very well I will do more for you than this. And how much will you do for me, Galors?"

"Ask and see," said Galors.

"I too may have accounts to settle."

"You will find me a good bailiff, Maulfry. Punctual at the audit."

Maulfry laughed again as she looked up at her armour. Galors' look followed hers.

"Choose, Galors," she said; "choose, my champion. Choose, Sir Galors de Born!"

Galors took a long and deliberate survey.

"I will go in black," said he, "and for the rest, since I am no man of race, the coat is indifferent to me." So he began to read and comment upon his texts. "*Je tiendray*—why, so I shall, but it savours of forecast, brags a little."

"None the worse for my knight," said Maulfry.

"No, no," he laughed, "but let me get something of which to brag first. Hum. *Dieu m'en garde*—we will leave God out of the reckoning, I think. *Designando*—I will do more than point out, by the Rood!*Jesus, Amor, Ma Dame*—I know none of these. *Entra per me*—Oh brave, brave! 'Tis your latest, dame?"

Maulfry's eyes grew hard and bright. "Choose it, choose, my Galors!" she cried. "And if with that you beat down the red feather, and blind the hooded hawk, you will serve me more than you dream. Oh, choose, choose!"

"*Entra per me* pleases me, I confess. But what are the arms? Wickets?"

"Three white wicket-gates on a sable field. It was the coat of Salomon de Montguichet."

"Salomon?" said Galors all in a whisper. "Never Salomon? Do you not remember?"

Maulfry laughed. "I should remember, I think. But there is no monopoly. What we choose others can choose. The name is free to the world, and a great name."

Galors, visibly uneasy; thought hard about it. Then he swore. "And I go for great deeds, by Heaven! Give it me, Dame. I will have it. *Entra per me*! And shut the wickets when I am in!"

He kissed Maulfry then and there, and they went to bed.

CHAPTER VIII

THE SALLY AT DAWN

On the morning after his strange wedding Prosper rose up early, quite himself. He left Isoult asleep in the bed, but could see neither old man, old woman, nor friar; so far as he could tell, he and his wife were alone in the cottage. Now he must think what to do. He admitted freely enough to himself that he had not been in a condition for this overnight; the girl's mood had exalted him; he had acted, and rightly acted (he was clear about this); now he must think what to do. The first duty was plain: he went out into the air and bathed in a pool; he took a quick run and set his blood galloping; then he groomed and fed his horse; put on his armour, and said his prayers. In the course of this last exercise he again remembered his wife, on whose account he had determined to make up his mind. He rose from his knees at once and walked about the heath, thinking it out.

"It is clear enough," he said to himself, "that neither my wife nor I desired marriage. We are not of the same condition; we have not—I speak for myself and by implication for her also—we have not those desires which draw men and women towards each other. Love, no doubt, is a strange and terrible thing: it may lead a man to the writing of verses and a most fatiguing search for words, but it will not allow him to be happy in anything except its own satisfaction; and in that it seems absurd to be happy. Marriage is in the same plight: it may be a good or a bad thing; without love it is a ridiculous thing. Nevertheless my wife and I are of agreement in this, that we think marriage better than being hanged. I do not understand the alternatives, but I accept them, and am married. My wife will not be hanged. For the rest, I shall take her to Gracedieu. The devout ladies there will no doubt make a nun of her; she will be out of harm's way, and all will be well."

He said another prayer, and rose up much comforted. And then as he got up Isoult came out of the cottage.

She ran towards him quickly, knelt down before he could prevent her, took his hand and kissed it. She was very shy of him, and when he raised her up and kissed her forehead, suffered the caress with lowered eyes and a face all rosy. Prosper found her very different from the tattered bride of over-night. She had changed her rags for a cotton gown of dark blue, her clouds of hair were now drawn back over her ears into a knot and covered with a silk hood of Indian work. On her feet, then bare, he now saw sandals, round her waist a leather belt with a thin dagger attached to it in a silver sheath. She looked very timidly, even humbly up at him whenever he spoke to her—with the long faithfulness of a dog shining in her big eyes: but she looked like a girl who was to be respected, and even Prosper could not but perceive what a dark beauty she was. Pale she was, no doubt, except when she blushed; but this she did as freely as hill-side clouds in March.

"Where is your wedding-ring, my child?" he asked her, when he had noticed that it was not where he had put it.

"Lord, it is here," said she, blushing again. She drew from her neck a fine gold chain whereon were the ring and another trinket which beamed like glass.

"Is that where you would have it, Isoult?"

"Yes, lord," she answered. "For this present it must be there."

"As you will," said Prosper. "Let us break our fast and make ready, for we must be on our journey before we see the sun." Isoult went into the cottage as Brother Bonaccord came out with good-morning all over his puckered face.

Isoult brought bread and goats'-milk cheese, and they broke their fast sitting on the threshold, while the sun slowly rose behind the house and lit up the ground before them—a broken moorland with heather-clumps islanded in pools of black water. The white forest mist hid every distance and the air was shrewdly cold; but Prosper and the friar gossiped cheerfully as they munched.

"We friars," said Brother Bonaccord, "have been accused of a foible for wedding-rings. I grant you I had rather marry a healthy couple than leave them aching, and that the sooner there's a christening the better I am pleased. Another soul for Christ to save; another point against the devil, thinks I! I have heard priests say otherwise: they will christen if they must, and marry if it is not too late; but they would sooner bury you any day. Go to! They live in the world (which I vow is an excellent place), and eat and drink of it; yet they shut their eyes, pretending all the time that they are not there, but rather in skyey mansions. If this is not a fit and proper place for us men, why did God Almighty take six days a-thinking before He bid it out of the cooking pot? For a gift to the devil? Not He! 'Stop bubbling, you rogue,' says He; 'out of the pot with you and on to the platter, that these gentlemen and ladies of mine may cease sucking their fingers and dip in the dish!' Pooh! Look at your mother Mary and your little brother Gesulino. There was a wedding for you, there was a sacring! Beloved sons are ye all, young men; full of grace are ye, young women! God be good, who told me to couple ye and keep the game a-going! Take my blessing, brother, and the sleek and tidy maid you have gotten to wife; I must be on the road. I am for Hauterive out of the hanging Abbot's country. He'll be itching about that new gallows of his, thinking how I should look up there."

He kissed them both very heartily and trudged out into the mist, waving his hand.

"There goes a good soul," said Prosper. "Give me something to drink, child, I beseech you."

Isoult brought a great bowl of milk and gave it into his hands, afterwards (though he never saw her) she drank of it from the place where he had put his lips. Then it was time for them also to take the road. Isoult went away again, and returned leading Prosper's horse and shield; she brought an ass for herself to ride on. Curtseying to him she asked—

"Is my lord ready?"

"Ready for anything in life, my child," said he as he took her up and put her on the ass. Then he mounted his horse. They set off at once over the heath, striking north. None watched them go.

The sky was now without cloud. White all about, it swam into clear blue overhead. A light breeze, brisk and fresh, blew the land clear, only little patches of the morning mist hung torn and ragged about the furze-bushes. The forest was still densely veiled, but the sun was up, the larks afloat; the rains of over-night crisped and sparkled on the grass: there was promise of great weather. Presently with its slant roofs shining, its gilded spires and cross, Prosper saw on his left the great Abbey of Holy Thorn. He saw the river with a boat's sail, the village of Malbank Saint Thorn on the further bank and the cloud of thin blue smoke over it; far across the heath came the roar of the weirs. Behind it and on all sides began to rise before him the dark rampart of trees—Morgraunt.

Prosper's heart grew merry within him at the sight of all this freshness, the splendour of the morning. He was disposed to be well contented with everything, even with Isoult, upon whom he looked down once or twice, to see her pacing gently beside him, a guarded and graceful possession. "Well, friend," he said to himself, "you have a proper-seeming wife, it appears, of whom it would be well to know something."

He began to question her, and this time she told him everything he asked her, except why she was called Isoult la Desirous. As to this, she persisted that she could not tell him. He took it good-temperedly, with a shrug.

"I see something mysterious in all this, child," said he, "and am not fond of mysteries. But I married thee to draw thee from the hangman and not thy secrets from thee. Keep thy counsel therefore."

She hung her head.

To all other questions she was as open as he could wish. From her earliest childhood, he learned, she had known servitude, and been familiar with scorn and reproach. She had been swineherd, goose-girl, scare-crow, laundress, scullery-wench, and what not, as her mother could win for her. She could never better herself, because of the taint of witchcraft and all the unholiness it brought upon her. As laundress and scullery-maid she had been at the Abbey; that had been her happiest time but for one circumstance, of which she told him later. Of her father she spoke little, save that he had often beaten her; of her mother more tenderly—it seemed they loved each other—but with an air of constraint. Her parents were undoubtedly in ill-savour throughout the tithing; her father, a rogue who would cut a throat as easily as a purse, her mother, a wise woman patently in league with the devil. But she said that, although she could not tell the reason of it, the Abbot had protected them from judgment many a time—whether it was her father for breaking the forest-law, deer-stealing, wood-cutting, or keeping running dogs; or her mother from the hatred and suspicion of the Malbank people, on account of her sorceries and enchantments. More especially did the Abbot take notice of her, and, while he never hesitated to expose her to every infamous reproach or report, and (apparently) to take a delight in them, yet guarded her from the direct consequences as if she had been sacred. This her parents knew very well, and never scrupled to turn to their advantage. For when hard put to it they would bring her forward between them, set her before the Abbot, and say, "For the sake of the child, my lord, let us go." Which the Abbot always did.

Cried Prosper here, "What did he want, this fatherly Abbot?"

"My lord," said Isoult, "he sought to have me put away."

"Well, child," Prosper chuckled, "he has got his wish."

"He wished it long ago, lord," she said; "before I was marriageable."

"And it was not to thy taste?"

"No, lord."

"It was not of that then that thou wert La Desirous?"

"No, lord," said Isoult in a low voice.

"So I thought," was Prosper's comment to himself. "The friar was out."

She went on to tell him of her service with the Abbey as laundry-maid, then as scullery-girl; then she spoke of Galors. She told him how this monk had seen her by chance in the Abbey kitchen; how he sought to get too well acquainted with her; how she had fled the service and refused to go back. Nevertheless, and in spite of that, she had had no peace because of him. He chanced upon her again when she was among the crowd at the Alms Gate waiting for the dole, had kept her to the end, and spoken with her then and there, telling her all his desire, opening all his wicked heart. She fled from him again for the time; but every day she must needs go up for the dole, so every day she saw him and endured his importunities. This had lasted up to the very day she saw Prosper: at that time he had nearly prevailed upon her by his own frenzy and her terror of the Abbot's, threat. She never doubted the truth of what he told her, for the Abbot's privy mind had been declared to much the same purpose to Mald her mother.

"But this privy mind of his," said Prosper, "must have swung wide from its first leaning, which seems to have been to preserve thee. Could he not have ruined thee without a charter? An Abbot and a cook-maid! Could he not have ruined thee without a rope?"

"My lord," she replied, "I think he was merciful. I was to be hanged by his desire; but there was worse with Galors."

"Ah, I had forgotten him," Prosper said.

She had spoken all this in a low voice through which ran a trembling, as when a great string on a harp is touched and thrills all the music. Prosper thought she would have said more if she dared. Although she spoke great scorn of herself and hid nothing, yet he knew without asking that she had been truthful when she told him she was pure. He looked at her again and made assurance double; yet he wondered how it could be.

"Tell me, Isoult," he said presently, "when thou sawest me come into the quarry, didst thou know that I should take thee away?"

"Yes, lord," said she, "when I saw your face I knew it."

"What of my face, child? Hadst thou seen me before that day?"

She did not answer this.

"It is likely enough," he went on. "For in my father's day we often rode, I and my brothers, with him in the Abbey fees, hawking or hunting the deer. And if thou wert gooseherd or shepherdess thou mightest easily have seen us."

Isoult said, "My lord, if I had seen thee twenty times before or none, I had trusted thee when I saw thy face."

"How so, child?" asked he.

For answer to this she looked quickly up at him for a moment, and then hung her head, blushing. He had had time to see that dog's look of trust again in her eyes.

"My wife takes kindly to me!" he thought. "Let us hope she will find Gracedieu even more to her mind."

They rode on, being now very near the actual forest. Prosper began again with his questions.

"What enmity," he said, "the Abbot had for thee, Isoult, or what lurking pity, or what grain of doubt, I cannot understand. It seems that he wished thy ruin most devoutly, but that being a Christian and a man of honour he sought to compass it in a Christian and gentlemanly way. Might not marriage have appeared to him the appointed means? And should I not tell him that thou art ruined according to his aspirations?"

"Lord," said she, "he will know it."

"Saints and angels!" Prosper cried, "who will tell him? Not Brother Bonaccord, who loves no monks."

"Nay, lord, but my mother will tell him for the ruin of Galors, who hates her and is hated again. Moreover, there are many in Malbank who will find it out soon enough."

"How is that, child?"

"Lord, many of them sought to have me."

"I can well believe it," said Prosper; and after a pause he said again—"I would like to meet this Galors of thine out of his frock. He looked a long-armed, burly rogue; it seemed that there might be some fighting in him. Further, some chastisement of him, if it could conveniently be done, would seem to be my duty, since he has touched at thy honour, which is now mine. I should certainly like to meet him unfrocked."

"Lord,'" answered the girl, "that will come soon enough. I pray that thine arm be strong, for he is very fierce, and a terrible man in Malbank, more often armed than in his robe."

"He must be an indifferent monk," Prosper said; "God seems not well served in such a man's life. Holy Church would be holier without him."

"He is a great hunter, my lord," said Isoult.

"It would certainly seem so," said Prosper grimly. "Where should I find him likeliest?"

"Lord, look for him in Martle Brush."

"Ah! And where is that?"

"Lord, it is here by," said Isoult.

Prosper looked about him sharply. He found that they had left the heath, and were riding down a smooth grassy place into a deep valley. The decline was dotted with young oak-trees, sparse at the top but thickening in clusters and ranks lower down. Between the stems, but at some distance, he could see a herd of deer feeding on the rank grass by a brook at the bottom. Beyond the brook again the wood grew still thicker with holly trees and yews interspersed with the oaks: the land he could see rose more abruptly on that side, and was densely wooded to the top of another ridge as high as that which he and Isoult descended. The ridge itself was impenetrably dark with a forest gloom which never left it at this season of the year. As he studied the place, Martle Brush as he supposed it to be, he saw a hart in the herd stop feeding and lift his head to snuff the air, then with his antlers thrown back, trot off along the brook, and all the herd behind him. This set him thinking; he knew the deer had not winded him. The breeze set from them rather, over the valley, from the north-east. He said nothing to his companion, but kept his eyes open as they began to descend deeper into the gorge. Presently he saw three or four crows which had been wheeling over the tops of the trees come and settle on a dead oak by the brook-side. Still there was no sign of a man. Again he glanced down at Isoult; this time she too was alert, with a little flush in her cheeks, but no words on her lips to break the silence they kept. So they descended the steep place, picking their way as best they could among the loose rocks and boulders, with eyes painfully at gaze, yet with no reward, until they reached a place where the track went narrowly between great rooted rocks with holly trees thick on either side. Immediately before them was the brook, shallow and fordable, with muddy banks; the track ran on across it and steeply up the opposite ridge. Midway of this Prosper now saw a knight fully armed in black (but with a white plume to his helmet), sitting a great black horse, his spear erect and his shield before him. He could even make out the cognizance upon it—three white wicket-gates argent on a field sable—but not the motto. The shield set him thinking where he could have seen it before, for he knew it perfectly well. Then suddenly Isoult said, "Lord, this is Galors the Monk."

"Ho, ho!" said Prosper, "is this Galors? I like him better than I did."

"Lord," she asked in a tremble, "what wilt thou do?"

"Do!" he cried; "are there so many things to do? You are not afraid, child?"

"No, lord, I am not afraid," she replied, and looked down at her belt.

"Now, Isoult," said Prosper, "you are to stay here on your beast while I go down and clear the road."

She obeyed him at once, and sat very still looking at Galors and at Prosper, who rode forward to the level ground by the ford. There he stopped to see what the other man would be at. Galors played the impenetrable part which had served him so well with the Abbot Richard, in other words, did nothing but sit where he was with his spear erect, like a bronze figure on a bridge. Impassivity had always been the strength of Galors; women had bruised themselves against it: but Prosper had little to do with women's ways.

"Sir, why do you bar my passage?" he sang out, irrepressibly cheerful at present. Galors never answered him a word. Prosper divined him at this; he was to climb the hill, and so be at the double disadvantage of having no spear and of being below him that had one. "The pale rascal means to make this a game of skittles," he thought to himself. "We shall see, my man. In the mean time I wish I knew your shield." So saying he forded the brook, stayed, called out again, "Whose shield is that, Galors?" and again got no reply. "Black dog!" cried he in a rage, "take your vantage and expect no more." Whereupon he set his horse at the hill and rode up with his shield before him.

The black knight feutred his spear, clapped spurs to his horse's flanks, and bore down the hill. He rode magnificently: horse and man had the impetus of a charging bull, and it looked ill for the man below. But Prosper had learned a trick from his father, which he in turn had had at Acre from the Moslems in one of the intervals of the business there. In those days men fought like heroes, but between whiles remembered that they were gentlemen and good fellows pitted against others equally happy in these respects.

The consequence was that many a throat was cut by many a hand which the day before had poured out wine for its delight, and nobody was any the worse. The infidels loved Mahomet, but they loved a horse too, and Baron Jocelyn was not the man to forget a lesson in riding. So soon, therefore, as Galors was upon him, Prosper slid his left foot from the stirrup and slipt round his horse almost to the belly, clinging with his shield arm to the bow of the saddle. The spear struck his shield at a tangent and glanced off. It was a bad miss for Galors, since horse and man drove down the incline and were floundering in the brook before they could stay. Prosper whipped round to see Galors mired, was close on his quarter and had cut through the shank of the spear, close to the guard, in a trice.

"Fight equal, my friend, and you will fight more at ease in the long run," was all he said. Galors let fly an oath at him, furious. He drew his great sword and cut at him with all his force; Prosper parried and let out at his shoulder. He got in between the armour plates; first blow went to him. This did not improve Galors' temper or mend his fighting. There was a sharp rally in the brook, some shrewd knocks passed. The lighter man and horse had all the advantage; Galors never reached his enemy fairly. He set himself to draw Prosper out of the slush of mud and water, and once on firmer ground went more warily to work. Then a chance blow from Prosper struck his horse on the crest and went deep. The beast stumbled and fell with his rider upon him both lay still.

"A broken neck," thought Prosper, cursing his luck. Galors never moved. "What an impassive rogue it is!" Prosper cried, with all his anger clean gone from him. He dismounted and went to where his man lay, threw his sword on the grass beside him, and proceeded to unlace Galors's hauberk. Galors sprang up and sent Prosper flying; he set his heel on the sword blade and broke it short. Then he turned his own upon the unarmed man. "By God, the man is for a murder!" Prosper grew white with a cold rage: he was on his feet, the flame of his anger licked up his poverty: Galors had little chance. Prosper made a quick rush and drove at the monk with his shield arm, using the shield like an axe; he broke down his guard, got at close quarters, dropt his shield and caught Galors under the arms. They swayed and rocked together like storm-driven trees, Prosper transported with his new-lighted rage, Galors struggling to justify his treachery by its only excuse. Below his armpits he felt Prosper's grip upon him; he was encumbered with shield and sword, both useless—the sword, in fact, sawing the air. Then they fell together, Prosper above; and that was the end of the bout. Prosper slipped out his poniard and drove it in between the joints of the gorget. Then he got up, breathing hard, and looked at his enemy as he lay jerking on the grass, and at the bright stream coming from his neck.

"The price of treachery is heavy," said he. "I ought to kill him. And there are villainies behind that to be reckoned with, to say nothing of all the villainies to do when that hole shall be stuffed. The shield—ah, the shield! No, monk, on second thoughts, I will not kill you yet. It would be dealing as you dealt, it would prevent our meeting again; it would cut me off all chance of learning the history of your arms. White wicket-gates! Where, under heaven's eye, have I been brought up against three white wicket-gates? Ha! there is a motto too." *Entra per me*, he read, and was no wiser. "This man and I will meet again," he said. "Meantime I will remember *Entra per me*." He raised his voice to call to Isoult—"Come, child; the way is clear enough."

She came over the brook at once, alighted on the further side, and came creeping up to her husband to kneel before him as once before that morning; but he put his hand on her shoulder to stay her. "Come," he said, smiling, "no more ceremony between you and me, my dear. Rather let us get forward out of the reach of hue-and-cry. For when the foresters find him that will be the next move in the game." To Galors he turned with a "By your leave, my friend," and took his sword; then having put Isoult upon her donkey and mounted his own beast, he led the way up the ridge wondering where they had best turn to avoid hue-and-cry. Isoult, who guessed his thoughts, told him of the minster at Gracedieu.

Sanctuary attached to the Church, she said, as all the woodlanders knew.

"Excellent indeed," Prosper cried; "that jumps with what I had determined on before. Moreover, I suppose that Gracedieu is outside the Malbank fee?"

"Yes, lord, it is far beyond that."

"And how far is it to Gracedieu?"

"It is the journey of two days and nights, my lord."

"Well," said he, "then those nights we must sleep in the forest. How will that suit you, child?"

"Ah, my lord," breathed the girl, "I have very often slept there."

"And what shall we do for food, Isoult?"

"I will provide for that, my lord."

CHAPTER IX

THE BLOOD-CHASE AND THE LOVE-CHASE

It was by this time high noon, hot and still. Having climbed the ridge, they found themselves at the edge of a dense beech-wood, to which there appeared no end. From their vantage-ground they could see that the land sloped very gradually away into the distance; upon it the giant trees stood like pillars of a church, whose floor was brown with the waste and litter of a hundred years. Long alleys of shade stretched out on all sides of them into the dark unknown of Mid-Morgraunt; there seemed either no way or countless ways before them, and one as good as the other. They rested themselves in sheer bewilderment, ate of the bread and apples which Isoult had brought with her; then Prosper found out how tired he was.

"Wife," said he, "if all the devils in Christendom were after me it would not keep me awake. I must sleep for half-an-hour."

"Sleep, sleep, my lord; I will take the watch," said Isoult, longing to serve him.

He unlaced his helm and body-armour without more ado, and laid his head in the girl's lap. She had very cool and soft hands, and now she put one of them upon his forehead for a solace, peering down nervously to see how he would take such daring from his servant. What she saw comforted her not a little, indeed she thought herself like to die of joy. He wondered again that such delicate little hands should have been reared on Spurnt Heath, and endured the service of the lowest; it was a half-comical content that made him send her a smiling acknowledgment; but she took it for a friendly message between them, and though the laughter in his eyes brought a mist over hers she was content. Prosper dropped asleep. Through the soft veil of her happiness she watched him patiently and still as a mouse. She was serving him at last; she could dare look tenderly at him when he was asleep—and she did. Something of the mother, something of the manumitted slave, something of the dumb creature brought up against a crisis which only speech can make tolerable,—something of these three lay in her wet eyes; she wanted ineffably more, but she was happy (she thought). She was not apt to look further than this, that she was in love, and suffered to serve her master. The dull torment of her life past, the doubts or despair which might beset and perplex her life to come, were all blurred and stilled by this boon of service, as a rosy mist makes beautiful the space of time between a day of storms and a dripping night. When the roaring of the wind dies down and the sun rays out in a clear pool of heaven, men have ease and forget their buffetings; they walk abroad to bathe their vexed souls in the evening calms. So now Isoult la Desirous, with no soul to speak of, bathed her quickened instincts. She felt at peace with a world which had used her but ill so long as she was in touch with all that was noble in it. This glorious youth, this almost god, suffered her to touch his brow, to look at him, to throne his head, to adore him. Oh, wonderful! And as tears are never far from a girl's eyes, and never slow to answer the messages of her heart, so hers flowed freely and quietly as from a brimming well; nor did she check them or wish them away, but let them fall where they would until they encroached upon the privileged hand. *Lèse majesté!* She threw her head back and shook them from her; she was more guarded how she did after that.

Then she heard something over the valley below which gave her heart-beats a new tune. A great ado down there, horses, dogs, voices of men shouting for more. She guessed in a moment that the foresters had come upon the body of Galors, knew that hue-and-cry was now only a question of hours, and all her joys at an end. She took her hand from Prosper's forehead, and he awoke then and there, and smiled up at her.

"Lord," said she, "it is time for us to be going, for they have found Dom Galors; and at the Abbey they have many slot-hounds."

"Good, my child," he answered. "I am ready for anything in the world. Let us go."

He got up instantly and armed himself; they mounted their animals and plunged into the great shade of the beeches. All the steering they could do now was by such hints of the sun as they could glean here and there. Prosper by himself would have been fogged in a mile, but Isoult had not lived her fifteen years of wild life for nothing: she had the fox's instinct for an earth, and the hare's for doubling on a trail. The woods spoke to her as they spoke to each other, as they spoke to the beasts, or the beasts among themselves. What indeed was this poor little doubtful wretch but one of those, with a stray itching to be more? Soul or none, she had an instinct which Prosper discovered and learned to trust. For the rest of the day she tacitly led the knight-at-arms in the way he should go.

But with all her help they made a slow pace. The forest grew more and more dense; there seemed no opening, no prospect of an opening. She knew what must be in store for them if the Abbot had uncoupled his bloodhounds, so she strained every nerve in her young body, listened to every murmur or swish of the trees, every one of the innumerable, inexplicable noises a great wood gives forth. She suffered, indeed, intensely; yet Prosper never knew it. He played upon her, quite unconsciously, by wondering over the difficulties of the road, the slowness of their going, the probable speed of the Abbot's dogs and foresters, and so on. Her meekness and cheerful diligence delighted him. The nuns of Gracedieu, he promised himself, should know what a likely novice he was bringing them. He should miss her, *pardieu*! after two or three days' companionship. So they struggled on.

Towards the time of dusk, which was very soon in that gloomy solitude, Isoult heard in the far distance the baying of the dogs, and began to tremble, knowing too well what all that meant. Yet she said nothing. Prosper rode on, singing softly to himself as his custom was, his head carried high, his light and alert look taking in every dark ambush as a thing to be conquered—very lordly to look upon. The girl, who had never seen his like, adored him, thought him a god; the fact was, she had no other. Therefore, as one does not lightly warn the blessed gods, she rode silent but quaking by his side, with her ears still on the strain for the coming danger, and all her mind set on the fear that Prosper would find out. Above all she heard a sound which shocked her more, her own heart knocking at her side.

Then at last Prosper reined up, listening too. "Hush!" he said, "what is that?"

This was a new sound, more hasty and murmurous than any girl's heart, and much more dreadful than the music of the still distant hounds; it was very near, a rushing and pattering sound, as of countless beasts running. Isoult knew it.

"Wolves!" she said; "let be, there is no harm from them save in the winter."

As she spoke a grey bitch-wolf came trotting through the trees, swiftly but in pain, and breathing very short. She was covered with slaver and red foam, her tongue lolled out at the side of her mouth long and loose, she let blood freely from a wound in the throat, and one of her ears was torn and bleeding. She looked neither to right nor left, did not stay to smell at the scent of the horse; all her pains were spent to keep running. She broke now and again into a rickety canter, but for the most part trotted straight forward, with many a stumble and missed step, all picked up with indescribable feverish diligence; and as she went her blood flowed, and her panting kept pace with her padding feet. So she came and so went, hunted by what followed close upon her; the murmur of the host, the host itself—dogs and bitches in a pack, making great pace. They came on at a gallop, a sea of wolves that surged restlessly, yet were one rolling tide. Here and there a grinning head cast up suddenly out of the press seemed like the broken crest of some hastier wave impatient with his fellows; so they snarled, jostled, and snapped at each other. Then one, playing choragus, would break into a howl, and there would be a long anthem of howls until the forest rang with the terror; but the haste, the panting and the padding of feet were the most dreadful, because incessant; the thrust head would be whelmed, the sharp voice drowned in howls; the grey tide and the lapping of it never stopped.

The fugitives watched this chase, in which they might have read a parable of their own affair, sweep past them like a bad dream. In the dead hush that followed they heard what was a good deal more significant for them, the baying of the dogs.

"What now?" said Prosper to himself, "there are the dogs. If I make haste they can make it better; if I stay, how on earth shall I keep my convoy out of their teeth?"

It was too late to wonder; even at that moment Isoult gasped and caught at his arm, leaning from her saddle to cling to him as she had done once before. But this was a danger not to be shamed away by a man armed. He followed her look, and saw the first dog come on with his nose to the ground. A thought struck him. "Wait," he said.

Sure enough, the great dog hit on the line of the wolves and got the blood in his nostrils. He was puzzled, his tail went like a flag in a gale as he nosed it out.

Prosper watched him keenly, it was touch-and-go, but never troubled his breath. "Take your choice, friend," he said. The dog beat to and fro for some long minutes. He could not deny himself—he followed the wolves.

"That love-chase is like to be our salvation," said Prosper. "Wait now. Here are some more of the Abbot's friends." It was as good as a play to him—a hunter; but to Isoult, the wild little outcast, it was deadly work. Like all her class, she held dogs in more fear than their masters. You may cajole a man; to a dog the very attempt at it is a damning proof against you.

As Prosper had predicted, the dogs, coming on by twos and threes, got entangled in the cross-trail. They hesitated over it, circled about it as the first had done, and like him they followed the hotter and fresher scent. One, however, in a mighty hurry, ran clean through it, and singled out his own again. They saw him coming; in his time he saw them. He stopped, threw up his head, and bayed a succession of deep bell-notes at them, enough to wake the dead.

"I must deal with this beast," Prosper said. "Leave me to manage him, and stay you here." He dismounted, ungirt his sword, which he gave to Isoult to hold, then began to run through the wood as if he was afraid. This brought the dog on furiously; in fifty yards he was up with his quarry. Prosper went on running; the dog chose his time, and sprang for his throat. Prosper, who had been waiting for this, ducked at the same minute; his dagger was in his hand. He struck upwards at the dog as he rose, and ripped his belly open. "That was your last jump, my friend," quoth he, "but I hope there are no more of you. It is a game that not always answers."

It was while he was away upon this errand that Isoult thought she saw a tall woman in a black cloak half-hidden behind a tree. The woman, she could have sworn, stood there in the dusk looking fixedly at her; it was too dark to distinguish anything but the white disk of a face and the black mass she made in her cloak, yet there was that about her, some rigid aspect of attention, which frightened the girl. She turned her head for a moment to see Prosper homing, and when she looked again into the trees there was certainly no woman. She thought she must have fancied it all, and dismissed the thought without saying anything to Prosper.

They took up their journey again, safe from dogs for the time. The music had died away in the distance; they knew that if the wolf-pack were caught there would be work enough for more hounds than the Abbey could furnish. Then it grew dark, and Isoult weary and heavy with sleep. She swayed in her saddle.

"Ah," said Prosper, "we will stay here. You shall sleep while I keep watch."

"It is very still, my lord. Wilt thou not let me watch for a little?" she asked.

Prosper laughed. "There are many things a man's wife can do for him, my dear," he said, "but she cannot fight dogs or men. And she cannot sleep with one eye open Eat what you have, and then shut your pair of eyes. You are not afraid for me?"

Isoult looked at him quickly. Then she said—"My lord is—," and stopped confused.

"What is thy lord, my girl?" asked he.

"He is good to his servant," she whispered in her low thrilled voice.

They ate what bread was left, and drank a little water. Before all was finished Isoult was nodding. Prosper bestirred himself to do the best he could for her; he collected a heap of dried leaves, laid his cloak upon them, and picked up Isoult to lay her upon the cloak. His arms about her woke her up. Scarce knowing what she did, dreaming possibly of her mother, she put up her face towards his; but if Prosper noticed it, no errant mercy from him sent her to bed comforted. He put her down, covered her about with the cloak, and patted her shoulder with an easy—"Good-night, my lass." This was cold cheer to the poor girl, who had to be content with his ministry of the cloak. It was too dark to tell if he was looking at her as he stooped; and ah, heavens! why should he look at her? The dark closed round his form, stiffly erect, sitting on the root of the great tree which made a tent for them both, and then it claimed her soul. She lost her trouble in sleep; he kept the watch all night.

CHAPTER X

FOREST ALMS

Towards the grey of the morning, seeing that the whole forest was at peace, with no sign of dogs or men all that night, and now even a rest from the far howling of the wolves, Prosper's head dropt to his breast. In a few seconds he slept profoundly. Isoult awoke and saw that he slept: she lay watching him, longing but not daring. When she saw that he looked blue and pinched about the cheekbones, that his cheeks were yellow where they should be red, and grey where they had been white, she knew he was cold; and her humbleness was not proof against this justification of her desires. She crept out of her snug nest, crawled towards her lord and felt his hands; they were ice. "Asleep he is mine," she thought. She picked up the cloak, then crept again towards him, seated herself behind and a little above him, threw the cloak over both and snuggled it well in. She put her arms about him and drew him close to her bosom. His head fell back at her gentle constraint; so he lay like a child at the breast. The mother in her was wild and throbbing. Stooped over him she pored into his face. A divine pity, a divine sense of the power of life over death, of waking over sleep, drew her lower and nearer. She kissed his face—the lids of his eyes, his forehead and cheeks. Like an unwatched bird she foraged at will, like a hardy sailor touched at every port but one. His mouth was too much his own, too firm; it kept too much of his sovereignty absolute. Otherwise she was free to roam; and she roamed, very much to his material advantage, since the love that made her rosy to the finger-tips, in time warmed him also. He slept long in her arms.

She began to be very hungry.

"He too will be hungry when he wakes," she thought; "what shall I do? We have nothing to eat." She looked down wistfully at his head where it lay pillowed. "What would I not give him of mine?" The thought flooded her. But what could she do?

She heard the pattering of dry leaves, the crackle of dry twigs snapt, and looking up, saw a herd of deer feeding in a glade not very far off.

Idly as she watched them, it came home to her that there were hinds among them with calves. One she noticed in particular feed a little apart, having two calves near her which had just begun to nibble a little grass. Vaguely wondering still over her plight, she pictured her days of shepherding in the downs where food had often failed her, and the ewes perforce mothered another lamb. That hind's udder was full of milk: a sudden thought ran like wine through her blood. She slid from Prosper, got up very softly, took her cup, and went towards the browsing deer. The hind looked up (like all the herd) but did not start nor run. A brief gaze satisfied it that here was no enemy, neither a stranger to the forest walks; it fell-to again, and suffered Isoult to come quite close, even to lay her hand upon its neck. Then she stood for a while stroking the red hind, while all the herd watched her. She knelt before the beast, clasping both arms about its neck; she fondled it with her face, as if asking the boon she would have. Some message passed between them, some assurance, for she let go of the hind's neck and crawled on hands and knees towards the udder. The deer never moved, though it turned its head to watch her. She took the teat in her mouth, sucked and drew milk. The herd stood all about her motionless; the hind nuzzled her as if she had been one of its own calves; so she was filled.

Next she had to fill her cup. This was much more difficult. The hind must be soothed and fondled again, there must be no shock on either side. She started the flow with her mouth; then she knelt against the animal with her head pressed to its side, took the teat in her hand and succeeded. She filled the cup with Prosper's breakfast. She got up, kissed the hind between the eyes, stroked its neck many times, and went tiptoe back to her lord and master. She found him still sound asleep, so sat quietly watching him till he should wake, with the cup held against her heart to keep it warm.

Broad daylight and a chance beam of sun through the trees woke him at last. It would be about seven o'clock. He stretched portentously, and sat up to look about him; so he encountered her tender eyes before she had been able to subdue their light.

"Good-morning, Isoult," said he. "Have I been long asleep?"

"A few hours only, lord."

"I am hungry. I must eat something."

"Lord, I have milk for thee."

He took the cup she tendered, looking at her.

"Drink first, my child," he said.

"Lord, I have drunk already."

He drained the cup without further ado.

"Good milk," he said when he had done. He took these things, you see, very much as they came.

His next act was to kneel face to the sun and begin his prayers. Something made him stop; he turned him to his wife.

"Hast thou said thy prayers, Isoult?"

"No, lord," said she, reddening.

"Come then and pray with me. It is a good custom."

She obeyed him so far as to kneel down by his side. He began again. She had nothing to say, so he stopped again.

"Dost thou forget thy prayers since thou art a wife, Isoult?"

"Lord, I know none," said she with a shameful face.

"Thou art not a Christian then?"

"If a Christian prays, my lord, I am not a Christian."

"But thou hast been baptized?"

"Yes, lord."

"How knowest thou?"

"The Lord Abbot once reproached me before my parents that I had disgraced Holy Baptism; and my father beat me soundly for it, saying that of all his afflictions that was the hardest to bear. This he did in the presence of the Lord Abbot himself. Therefore I know that I have been beaten for the sake of my baptism."

Prosper was satisfied.

"It is enough, Isoult. Thou art certainly a Christian. Nevertheless, such an one should pray (and women as well as men), even though it may very well be that he knows not what he is saying. Prayer is a great mystery, look you. Yet this I know, that it is also a great comfort. For remember that if a Christian prays— knowing or not knowing the meaning of the act and the upshot of it—he is very sure it is acceptable to Saint Mary, and through her to God Almighty Himself. So much so, indeed, that he is emboldened thereafter to add certain impertinences and urgent desires of his own, which Saint Mary is good enough to hear, and by her intercession as often as not to win to be accepted. Some add a word or two to their saint or guardian, others invoke all the saints in a body; but it is idle to do one or any of these things without you have prayed first. So you must by all means learn to pray. Sit down by me here and I will teach you."

She sat as close to him as she dared on the trunk of the beech, while he taught her to say after him, *"Pater noster qui es in coelis"*, and *"Ave Maria gratia plena."* In this way they spent a full hour or more, going over and over the Latin words till she was as perfect as he. In the stress of the task, which interested Prosper vastly, their hands met more than once; finally Prosper's settled down over hers and held it. In time he caught the other. Isoult's heart beat wildly; she had never been so happy. When she had all the words pat they knelt down and prayed together, with the best results.

"Now, child," said Prosper, "you may add what you choose of your own accord; and be sure that our Lady will hear you. It is a great merit to be sure of this. The greater the Christian the surer he is. I also will make my petition. You have no patron?"

"No, lord, I have never heard of such an one."

"I recommend you to Saint Isidore. His name is the nearest to yours that I can remember. For the rest, he is very strong. Ask, then, what you will now, my child, and doubt nothing."

Isoult bent her head and shut her eyes for the great essay. What could she say? What did she want? She was kneeling by Prosper's side, his hand held hers a happy prisoner.

"Mary, let him take me! Saint Isidore, let him take me—all, all, all!" This was what she panted to Heaven.

Prosper prayed, "My Lady, I beseech thee a good ending to this adventure which I have undertaken lightly, it may be, but with an honest heart. Grant also a good and honourable end to myself, and to this my wife, who is a Christian without knowing it, and by the help of thy servants at Gracedieu shall be a better. *Per Christum dominum*, etc."

Then he crossed himself, and taught Isoult to do the same, and the great value of the exercise.

"Now, child," he said, "I have done thee a better turn in teaching thee to pray and sign thyself meekly and devoutly than ever I did by wedding thee in the cottage. Thy soul, my dear, thy soul is worth a hundred times thy pretty person. Saint Bernard, I understand, says, 'My son, think of the worms when thou art disposed to cherish thyself in a looking-glass.' It is to go far. Saint Bernard was a monk, and it is a monk's way to think of nastiness; but he was right in the main. Your soul is the chief part of you. Now to finish: when we are at Gracedieu thou shalt confess and go to Mass. Then thou wilt be as good a Christian as I am."

"Lord, is that all I must do?" she asked meekly.

Prosper grew grave. He put his hand on the girl's shoulder, as he said—

"Deal justly, live cleanly, breathe sweet breath. Praise God in thy heart when He is kind, bow thy head and knees when He is angry; look for Him to be near thee at all times. Do this, and beyond it trust thy heart."

"Lord, I will do it."

"Thou art a good child, Isoult. I am pleased with thee," he said, and kissed her. She turned her face lest he should see that she was crying. Soon afterwards they set off towards Gracedieu.

The day, the night, the next morning found them on the journey. They had to travel slowly, could indeed have made better pace on foot; for Mid-Morgraunt is a tangle of brush and undergrowth, and the swamps (which are many and of unknown depth) have all to be circled.

There seemed, however, to be no further pursuit; they could go at their ease, for they met nobody. On the other hand, they met with no food more solid than milk. There were deer in plenty. Isoult was able to feed herself and her husband, and keep both from exhaustion, without suspicion from him or much cost to herself. The second time of doing it, it is true, she went tremblingly to work, and was like to bungle it. What one may do on the flood one may easily miss on the ebb; moreover, it was night-time, she was tired, and not sure of herself. Nevertheless, she was fed, and Prosper was fed. Next morning she was as cool as you choose, singled out her hind as she walked into the herd, went on all fours and sucked like a calf. She grew nice, indeed. The beast she tried first had rough milk; this would do for her well enough, but my lord must have of the best. She chose another with great care, played milk-maid to her, and drew Prosper full measure.

He, her sovereign, took every event with equal mind, and placidly, whether it was a wedding, a fight, or a miraculous fountain of milk. If she had drawn his food from herself he would not have questioned her; if it had been her last ounce of life he would not have thanked her the more. You cannot blame him for this. To begin with, he knew nothing of her or her doings when he was asleep or on the watch. And a young man is a prodigal always, of another's goods besides his own, while a young woman is his banker, never so rich as when he overdraws. Deprived of him by her own act, his wife in name, she was his servant in reality. His servant and, just now, his sumpter-beast. Very wistfully she served him, but very diligently, only asking that he should neither thank nor blame her. It very seldom occurred to him to do either; but so sure as he threw a "good child" at her, she had a lump in her throat and smarting eyes. True, she had her little rewards, to be enjoyed when he could not guess that her heart was all in a flutter, or see that her cheeks were wet. Night and morning they said their *Pater Noster* and *Ave Maria*, out of which (although she understood them as little as he did) she did not fail to suck the comfort he had promised her. She learned also to speak familiarly to Saint Isidore and Madonna. This served her in good stead later in her career. Meantime, night and morning they knelt side by side, their arms touched, sometimes their hands strayed and joined company. Then hers ended by resting where they were, as in a warm nest. Pray what more could a girl ask of the Christian faith?

By sunset of the second day passed in this fashion they were before the great west front of Gracedieu Minster, knocking at the Mercy Door. It opened. They were safe for the present, and Prosper felt his horizon enlarged.

CHAPTER XI

SANCTUARY

After Vespers that day Prosper demanded an audience of the Lady Abbess, and had it. He found her a handsome, venerable old lady, at peace with all the world and, so far as that comported with her religion, a woman of it. She had held high rank in it by right of birth; she knew what it could do, and what not do, of good and evil. Now that she was old enough to call its denizens her children, she folded her hands and played grandmother. Naturally, therefore, she knew Prosper by name; for that, as much as his frank looks, she made him welcome. She did not ask it, but he could see that she expected to be enlightened upon the subject of Isoult—doubtful company for a knight; so having made up his mind how much he could afford to tell her, he did not waste time in preliminaries.

"Madam," said he, after the first greetings of good company, "a knight adventuring in this forest cannot see very far before his face, and may make error worse by what he does to solve error. If by mischance such a thing should befall him, he must not faint, but persist until he has loosed not only the knot he has tied himself, but that as well which he has made more inexorable."

The Lady Abbess bowed very graciously, waiting for him to be done with phrases. Prosper went on—

"I found this damsel in the hands of a knave, who offered her a choice of death

64

or dishonour. I took her into my own, and so far have spared her either. The rascal who had her now lies with a split gullet many leagues from here, in such a condition that he will trouble her no more I hope. Add to this, that I have questioned her, and find her honest, meek, and a Christian. She is, as you, will see for yourself, very good-looking: it was near to be her undoing. I cannot tell you, nor will you ask me, first, her name (for I am not certain of it), second, the name of her enemy (for that would involve a great company whereof he is a most unworthy member), nor third, what means I employed to insure immunity for her body, and honour for my own as well as hers; for this would involve us all. In time I shall certainly achieve the adventure thus thrust upon me, but for the present my intention is for High March Castle, and the Countess of Hauterive, who was a friend of my father's, and is, as I know, one of yours. If you will permit it I will leave Isoult with you. She will serve you well and faithfully in a hundred ways; she is very handy and quick, a good girl, anxious to be a better. If you can make a nun of her, well and good: by that means the adventure will achieve itself. I leave you to judge, however; but if you cannot help me there, let her stay with you for a year. After that I will fetch her and achieve the adventure otherwise."

The Abbess smiled at the young man's judicial airs, which very ill concealed the elevation of his mind. She only said that she would gladly help him in the honourable task he had set himself, and doubted not but that the girl would prove a good and useful servant to the convent. But she added—

"It is easy to see, sir, that as a Christian your part is of the Church militant. I would remind you that a nun is not made in a year."

"I mentioned a year because it was a long time, and for the sake of an example of what I had designed," said Prosper calmly. "However, if it takes longer, and you think well of it, I shall not complain."

"And what does the girl say?" the Abbess inquired. "For some sort of vocation is necessary for the religious life, you must understand."

"I have not yet spoken to Isoult about it," he replied. "She will do what I tell her. She is a very good girl."

"I think I should speak to her myself," said the Abbess, not without decision.

"So you shall," Prosper agreed; "but it will be better that I prepare her. If you will allow me I will do so at once, as I should leave early to-morrow."

"There goes a young man who should climb high," said the Lady Abbess, as her guest paid his respects.

Prosper went into the cloister, and found Isoult sitting with the mistress of the novices and her girls who were at work there. She looked tired and constrained, but lit up when he came in, firing a girl's signals in her cheeks. As for her eyes, the moment Prosper appeared they never wavered from him.

He excused himself to the nun, saying that he had business with Isoult, which by leave of the Abbess he might transact in the guest chamber. One of the novices conducted him; Isoult followed meekly.

Once alone with her, Prosper sat down by the fire and told Isoult to fetch a stool and sit by him. She did as she was bid, sat at his knee, folded her hands in her lap, and waited for him to begin, looking thoughtfully into the fire. Prosper laid a hand upon her shoulder.

"Isoult," he said, "We have got our sanctuary, as you see, and for all that appears need neither have sought nor claimed it. We have had no pursuit worthy the name. It is evident to me that they have calculated the deserts of Master Galors at Malbank, and put it at our figure. Nevertheless, I am glad to be at Gracedieu, for I had decided upon it before ever we met and drubbed that monk. When I saved you from being hanged I saved your body; now I shall think of your soul's health, which (the Church tells us) is far more precious. For it would seem that a man can do without a body, but by no means without a soul. Now, I have married you, Isoult, and by that act saved your body; but I have not as yet done any more, for though I have heard many things of marriage, I never heard that it was good for the soul. Moreover, for marriage to be tolerable, I suppose love is necessary,"—Isoult started,—"and that we certainly know nothing about it." Isoult shivered very slightly, so slightly that Prosper did not notice it. "I have thought a great deal about you, my child," he continued, "since I married you, and something also of myself, my destinies, and duties as a knight and good Christian. I have decided to go at once to High March, where I shall find the Countess Isabel. She, being an old friend of my family's, will no doubt take me into her service. I shall fight for her of course, I shall win honour and renown, very likely a fief. With that behind me I shall go to Starning and trounce my brother Malise, baron or no baron. I shall bring him to his knees in a cold sweat, and then I shall say—`Get up, you ass, and learn not to meddle again with a gentleman, and son of a gentleman.'

"In addition to that business I have a certain matter to inquire into concerning a lady whom I met in the purlieus of this forest, and a dead man she had with her. I do not like the looks of that case. Certainly I must inquire into it, and do what pertains. There may be other things needing my direction, but if there are I have forgotten them for the moment.

"You will think that in all this I have also forgotten you, child. Far from it. Listen now. You cannot of course go to High March. You would not be happy there, nor am I in a position to make you happy. No, no; you shall stay here with the good nuns, and be useful to them, and happy with them. You shall learn to serve God, so that in time you may become a nun yourself. You know my thoughts about monks, that I do not like them. But nuns are quite otherwise. Our Lord Jesus was served by two women, of whom Mary was assuredly a nun, and Martha a religious woman equally, probably of the begging order—a sister of Saint Clare, or of the order of Mount Carmel. The point is, I believe, still in doubt. So you see that you have excellent examples before you to persevere. When I have put my affairs in train at High March I will come and see you; and as you are my wife, if any trouble should come about you, any sickness, or threatening from without, or any private grief, send me word, and I will never fail you. Moreover, have no doubts of my fidelity: I am a gentleman, Isoult, as you know. And indeed such pranks are not to my taste."

He stopped talking, but not patting the girl's shoulder. It was almost more than she could endure. At first her blank and sheer dismay had been almost comical; she had looked at him as if he was mad, or talking gibberish. The even flow of his reasoning went on, and with it a high satisfaction in all his plans patent even to her cloudy intellect; gradually thus the truth dawned upon her, and as he continued she lost the sense of his spoken thoughts in the mad cross-tides of her own unuttered. Now her crying instinct was for rescue at all costs, at any hazard. Prayers, entreaties, cravings for reprieve thronged unvoiced and not to be voiced through every fibre of her body. Could he not spare her? Could he not? If she could turn suddenly upon him, clasp his knees, worm herself between his arms, put her face—wet, shaking, tremulous, but ah, Lord! how full of love—near to his! If she could! She could not; shame froze her, choked not speech only but act; she was dumb through and through—a dumb animal.

"Well, Isoult, what do you say?" he asked in his cheerful voice. He could hardly hear her answer, it came so low.

"I will do thy pleasure, lord," she murmured.

He stooped and kissed her forehead, not noticing how she shook.

"Good child," he said, "good child! I am more than satisfied with you, and hope that I may have proved as pleasant a traveller as I have found you to be. My salute must be for good-night and farewell, Isoult, for to-morrow morning I shall be gone before you have turned your side in bed. That is where you should be now, my dear. Your head is very hot—a sign that you are tired. Forget not what I have said to you in anything; forget not to trust me. They will show you your bed. Good-bye, Isoult."

She muttered something inaudible with her lips, and went out without looking at him again. Every bone in her body ached so cruelly that she could hardly drag herself along. She could neither think nor cry out; what strength she had went towards carrying this new load, which, while it paralyzed, for the present numbed her as well. The mistress of the novices was shocked to see her white drawn face, heavily-blacked eyes, and to hear a dead voice come dully from such pretty lips.

"My dear heart," said the good woman, "you are tired to death. Come with me to the still-room; I will give you a cordial." The liquor at least sent some blood to her face and lips, with whose help she was able to find her bed. For that night she had for bedfellow a fat nun, who snored and moaned in her sleep, was fretful at the least stir, and effectually prevented her companion from snoring, in turn, if she had been afflicted with that disease. Isoult stirred little enough: being worn out with grief entirely new to her, to say nothing of her fatigue of travel, she lay like a log and (what she had never done before) dreamed horribly. Very early, before light, she was awake and face to face with her anguish again. She lay in a waking stupor, fatally sensible, but incapable of responsible action. She had to hear Prosper's voice in the courtyard sharply inquiring of the way, his words to his horse, all his clinking preparations; she heard his high-sung "Heaven be with you; pray for me," and the diminishing chorus of Saracen's hoofs on the road. She trembled so much during this torment that she feared to shake the bed. Very weakness at last took pity on her; she swooned asleep again, this time dreamless. The fat nun getting up for Prime, also took enough pity upon her to let her he. So it was that Prosper left Gracedieu.

CHAPTER XII

BROKEN SANCTUARY

Through the days of rain and falling leaves, when all the forest was sodden with mist; through the dark days of winter, hushed with snow, she stayed with the nuns, serving them meekly in whatever tasks they set her. She was once more milk-maid and cowherd, laundress again, still-room maid for a season, and in time (being risen so high) tire-woman to the Lady Abbess herself. Short of profession you can get no nearer the choir than that. It was not by her tongue that she won so much favour—indeed she hardly spoke at all; as for pleasantness she never showed more than the ghost of a smile. "I am in bondage," she said to herself, "in a strange house, and no one knows what treasure I hide in my bosom." There she kept her wedding-ring. But if she was subdued, she was undeniably useful, and there are worse things in a servant than to go staidly about her work with collected looks and sober feet, to have no adventurous traffic with the men-servants about the granges or farms, never to see nor hear what it would be inconvenient to know—in a word, to mind her business. In time therefore—and that not a long one as times go—her featness and patience, added to her beauty (for it was not long before the gentler life or the richer possession made her very handsome), won her the regard of everybody in the house.

The Abbess, as I have told you already, took her into high favour before Christmas was over—actually by Epiphany she could suffer no other to dress her or be about her person.

She loved pretty maids, she said, when they were good. Isoult was both, so the Abbess loved her. The two got to know each other, to take each other's measure —to their reciprocal advantage. Isoult was very guarded how she did; what she said was always impersonal, what she heard never went further. The Abbess was pleased. She would often commend her, take her by the chin, turn up her face and kiss her. A frequent strain of her talk was openly against Prosper's ideas: the Abbess thought Prosper a ridiculous youth.

"Child," she would say—and Isoult thrilled at the familiar word (Prosper's!) —"Child, you are too good-looking to be a nun. In due season we must find you a husband. Your knight seemed aghast at the thought that salvation could be that way. Some fine morning the young gentleman will sing a very different note. Meantime he is wide of the mark. For our blessed Lord loveth not as men love (who love as they are made), nor would He have them who are on the earth and of it do otherwise than seek the fairest that it hath to give them. Far from that, but He will draw eye to eye and lip to lip, so both be pure, saying, 'Be fruitful, and plenish the earth.' But to those not so favoured as you are He saith, 'Come, thou shalt be bride of Heaven, and lie down in the rose-garden of the Lamb.' So each loves in her degree, and according to the measure of her being; and it is very well that this should be so, in order that the garners of Paradise may one day be full."

This sort of talk, by no means strange on the old lady's part, sometimes tempted Isoult to tell her story—that she was a wife already. No doubt she would have done it had not a thought forborne her. Prosper did not love her; their relations were not marital—so much she knew as well as anybody. She would never confess her love for him, even to Prosper himself; she could not bring herself to own that she loved and was unloved. She thought that was a disgrace, one that would flood her with shame and Prosper with her, as her husband though only in name. She thought that she would rather die than utter this secret of hers; she believed indeed that she soon would die. That was why she never told the Abbess, and again why she made no effort nor had any temptation to run away and find him out. It seemed to her that her mere appearance before him would be a confession of deep shame.

But she never ceased for an hour to think of him, poor miserable. In bed she would lie for whole watches awake, calling his name over and over again in a whisper. Her ring grew to be a familiar, Prosper's genius. She would take it from her bosom and hold it to her lips, whisper broken words to it, as if she were in her husband's arms. With the same fancy she would try to make it understand how she loved him. That is a thing very few girls so much as know, and still fewer can utter even to their own hearts; and so it proved with her. She was as mute and shamefaced before the ring as before the master of the ring. So she would sigh, put it back in its nest, and hide her face in the pillow to cool her cheeks. At last in tears she would fall asleep. So the days dragged.

In February, when the light drew out, when there was a smell of wet woods in the air, when birds sang again in the brakes, and here and there the bushes facing south budded, matters grew worse for her. She began to be very heavy, her nightly vigils began to tell. She could not work so well, she lagged in her movements, fell into stares and woke with starts, blundered occasionally. She had never been a fanciful girl, having no nurture for such flowering; but now her visions began to be distorted. Her love became her thorn, her side one deep wound. More and more of the night was consumed in watchings; she cried easily and often (for any reason or no reason), and she was apt to fall faint. So February came and went in storms, and March brought open weather, warm winds, a carpet of flowers to the woods. This enervated, and so aggravated her malady: the girl began to droop and lose her good looks. In turn the Abbess, who was really fond of her, became alarmed. She thought she was ill, and made a great pet of her. She got no better.

She was allowed her liberty to go wherever she pleased. In her trouble she used to run into the woods, with a sort of blind sense that physical distress would act counter to her sick soul. She would run as fast as she could: her tears flew behind her like rain. Over and over to herself she whispered Prosper's name as she ran—"Prosper! Prosper le Gai! Prosper! Prosper, my lord!" and so on, just as if she were mad. It was in the course of these distracted pranks that she discovered and fell in love with a young pine tree, slim and straight. She thought that it (like the ring) held the spirit of Prosper, and adored him under its bark. She cut a heart in it with his name set in the midst and her own beneath. Ceremony thereafter became her relief and all she cared about. She did mystic rites before her tree (in which the ring played a part), forgetting herself for the time. She would draw out her ring and look at it, then kiss it. Then it must be lifted up to the length of its chain as she had seen the priest elevate the Host at Mass; she genuflected and fell prone in mute adoration, crying all the time with tears streaming down her face. She was at this time like to dissolve in tears! Without fail the mysteries ended with the *Pater Noster*, the *Ave*, a certain Litany which the nuns had taught her, and some gasping words of urgency to the Virgin and Saint Isidore. Love was scourging her slender body at this time truly, and with well-pickled rods.

On a certain day of mid-March,—it would be about the twelfth,—as she was at these exercises about the mystic tree, a tall lady in Lincoln green and silver furs came out of a thicket and saw Isoult, though Isoult saw not her. She stood smiling, watching the poor devotee; then, choosing her time, came quietly behind her, saw the heart and read the names. This made her smile all the more, and think a little. Then she touched Isoult on the shoulder with the effect of bringing her from heaven to dull earth in a trice. By some instinct—she was made of instincts, quick as a bird—the girl concealed her ring before she turned.

"Why are you crying, child?" said this smiling lady.

"Oh ma'am!" cried the girl, half crazy and beside herself with her troubles —"Oh, ma'am! let me tell you a little!"

She told her more than a little: she told her in fact everything—in a torrent of words and tears—except the one thing that might have helped her. She did not say that she was married, though short of that she gulped the shame of loving unloved.

"Poor child!" said the lady when she had heard the sobbed confession, "you are indeed in love. And Prosper le Gai is your lover? And you are Isoult la Desirous? So these notches declare at least: they are yours, I suppose?"

"Yes, indeed, ma'am," said Isoult; "but he is not my lover. He is my master."

"Oh, of course, of course, child," the lady laughed—"they are always the master. If we are the mistress we are lucky. And do you love him so much, Isoult?"

"Yes, ma'am," said she.

"Silly girl, silly girl! How much do you love him now?"

"I could not tell you, ma'am."

"Could you tell him then?"

"Ah, no, no!"

"But you have told him, silly?"

"No, ma'am, indeed."

"It needs few words, you must know."

"They are more than I can dare, ma'am."

"It can be done without words at all. Come here, Isoult. Listen."

She whispered in her ear.

Isoult grew very grave. Her eyes were wide at this minute, all black, and not a shred of colour was left in her face.

"Ah, never!" she cried.

Maulfry laughed heartily.

"You are the dearest little goose in the world!" she cried. "Come and kiss me at once."

Isoult did as she was told. Maulfry did not let her go again.

"Now," she went on, with her arms round the girl's waist and her arch face very near, "now you are to know, Isoult, that I am a wonderful lady. I am friends with half the knights in the kingdom; I have armour of my own, shields and banneroles, and halberts and swords, enough to frighten the Countess Isabel out of her three shires. I could scare the Abbot Richard and the Abbess Mechtild by the lift of a little finger. Oh, I know what I am saying! It so happens that your Prosper is a great friend of mine. I am very fond of him, and of course I must needs be interested in what you tell me. Well now—come with me and find him. Will you? I dare say he is not very far off."

Isoult stared at her without speaking. Doubt, wonder, longing, prayer, quavered in her eyes as each held the throne for a time.

"He told me to stay at Gracedieu," she faltered. It seemed to her that she was maiming her own dream.

"He tells me differently then," said Maulfry, smiling easily; "I suppose even a lover may change his mind."

"Oh! Oh! you have seen him?

"Certainly I have seen him."

"And he says—"

"What do you think he says? Might it not be, Come and find me?"

"He is—ah, he is ill?"

"He is well."

"In danger?"

"I know of none."

"I am to leave Gracedieu and come with you, ma'am?"

"Yes. Are you afraid?"

For answer Isoult fell flat down and kissed Maulfry's silver hem.

"I will follow you to death!" she cried.

Maulfry shivered, then arched her brows.

"It will not be so bad as all that," she said. "Come then, we will find the horses."

Isoult looked down confusedly at her grey frock.

"You little jay bird, who's to see you here among the trees? Come with me, I'll set you strutting like a peacock before I've done with you," said Maulfry, in her mocking, good-humoured way.

They went together. Maulfry had hold of Isoult by the hand. Presently they came to an open glade where there were two horses held by a mounted groom. As soon as he saw them coming the groom got off, helped Isoult first, then his mistress. They rode away at a quick trot down the slope; the horses seemed to know the way.

Maulfry was in high spirits. She played a thousand tricks, and enveigled from the brooding girl her most darling thoughts. Before they had made their day's journey she had learnt all that she wanted to know, or rather what she knew already. It confirmed what Galors had told her: she believed his story. For her part Isoult, having once made the plunge, gave her heart its way, bathed it openly in love, and was not ashamed. To talk of Prosper more freely than she had ever dared even to herself, to talk of loving him, of her hopes of winning him! She seemed a winged creature as she flew through the hours of a forest day. It pleased her, too, to think that she was being discreet in saying nothing of her marriage. If Prosper had not thought fit to reveal it to his accomplished friend she must keep the secret by all means—his and hers. Instead of clouding her hopeful visions this gave them an evening touch of mystery. It elevated her by making her an accomplice. He and she were banded together against this all-wise lady. No doubt she would learn it in time—in his time; and then Isoult dreamed (and blushed as she dreamed) of another part, wherein she would snuggle herself into his arm and whisper, "Have I not been wise?" Then she would be kissed, and the lady would laugh to learn how she had been outwitted by a young girl. Ah, what dreams! Isoult's wings took her a far flight when once she had spread them to the sun.

Journeying thus they reached a road by nightfall, and a little House of Access. To go direct to Tortsentier they should have passed this house on the left-hand, for the tower was south-east from Gracedieu. But there was a reason for the circuit, as for every other twist of Maulfry's; the true path would have brought them too nearly upon that by which Prosper and Isoult had come seeking sanctuary. Instead they struck due east, and hit the main road which runs from High March to Market Basing; then by going south for another day they would win Tortsentier. Isoult, of course, as a born woodlander would know the whereabouts of Maulfry's dwelling from any side but the north. She was of South Morgraunt, and therefore knew nothing of the north or middle forest. All this Maulfry had calculated. At the House of Access the girl was actually a day's journey nearer Prosper than she had been at the convent, but she knew nothing of it. Consequently her night's rest refreshed her, waking dreams stayed the night, and left traces of their rosy flames in her cheeks next morning. Maulfry, waking first, looked at her as she lay pillowing her cheek on her arm, with her wild hair spread behind her like a dark cloud. Maulfry, I say, looked at her.

"You are a little beauty, my dear," she thought to herself. "Countess or bastard, you are a little beauty. And there is countess in your blood somewhere, I'll take an oath. Hands and feet, neck and head, tell the story. There was love and a young countess and a hot-brained troubadour went to the making of you, my little lady. A ditch-full of witches could not bring such tokens to a villein. Galors, my dear friend, if I owed nothing to Master le Gai, I doubt if I should help you to this. 'Tis too much, my friend, with an earldom. She needs no crown, pardieu!"

She knew her own crown had toppled, and grew a little bleak as she thought of it. There was no earldom for her to fall back upon. She looked older when off her guard. But she had determined to be loyal to the one friend she had ever had. The worst woman in the world can do that much. Therefore, when Isoult woke up she found herself made much of. The sun of her day-dreaming rose again and shone full upon her. By the end of the day they had reached Tortsentier. Isoult was fast in a prison that had no look of a prison, where Galors was mending his throat in an upper chamber.

Maulfry came and sat on the foot of his bed. Galors, strapped and bandaged till he looked like a mewed owl in a bush, turned his chalk face to her with inquiry shooting out of his eyes. He had grown a spiky black beard, from which he plucked hairs all day, thinking and scheming.

"Well," was all he said.

Maulfry nodded. "The story is true. She has the feet and hands. She is a little beauty. You have only to shut the hole in your neck."

Galors swore. "Let God judge whether that damned acrobat shall pay for his writhing! But the other shall be my first business. So she is here—you have seen her? What do you think of her?"

"I have told you."

The man's appetite grew as it fed upon Maulfry's praise of his taste.

"Ah—ah! Dame, I'm a man of taste—eh?"

Maulfry said nothing. Galors changed the note.

"How shall I thank you, my dear one?" he asked her.

"Ah," said she, "I shall need what you can spare before long."

Then she left him.

CHAPTER XIII

HIGH MARCH, AND A GREAT LADY

In the weeping grey of an autumn morning, but in great spirits of his own, Prosper left Gracedieu for High March. The satisfaction of having braved the worst of an adventure was fairly his; to have made good disposition of what threatened to fetter him by shutting off any possible road from his advance; and to have done this (so far as he could see) without in any sense withdrawing from Isoult the advantages she could expect—this was tunable matter, which set him singing before the larks were off the ground. He felt like a man who has earned his pleasure; and pleasure, as he understood it, he meant to have. The zest for it sparkled in his quick eyes as he rode briskly through the devious forest ways. Had Galors or any other dark-entry man met him now and chanced a combat, he would have bad it with a will, but he would have got off with a rough tumble and sting or two from the flat of the sword. The youth was too pleased with himself for killing or slicing.

However, there was nobody to fight. North Morgraunt was pretty constantly patrolled by the Countess's riders at this time. A few grimy colliers; some chair-turners amid their huts and white chips on the edge of a hidden hamlet; drovers with forest ponies going for Waisford or Market Basing; the hospitality and interminable devotions of a hermit by a mossy crucifix on Two Manors Waste; one night alone in a ruined chapel on the top of a down:—of such were the encounters and events of his journey. He was no Don Quixote to make desperadoes or feats of endurance out of such gear; on the contrary, he persistently enjoyed himself. Sour beer wetted his lips dry with talking; leaves made a capital bed; the hermit, in the intervals of his prayers, remembered his own fighting days in the Markstake, and knew what was done to make Maximilian the Second safely king. Everything was as it should be.

On the third day he fell in with a troop of horse, whose spears carried the red saltire of the house of Forz on their banneroles. Since they were bound as he was for the Castle, he rode in their company, and in due course saw before him on a height among dark pines the towers of High March, with the flag of the Lady Paramount afloat on the breeze. It was on a dusty afternoon of October and in a whirl of flying leaves, that he rode up to the great gate of the outer bailey, and blew a blast on the horn which hung there, that they might let down the bridge.

When the Countess Isabel heard who and of what condition her visitor was she made him very welcome. The Forz and the Gais were of the same country and of nearly the same degree in it. She had been a Forz before she married, and she counted herself so still, for the earldom of Hauterive was hers in her own right; and though she was Earl Roger's widow (and thus a double Countess Dowager) she could not but remember it. So she did Prosper every honour of hospitality: she sent some of her ladies to disarm him and lead him to the bath; she sent him soft clothing to do on when he was ready for it; in a word, put him at his ease. When he came into the hall it was the same thing she got up from her chair of estate and walked down to meet him, while all the company made a lane for the pair of them. Prosper would have knelt to kiss her hand had she let him, but instead she gave it frankly into his own.

"You are the son of my father's friend, Sir Prosper," she said, "and shall never kneel to me."

"My lady," said he, "I shall try to deserve your gracious welcome. My father, rest his soul, is dead, as you may have heard."

"Alas, yes," the Countess replied, "I know it, and grieve for you and your brothers. Of my Lord Malise I have also heard something."

"Nothing good, I'll swear," interjected Prosper to himself.

The Countess went on—

"Well, Sir Prosper, you stand as I stand, alone in the world. It would seem we had need of each other."

Prosper bowed, feeling the need of nobody for his part. Remember he was three-and-twenty to the Countess's thirty-five; and she ten years a widow. She did not notice his silence, but went on, glowing with her thoughts.

"We should be brother and sister for the sake of our two fathers," she said with a gentle blush.

"I never felt to want a sister till now," cried Master Prosper, making another bow. So it was understood between them that theirs was to be a nearer relationship than host and guest.

The Countess Isabel—or to give her her due, Isabel, Countess of Hauterive, Countess Dowager of March and Bellesme, Lady of Morgraunt—was still a beautiful woman, tall, rather slim, pale, and of a thoughtful cast of the face. She had a very noble forehead, level, broad, and white; her eyes beneath arched brows were grey—cold grey, not so full nor so dark as Isoult's, nor so blue in the whites, but keener. They were apt to take a chill tinge when she was rather Countess of Hauterive than that Isabel de Forz who had loved and lost Fulk de Bréauté. She never forgot him, and for his sake wore nothing but silk of black and white; but she did not forget herself either; within walls you never saw her without a thin gold circlet on her head. Even at Mass she, would have no other covering. She said it was enough for the Countess of Hauterive, whom Saint Paul probably had not in his mind when he wrote his epistle. Her hair was a glory, shining and very abundant, but brown not black. Isoult, you will perceive, was a warmer, tenderer copy of her mother, owing something to Fulk. Isoult, moreover, had not been born a countess. Both were inaccessible, the daughter from the timidity of a wild thing, the mother from the rarity of her air. Being what she was, twice a widow, bereft of her only child, and burdened with cares which she was much too proud to give over, she never had fair judgment she was considered hard where she was merely lonely. Her greatness made her remote, and her only comforter the worst in the world—herself. Her lips drooped a little at the corners; this gave her a wistful look at times. At other times she looked almost cruel, because of a trick she had of going with them pressed together. As a matter of fact she was shy as well as proud, and fed on her own sorrows from lack of the power to declare them abroad. It was very seldom she took a liking for any stranger; doubtful if Prosper's lineage had won her to open to him as she had done. His face was more answerable; that blunt candour of his, the inquiring blue eyes, the eager throw-back of the head as he walked, above all the friendly smile he had for a world where everything and everybody seemed new and delightful and specially designed for his entertainment—this was what unlocked the Countess's darkened treasury of thought.

Once loosed she never drew back. Brother and sister they were to be. She made him hand her in to supper; he must sit at her right hand; her own cup-bearer should fill his wine-cup, her own Sewer taste all his meats. At the end of supper she sent for a great cup filled with wine; it needed both her hands. She held it up before she drank to him, saying, "Let there be love and amity between me and thee." The terms of this aspiration astonished him; he accepted honours easily, for he was used to observances at Starning; but to be thee'd and thou'd by this lady! As he stood there laughing and blushing like a boy she made him drink from the cup to the same wish and in the same terms. When once your frozen soul opens to the thaw all the sluices are away, truly. Prosper went to bed that night very well content with his reception. He saw his schemes ripening fast on such a sunny wall as this. His head was rather full, and of more than the fumes of wine; consequently in saying his prayers he did not remember Isoult at all. Yet hers had been sped out of Gracedieu Minster long before, and to the same gods. Only she had had Saint Isidore in addition; and she had had Prosper. Hers probably went nearer the mark. Until you have made a beloved of your saint or a saint of your beloved—it matters not greatly which—you will get little comfort out of your prayers.

It was, however, heedlessness rather than design which brought it about, that as the days at High March succeeded each other Prosper did not tell the Countess either of his adventure or of his summary method of achieving it. Design was there: he did not see his way to involving the Abbot, who was, he knew, a dependant of his hostess, and yet could not begin the story elsewhere than at the beginning. Something, too, kept the misfortunes of his wife from his tongue—an honourable something, not his own pride of race. But he, in fact, forgot her. The days were very pleasant. He hunted the hare, the deer, the wolf, the bear. He hunted what he liked best of all to hunt, the man; and he got the honour which only comes from successful hunting in that sort-the devout admiration of those he led. So soon as it was found out where his tastes and capacities lay he had as much of this work as he chose. High March was on the northern borders of the Countess's country; not far off was the Markstake, stormy, debatable land, plashy with blood. There were raids, there were hornings and burnings, lifting of cattle and ravishment of women, to be prevented or paid for. Prosper saw service. The High March men had never had a leader quite like him-so young, so light and fierce, so merry in fight. Isoult might eat her heart out with love; Prosper had the love of his riders, for by this they were his to a man.

There were other influences at work, more subtle and every bit as rapacious.

There were the long hours in the hall by the leaping light of the fire and the torches, feasts to be eaten, songs to sing, dances, revels, and such like. Prosper was a cheerful, very sociable youth. He had the manners of his father and the light-hearted impertinence of a hundred ancestors, all rulers of men and women. He made love to no one, and laughed at what he got of it for nothing—which was plenty. There were shaded hours in the Countess's chamber, where the songs were softer and the pauses of the songs softer still; morning hours in the grassy alleys between the yew hedges; hours in the south walk in an air thick with the languors of warm earth and garden flowers; intimate rides in the pine wood; the wild freedom of hawking in the open downs; the grass paths; Yule; the music, the hopes of youth, the sweet familiarity, the shared books, the timid encroachments and gentle restraints, half-entreaties, half-denials:—no young man can resist these things unless he thinks of them suspectingly (as Prosper never did), and no woman wishes to resist them. If Prosper found a sister, Isabel began to find more than a brother. She grew younger as he grew older. They were more than likely to meet half way.

CHAPTER XIV

A RECORDER

In these delicate times of crisis Isoult found an advocate, a recorder, if you will be ruled by me. It was none too soon, for the brother and sister of High March had reached that pretty stage of intimacy when long silences are an embarrassment, and embarrassments compact equally of pleasure and pain. As far as the lady was concerned the pleasure predominated; the pain was reduced to sweet confusion, the air made tremulous with promise. I do not say that for Prosper the relationship did more than put him at his ease—but that is a good deal. Say the Countess was a fire and High March an armchair. Prosper had settled himself to stretch his legs and drowse. Poor Isoult was the wailing wind in the chimney—a sound which could but add to his comfortable well-being. It needs more than a whimper to tempt a man to be cold in your company. The recorder was timely.

Prosper and his Countess were hawking in the fields beyond the forest, and the sport had been bad. They had, in fact, their birds jessed and hooded and were turning for home, when Prosper saw some fields away a white bird—gull he thought—flying low. He sprang his tercel-gentle; the same moment the Countess saw the quarry and flew hers. Both hawks found at first cast; the white bird flew towards the falconers, circling the field in which they stood, with its enemies glancing about it. It gradually closed in, circling still round them and round, till at last it was so near and so low as almost to be in reach of Prosper's hand. He saw that it was not a gull, but a pigeon, and started on a reminiscence. Just then one of the towering falcons stooped and engaged. There was a wild scurry of wings; then the other bird dropt. The Countess cheered the hawks: Prosper saw only the white bird with a wound in her breast. Then as the quarry began to scream he remembered everything, and to the dismay of the lady leapt off his horse, ran to the struggling birds, and cuffed them off with all his might. He succeeded. The wounded bird fluttered, half flying, half hopping, across the grass, finally rose painfully into the air and soared out of sight. Meantime Prosper, breathless and red in the face, had hooded and bound the hawks. He brought hers back to the Countess without a word.

"My dear Prosper," said she, "you will forgive me for asking if you are mad?"

"I must seem so," he replied. "But I suppose every one has his tender part which some shaft will reach. Mine is reached when two hawks wound a white bird in the crop."

He spoke shortly, and still breathed faster than his wont. The Countess was piqued.

"It seems to me, I confess, inconvenient in a falconer that he should be nice as to the colour of his quarry. There must be some reason for this. I will forgive you for making a bad day's sport worse if you will tell me your story."

Prosper was troubled. He connected his story with Isoult, though he could hardly say why. He had merely seen a white bird before his marriage; yet without that sequel the story could have no point. He did not wish to speak of his marriage, if for no other reason than that it was much too late to speak of it. The other reasons remained as valid as ever; but he was bound to confess the superior cogency of this present one. Meanwhile the Countess clamoured.

"The story, Prosper, the story!" she cried. "I must and will have the story. I am very sure it is romantic; you are growing red. Oh, it is certainly romantic; I shall never rest without the story."

Prosper in desperation remembered a hawking mishap of his boyhood, and clutched at it.

"This is my story," he said. "When I was a boy with my brothers our father used to take us with him hawking on Marbery Down. There is a famous heronry in the valley below it whence you may be sure of a kill; but on the Down itself are great flocks of sheep tended by shepherds who come from all parts of the country round about and lie out by their fires. One day—just such a windy morning as this—my father, my brother Osric, and I were out with our birds, and did indifferently well, so far as I can remember. I had new falcon with me— a haggard of the rock which I had mewed and manned myself. It was the first time I had tried her on the Down, and she began by giving trouble; then did better, but finally gave more trouble than at first, as you shall hear. Towards noon I found myself separate from our company on a great ridge of the Down where it slopes steeply to the forest, as you know it does in one place. The flocks were out feeding on the slopes below me, and their herds—three or four boys and girls—were lying together by a patch of gorse, but one of them stood up after a while and shaded her eyes to look over the forest. Then I saw a lonely bird making way for the heronry. I remember it plainly; in the sun it looked shining white. I flew my haggard out of the hood at her, sure of a kill. She raked off at a great pace, as this one did just now; but in mid air she checked suddenly, heeled over, beat up against the wind, stooped and fell headlong at the shepherds. I could not tell what had happened; it was as if the girl had been shot. But, by the Saviour of mankind, this is the truth: I saw the girl who was standing throw her arms up, I heard her scream; the others scattered. Then I saw the battling sails of my falcon. She was on the girl. I spurred my pony and went down the hill headlong to the music of the girl's screaming. Never before or since have I seen a peregrine engage at such a quarry as that. She had her with beak and claws below the left pap. She had ripped up her clothes and drawn blood, sure enough. The poor child, who looked very starved, was as white as death: I cannot think she had any blood to spare. As for her screaming, I have not forgotten it yet—in fact, the bird we struck to-day reminded me of it and made me act as I did. To cut down my story, I pulled the hawk off and strangled it, gave the girl what money I had, said what I could to quiet her, and left her to be patched up by her friends. She was more frightened than hurt, I fancy. As I told you, I was a boy at the time; but these things stay by you. It is a fact at least that I am queasy on the subject of white birds. Before I came to High March, indeed it was almost my first day in Morgraunt, I saw and rescued a white bird from two hen-harriers; and now I have been troubled by another. I seem beset by white birds!"

"It is fortunate you have other hues to choose from," said the Countess with a smile, "or otherwise you would be no falconer. But your story is very strange. Have you ever consulted about it?"

"I have said very little about it," Prosper replied, remembering as he spoke the forest Mass which he had heard, and that he had discoursed upon this adventure with Alice of the Hermitage.

"The hawk pecked at the girl's heart," said the lady.

"It did not get so far as that, Countess."

"You speak prose, my friend."

"I am no troubadour, but speak what I know."

"The heart means nothing to you, Prosper!"

"The heart? Dear lady, I assure you the girl was not hurt. She is a young woman by now, probably wife to a clown and mother of half-a-dozen."

"Prosper, you disappoint me. Let us ride on. I am sick of these shivering grey fields."

The Countess was vexed, for the life of him he could not tell why. He made peace at last, but she would not tell him the cause of her morning's irritation.

That was not the only reminder he had that day—in fact, it was but the first. In the evening came another.

He was in the Countess's chamber after supper. She was embroidering a banner, and he had been singing to her as she worked. After his music the Countess took the lute from him, saying that she would sing. And so she did, but in a voice so low and constrained that it seemed more to comfort herself than any other.

Prosper sat by the table idly turning over a roll of blazonry—the coats of all the knights and gentlemen who had ever been in the service of High March. It was a roll carefully kept by the pursuivant, very fine work. He saw that his own was already tricked in its place, and recognized many more familiar faces. Suddenly he gave a start, and sat up stiff as a bar. He looked no further, but at the end of the Countess's song said abruptly—

"Tell me, Countess, whose are these arms?"

She looked at the coat—sable, three wicket-gates argent. "There is a story about that," she said.

"I beg you to tell it to me," said Prosper; "story for story."

"That is only fair," she laughed, having quite recovered her easy manner with him. "Come and sit by the fire, and you shall hear it. The arms," she began, "are those which were assumed by a young knight after a very bold exploit in my service. He came to me as Salomon de Born, and I think he was but eighteen—a mere boy."

Prosper, from the heights of his three-and-twenty years, nodded benignly.

"So much so," said the Countess, "that I fear I must have wounded his vanity by laughing away what he asked of me. This was no less than to lead a troop of my men against Renny of Coldscaur, an enemy and slanderer of mine, but none the less as great a lord as he was rascal. However, he begged so persistently that I gave in, finding other things about him—a mystery of his birth and upbringing, a steadfastness also and gravity far beyond his years—which drew me to put him to the proof of what he dared. He went, therefore, with a company of light horse, some fifty men. He was away eight weeks, and then came back—with but six men, it is true; but youth is prodigal of life, knowing so little of it."

"Life is given us to spend," quoth Prosper here.

"He came back with six men. But he brought the tongue of Blaise Renny in a silver cup, and three wicket-gates, which took two men apiece to carry."

"He had saved just enough men. That was wise of him, and like the king his namesake," Prosper said, approving of Salomon.

"It was what he said himself", pursued the Countess, "that it was a fortunate circumstance."

"And how did he win his adventure, and what had the wicket-gates to do with the business?"

"You shall hear. It seems that Coldscaur, which is in North Marvilion beyond the Middle Shires, stands on a fretted scarp. It is strongly defended by art as well as nature, for there are three ravines about it with a stepped path through each up to the Castle. These were defended about midway of each by a wicket-gate and a couple of towers. The gorges are so narrow that there is barely room for a man and horse to get through; the gates of course correspond."

"Fine defences," said Prosper.

"Very. Well, Salomon de Born with my fifty men seized and occupied a village at the foot of the scarp one night. In the morning there were his defences thrown up man-high, and my standard on the church tower. Renny was furious, and despatched a stronger force than he could afford to re-take the village. Salomon, counting upon this, had left two men in it to be killed; with the rest he scaled the scaur and waited in hiding to see what force Renny took out. He knew to a nicety the strength of the garrison, saw what there was to see, made his calculations, and thought he would venture it. He got over the rock, he and his men, by some means; came down the gorges from the top, secured the defences, and posted a couple of men at each wicket. With the rest he surprised the Castle. I believe, indeed, that all the men in it were killed as well as most of mine. Yet for three or four hours Coldscaur was in my hands."

"It should have been yours now," said Prosper, "with fifty of your men once in it."

"My friend, I didn't need Coldscaur. I have castles enough. But it was necessary to punish Renny."

"And that was done?"

"It was done. Salomon posted his men in the towers by the wicket-gates, and waited for Renny to return from the village. Luckily for him it grew dusk, but not dark, before he could be certain by which gorge Renny himself was coming in. When he had made sure of this he took all three wickets off their hinges, and sent six men to carry them home to High March. With the rest he waited for Renny. Finally he saw him riding up the stepped way, and, as his custom was, far ahead of his troop. You must know that these people are besotted with pride; the state they kept (and still keep, I suppose) was more than royal. No one must ride, walk, or stand within a dozen yards of Renny of Coldscaur. Salomon had calculated upon it. Well, it was dark before Renny reached the wicket. Someone (Salomon, no doubt) called for the word. Renny gave it; but it was his last. Salomon stabbed him at the same instant and pulled him off his horse out of the way. He sent the horse clattering up the hill. Renny's men followed it, nothing doubting. I might have had the better part of my men but for the subsequent foppery of the youth. He had Renny dead. He had Renny's tongue. He must needs have a silver dish to put it in, so as to present it honourably to me. He went to the Castle to get this. He got it; but he was discovered and pursued, and only he escaped—he and the six bearers of the wicket-gates. That is my story of the coat in return for yours of the bird. The hero of it took the name of Salomon de Montguichet after this performance, and my pursuivant devised him a blazon, with the legend, *Entra per me*."

"He did very well," said Prosper, "though he should have fought with Renny, and not stabbed him in the dark. But why did he bring the wicket-gates?"

"He said that since they had for once been held by honest men, he could not let them backslide. Moreover, they were in his way, and he knew not what else to do with them."

"And why did he take the man's tongue?"

"He said that the head must stay tongueless at Coldscaur to warn all traducers of me. True enough, the man has come to be remembered as Blaise Sanslang."

"I should have done otherwise," said Prosper.

"What would you have made of it, Prosper?"

"I should have brought the man alive to your feet; I should have advised you to give him a whipping and let him go."

"That would have been more merciless to Renny, my friend, than what Salomon de Montguichet did. I have told you that they are the proudest family in Christendom."

"I never thought of Renny," he answered; "I was thinking of myself in Salomon's place."

"Montguichet thought of me, Prosper."

"I also was thinking of you, Countess."

Presently he grew keen on his own thoughts again and asked—

"What became of Salomon de Born?"

"I cannot tell you," she replied, "except this, that he took service under the King of the Romans and went abroad. Of where he is now, or how he fares, I know nothing."

"I think he is dead," said Prosper.

"What is your reason?"

"I have seen another carrying his arms."

"But it may have been the man himself. A thin man, hatchet-faced, with hot, large eyes; a pale man, who looked not to have the sinew he proved to have."

Prosper looked thoughtful, a little puzzled too. "The description is familiar to me. I may have seen the man. But certainly it was not he who carried the Montguichet shield."

Suddenly he sprang up with a shout. He stood holding the table, white and shaky. The Countess ran to him and put her arm on his shoulder: "Prosper, Prosper, you have frightened me! What is your thought? Are you ill? I entreat you to tell me, Prosper."

He collected himself at once to reassure her.

"The man is dead," he said, "and I buried him. I remember his face; I remember a badge on his breast; I remember it all. But I do not understand—I do not see clearly as yet. I must think. I beg you to let me leave you for the present. To-morrow I will go to avenge Salomon de Montguichet."

The youth was quite wild and out of breath.

"Prosper!" cried the Countess, clinging to him, "I conjure you to tell me what this means. You will never leave me this night without a word. You cannot know—"

She could not finish what she longed to say. As for Prosper, he was in another world; it is doubtful whether he heard her.

"Countess," he said, "I can tell you nothing as yet. I know but half of the truth. But I must find out the whole, and to-morrow I will tell you what I mean to do. You must have me excused for this night."

She knew that she could say nothing more, although she had never yet seen him in this mood. But he reminded her strongly of his father; she felt that he and she had changed places and ages. So she bowed her head, and when she lifted it he was gone.

Pacing his room Prosper tried to reason out his tangle. This was not so easy as fighting, for he was pulled two different ways. Salomon de Montguichet was the dead man whom the lady had in the wood—that was clear. Galors had Salomon de Montguichet's arms—that too was clear. The trouble was to connect the two strings. What had Galors to do with the lady? Which of them had killed Salomon de Montguichet, or de Born, to give him his real name? How did this threaten Isoult? For the massed events of the long day drove him at last face to face with Isoult. He had sworn upon all knightly honour to save her neck. He thought he had saved it, but now he was not so sure. There was something undefinably sinister, some foreboding about the turn matters had taken (matters so diverse in their beginning) that day. Was he sure he had saved her? He must certainly be sure, he thought. Had he not sworn? And after all, she was his wife. That should count for something. He was not disposed to rate marriage highly; he knew very little about it, but he felt that it should count for something. The honour of the man's wife touched the honour of the man. Again, she was a very good girl. He recalled her—submissive, patient, recollected, pacing beside him on her donkey, as they brushed their way through brown beechwoods and stained wet bracken. He remembered her at her prayers—how kindly she took to the devotion. She was different from the hour she was a good Christian, he swore. Ah, so he had given her more than a free neck! He had given her pride in herself; nay, he had quickened a soul languid for want of spiritual food. And she looked very well praying. She was good-looking, he thought. Oh, she was a good girl!

But surely she was well where she was, could hardly be better. Galors had a split throat; he would be in Saint Thorn, crying *peccavi* in chapter, and gaining salvation with every sting of the scourge. The woman in the wood he had distrusted from the first moment he saw her watching eyes. She was bad through and through; she might be a worse enemy than Galors, or a church-load of pursy monks. But it was impossible that she should have anything to do with Galors, clean impossible. And if she had—why, he was going to her to-morrow, and would find out. Meantime, he would go to bed. Yes, he might go to bed. Was not Gracedieu sanctuary? Ah, he had forgotten that! All was well.

He went to bed; but Tortsentier was not to see him on the morrow. All was not well. He had a dream which drew all the apprehensions and suspicions of the day into one head. The hidden things were made plain, and the crooked things straight; for the first time, it seemed, he was to see openly—when his eyes were shut. He had, in spite of himself, centred them one by one in Isoult, and now he dreamed of her as she was, and of them as they were. This was his dream. He and she were together, lying under the stars in the open wood with his drawn sword between them, set edgeways as it had always been. He lay awake, but Isoult was asleep, and moaning in her sleep. The sound was like voiced sighs which came quickly with her breath. He lay and watched her in the perfectly clear light there was, and presently the moaning ceased, and she opened her eyes to look at him. But though they were wide, they were blank; he knew that she slept still. She moved her lips to speak, but without sound; she strained out her arms to him, but he could not take her. And, leaning more and more towards him, the edge of the sword pressed her bare bosom, yet she seemed not to heed it; and presently it broke the skin, and she pressed it in deeper, as if glad of the sharp pain; and then the blood leapt out and flooded her night-dress. Her arms dropt, she sighed once, she closed her eyes languidly as if mortally tired. Then she lay very still, white to the lips, and Prosper knew that she was dead. So in his own dream he cried out and tried to come at her, but could not because of the red sword.

He woke in a cold sweat and lay trembling, blenched with fear. The dream had been so vivid that involuntarily he turned in his bed to look again at what haunted him, the dying eyes, the white body, and the blood. Terror, when once he had accepted the fact that she was dead, gave place to pity—a pity more intense than he had ever conceived. He had pitied her on the night of their marriage, but never to such a degree that he felt heart-broken at the mere knowledge of such things. And now, as the principal actor in a play, she grew in importance. He began to see that she was more than an incident; she was of the stuff of his life.

What was more odd was, that in the dream he had wanted her, as she him; and that he could look back upon it now and understand the desire. With all the shock that still crowded about him till the shadowy room seemed full of it, there was this one beam of remembrance, like sunlight in a dusty place. He too had held out his arms: he had wanted to take her, to hold her, white and unearthly though she might be—dying as she certainly was. Waking, this seemed very strange to him, for he had never wanted her before; and though (as I say) the remembrance brought a glow along with it, he did not want her in that way now. Supposing that she were alive and lying here, he knew that he should not want her. But the red sword! He shuddered and closed his eyes; there she was, pitifully dead of a wound in the breast. I suppose he was not more superstitious than most people of his day, but he knew that he must go to Gracedieu.

He got up at once to arm himself; he had made all his preparations before sunrise. Then he left word for the Countess that he would return in a day or two, and set out.

The journey could not be done under three days; that gave him two nights in the forest, each of which brought the same dream. He arrived at the convent late in the evening, and asked to see the Abbess at once. The tranquil monotony of the place, its bells and recurrent chimes, the subdued voices of the nuns chanting an office in choir, brought him like a beaten ship into haven. He was reassured before he saw the Abbess.

"Yes, indeed," said that lady in answer to his outburst of questions, "the child is well. Not so bright as during the winter season, it may be; but the spring is no easy time for young people. I may tell you, Sir Prosper, that we have grown very fond of her. Indeed, I am often saying that I wonder how to do without her. She is so diligent and of so toward a disposition. You will find her well cared for, sleek, and quite good-looking. We have great hopes for her future if she makes a happy choice. But you will wish to see her and prove my words. I will send for her this moment."

The Abbess had her hand-bell in her hand. If she had rung it she would have given Prosper justification of his hurry. But the complacent youth forestalled her.

"I beg you, mother, to do nothing of the kind," he said. "She is well, you tell me, she is happy: that is all I cared to know. I have no wish to unsettle her, but leave her cheerfully and confidently with you, being well assured that you will not fail to send me word at High March should need be."

"I understand you, sir, and agree with you. You may be quite easy about her. We are regular livers, as you may guess, and small events are great ones to us. So you return to High March? I will beg you to carry with you my humble duty to her ladyship the Countess. She is well?"

"She is very well," said Prosper, and took his leave.

A frantic Gracedieu messenger started half a night behind him, but was stopped on Two Manors Waste by a party of outlaws, robbed of his letters, and hanged. Prosper's dream visited him for two nights of his journey back, and four nights at High March; but as no word or other warning came from Gracedieu to give it point, he grew to have some strange liking for it, since he knew that it meant nothing. It gave him new thoughts of Isoult; it convinced him, for instance, that since the girl was so good she must be affectionate when you came to know her. His own share in the nightly performance he could now set in humorous comparison with his waking state. He found it difficult to believe in the self of his dream, and was almost curious to see Isoult that he might pursue his juxtapositions. At this rate she filled his waking thoughts as well as his nights. The Countess was not slow to perceive that Prosper was changed, and she affected. His songs came less willingly from him, his sallies were either languid or too polite to be from the heart of the youth, who could make hers beat so fast. Thinking that he wanted work, she devised an expedition for him which might involve some danger and the lives of a dozen men. But she counted that lightly. He went on the fourth day after his return from Gracedieu, and the expedition proved effectual in more ways than one.

The dream stopped, and he forgot it.

CHAPTER XV

THREE AT TORTSENTIER

At Tortsentier there was very little daylight, because the trees about it formed a thick wall. The branches of the pines tapped at the windows on one side; on the other they linked arms with their comrades, and so stood for a mile on all sides of the tower. Paths there were none, nor ways to come by unless you were free of the place. The winter storms moaned, lashed themselves above it, yet below were hushed down to a long sighing. The quiet visitations of the snow, the dripping of the autumn rains, the sun's force, the trap-bite of the frost, or that new breath that comes stealing through woodlands in spring, were all strangers alike to the carpet of brown needles about Maulfry's hold. No birds ever sang there. Death and a great mystery, the dark, air like a lake's at noon, kept fur and feather from Tortsentier, and left Maulfry alone with what she had.

Within, it was a spacious place. A great hall ran the whole height (although not the whole area) of it, having a gallery midway up whence you gained what other chambers there were. Below the gallery were deep alcoves hung with tapestry (of which Maulfry was a diligent worker), and thickened with curtains; between every alcove hung trophies of shields and arms. Mossy carpets, skins, and piled cushions were on the floor; the place smelt of musk: it was lighted by coloured torches and lamps, and warmed with braziers. It was by a spiral stair that you found the gallery and doors of the other rooms, or as many of them as it was fitting you should find. There were doors there which were no doors at all unless occasion served. These rooms had windows; but the hall had only a lantern in the roof, and its torches. From all this it will appear that Isoult was a prisoner, since a prisoner you are if, although you can go out, there is nowhere for you to go; if, further, your hostess neither goes out herself nor gives you occasion to leave her. Yet Maulfry made her guest elaborately free of the place.

"Child," she said, "you see how I live here. My trees, my birds—" she had many birds in cages—"my collections of arms and arras and odd books, are my friends for want of better. If you can help me to any such I shall be very much obliged to you. Other friends I have—yourself I may count among them, one other you know,—but they are of the world, and refuse to hang upon my walls. Sometimes they pay me a visit, stay for a little season, remonstrate, argue with me, shrug, and leave me gladder than I was to receive them. I am a hermit, my child, when all's said. These other friends, these more constant friends, on the other hand, suit me better. They talk to me when I bid them, are silent when I want to think. They have no vapours, unless I give them of mine, no airs but what I choose to find in them. And they are complaisant, they seek nothing beyond my entertainment. My friends from outside come to please themselves and to take what they can of my store. Sometimes they take each other. One of them (not unknown to my Isoult!) will come before long—he is overdue now—and find my store enriched. I doubt he will turn thief. You may well blush, child, for, apart that it becomes you admirably, thieving is a sin, and naturally you cannot approve of it. It is to be hoped he has rifled no treasury already. There, there, I have your word for it; but you know my way! Living alone in the woods at a distance from men, which makes them ants in a swarm for me, I become a philosopher. Can you wonder?"

To such harangues, delivered with a pretty air of mockery and extravagance, which was never allowed to get out of hand, Isoult listened as she had listened to the cheerful prophetics of the Abbess of Gracedieu, with her gentle smile and her locked lips. Maulfry talked by the hour together while she and Isoult sat weaving a tapestry. For the philosopher which it seemed she was, the subject of the piece was very pleasant. It was the story of Troilus and Cresseide, no less, wherein Sir Pandarus, (departing from the custom) was represented a young man of tall and handsome presence, and the triangle of lovers like children. Diomede was an apple-cheeked school-boy, Troilus had a tunic and bare legs, Cresseide in her spare moments dandled a doll. Calchas, for his part, kept a dame-school in this piece, which for the rest was treated with a singular freedom. Isoult, poor girl, was occasionally troubled at her part of the work; but the philosopher laughed heartily at her.

"What ails thee with the piece, child?" she would cry out in her hearty way.

"Dost thou think lovers are men and women, to be taken seriously? It is to be hoped they are not, forsooth! For if they are not innocent, what shall be said of their antics?" and more to the same tune.

While affecting to treat her with freedom, Maulfry kept in reality a steady rein.

"Go out?" she would cry in mock dismay, at the least hint of such a wish from the girl—"why under the sun should we go out? To see a thicket of twigs and breathe rotten vapours? Or do you think we have processions passing in and out of the tree-trunks? Ah, minx, 'tis a procession of one you would be spying for! Nay, nay, never look big eyes at me, child. I know your processioner better than you. He will come in his time; and whether he come through the door or down the stairs I cannot tell you yet. Who taught you, pray, that he was in the wood? Not I, I vow. Why should he not be skulking in the blue alcove awaiting the hour? You look thither; how you kindle at a word! Well, well, go and see for yourself if he is in the blue alcove."

Poor trembling Isoult went on tiptoe, was fool enough to peep through the curtains, but good soul enough to take Maulfry's railing in fair part. She got as much as she deserved, and the joke was none too good perhaps; but as a trick, it sufficed to keep her on the fine edge of expectation. She dared not go out for fear of missing Prosper. She grew so tight-strung as to doubt of nothing. Had Maulfry told her he would be with them to supper on such and such a night, she would have come shaking to the meal, rosy as a new bride, nothing doubting but that the next lift of her shy eyes would reveal him before her. Thus Maulfry by hints in easy degrees led her on; and not only did she not dare to go out, but she lost all wish to peer for him in the wood, because she had been led to the conviction that he was actually in the tower—a mysterious, harboured visitant who would appear late or soon, obedient to his destiny. A door even was pointed at, smiled and winked at, passed by light-foot as they went along the gallery. Maulfry had a biting humour which sometimes led her further than she was aware.

She kept Isoult in a fever by her tricks; by this particular trick she risked a different fire—jealousy. For of the four persons who made up the household, she alone went behind that door. Vincent, the young page, brought food and wine to the threshold; Maulfry came out and took them in. But there she was perfectly safe. Isoult could never be jealous of Prosper; she would despair, but would resent nothing he might do. Jealousy requires two things exorbitantly—self-love and a sensitive surface. Isoult loved Love and Prosper—the two in one glorious image; and as for her surface, that, like the rest of her, body and soul, was his when Love allowed. Nor was she even curious, at first. Many thrashings, acquaintance with her world which was close if not long, and a deeply-driven scorn of herself threw her blindly upon the discretion of the only man she had ever found to be at once splendid and humane. What he chose was the law and what he declared the prophets. But she might get curious on other grounds, on grounds where destiny and suchlike mannish appendages did not hold up a finger at her. And in fact she did.

* * * * *

Meantime Maulfry took charge of her body and will. Isoult was obedient in everything but one. Maulfry, who always saw the girl undress and go to bed, objected to her prayers.

"Pray!" she would call out, "for what and to what do you pray? Pray to your husband when you have one, and he will give you according to your deserts, which he alone can appraise. Trust him for that. But to crave boons you know little of, from a God of whom you know nothing at all, save that you made him in your own image—what profit can that be?"

To which Isoult replied, "He told me always to pray, ma'am, and I cannot disobey any of his words."

"Ah, I remember he was given to the game. Hum! And what else did he tell you, child?"

"Deal justly, live cleanly, breathe sweet breath," Isoult answered in a whisper, as if she were in church: "praise God when He is kind, bow head and knees when He is angry, look for Him to be near at all times. Do this, and beyond it trust to thine own heart."

Maulfry pished and pshawed at this hushed oracle. "You would do better to eat well and sleep softly. 'Twould bring you nearer your heart's desire. Men like a girl to be sleek."

But in this Isoult had her way, though she said her prayers in bed. In all else she was meek as a mouse. Maulfry made her dress to suit her own taste, and let down her hair. The dress was of thin silk, fitted close, and was cut low in the neck. Isoult, who had known pinned rags, and had gone feet and legs bare without a thought, went now as if she were naked, or clothed only in her shame. But it was the fashion Maulfry adopted towards her own person, and there were no others to convict her. Nanno the old serving-woman and Vincent the page, who was only a boy, made up the household-except for the closed door. Nanno never looked at anything higher than the ground; and as for Vincent, he was in love with Isoult, and would sooner have looked at Christ in judgment.

Of those two people Nanno was believed to be dumb; Isoult, at least, never got speech of her. Vincent, who was treated by Maulfry as if he had been a mechanism, was a very simple machine. If Maulfry had been less summary with him she might have prevented the inevitable; but like all people with brains she thought a simpleton was an ass, and kicks your only speech with such. Vincent and Isoult, therefore, became friends as the days went on. Maulfry's cagebirds drew their heads together, and in Vincent's case, at any rate, it was not long before the blood began to beat livelier for the contact. Isoult was as simple as he was, and concealed nothing from him that came up in their talks together. She knew much more than he about birds, about the woods, the country beyond the forest—great rolling sheep-pastures, dim stretches of fen, sleepy rivers, the heaths and open lands about Malbank. Of all these things which came to him through her voice almost with a breath of their own roving air, he knew absolutely nothing, whereas there was very little county-lore which she did not know. She seemed indeed to him a woodland creature herself, in touch with the birds and beasts. She could put her hand into a cage full of them; the little twinkling eyes were steady upon her, but there was no fluttering or beating at the bars. Her hand closed on the bird, drew it out: the next minute it was free upon her shoulder, peeping into her sidelong face. She could hold it up to her lips: it would take the seed from her. The horses knew her call and her speaking voice. They would go and come, stand or start, as she whispered in their pricked ears. Vincent thought she might easily be a fairy. But, "No, Vincent," she would say to that, "I am a very poor girl, poorer than you."

One day Vincent disputed this point.

"You go in silks and have pearls on your head."

"They are not mine, Vincent."

"My mistress loves you."

"Oh, in love I am very rich," said the girl.

"Everybody would love you, I think," he dared.

But she shook her head at this.

"I have not found that. I am not sure of anybody's love."

"I know of one person of whom you may be very sure," said the boy, out of breath.

"But I never meant that when I said I was rich. I meant that I was rich in love, not in being loved. Ah, no!"

"You ask not to be loved, Isoult?"

"Oh, it would be impossible to be loved as I mean, as I love."

"I would like to know that. Whom do you love?"

"Why, my lord, of course! Must I not love my lord?"

"Your lord!" stammered Vincent, red to the roots of his hair. "Your lord! I never knew that you loved a lord." He gulped, and went on at random—"And where is your lord?"

"I cannot tell. He may be in this castle. I only know that I shall see him when his time comes."

"If he is in this castle, Isoult," said Vincent, sober again, "his time is not yet."

She caught her breath.

"How do you know that?" she panted.

"I know that there is a great lord in the Red Chamber, him that Madam Maulfry tends with her own hands."

"Ah, ah! You have seen him?"

"No, I have never seen him. He is very ill."

Isoult gazed at him, shocked to the soul. Ill, and she not near by!

"Oh, Vincent," she whispered. "Oh, Vincent!"

"Yes, Isoult,"—Vincent had caught some breath of her horror, and whispered, —"Yes, Isoult, he is very ill. He has been ill since the autumn, with bleeding and bleeding and bleeding. I know that is true, though I have never seen him since he was brought here swathed up in a litter; but I once saw Madam Maulfry bury something in the wood, very early in the morning. And I was frightened. Ah! I have seen strange things here, such as I dare not utter even now. So I watched my time and dug up what she had concealed. They were bloody clothes, Isoult, very many of them, and ells long! So it is true."

Isoult swayed about like a broken bough. Vincent ran to catch her, fearing she would fall. He felt the shaking of her body under his hands. That frightened him. He began to beseech.

"Isoult, dear Isoult, I have hurt you, I who would rather die, I who—am very fond of you, Isoult. Look now, be yourself again—think of this. He may not be ill by now; he is likely much better. I will find out for you. Trust me to find it all out."

"No, no, no," she whispered in haste; "you must do nothing, can do nothing. This is mine. I will find out."

"Will you ask Madam Maulfry?" said Vincent. "She will kill me if she knows that I have told you. Not that I mind that," he added in his own excuse, "but you will gain nothing that way."

"No," Isoult answered curtly. "I will find out by myself. Hush! Some one is coming. Go now."

Vincent went slowly away, for he too heard the sweep of Maulfry's robe. There was a long looking-glass in the wall, flickering over which Isoult's eyes encountered their own woeful image-brooding, reproachful, haunted eyes; this would never do for her present business. Determined to meet craft with craft, she wried her mouth to a smile, she drove peace into her eyes, took a bosomful of breath, and turned to be actress for the first time in her life. This meant to realize and then express herself. She was like to become an artist.

Towards the end of that night her brain swam with fatigue. She had had to study, first Maulfry, second, her new self, third, her old self. In studying Maulfry she began unconsciously to prepare for the shock to come—the shock of a free-given faith, than which no crisis can be more exquisite for a child. So far, however, she had no cause to distrust her châtelaine's honour, nor even her judgment. Both, she doubted not, were in Prosper's keeping.

Maulfry was in a gay, malicious humour. She pinched Isoult's cheek when she met her.

"Tired of waiting, my minion?" she began.

"No, ma'am, I am not tired at all."

"That is well. I went by the eye-shine. So you are still patient for the great reward! Well, build not too high, my dear. All men are alike, as I find them."

"My reward is to serve, ma'am, not to win."

"It is a reward one may weary of with time. There may be too much service where the slave is willing, child. But to win gives an appetite for more winning; and so the game goes on."

Again, later on, she said—

"I should like him to see you tonight, child. He would be more malleable set near such a fire. Your cheeks are burning bright! As for your big eyes, I believe you burnish them. Do you know how handsome you are, I wonder?"

"No one has ever told me that but you, ma'am," said Isoult, demure.

"Pooh, your glass will have told you. They don't lie."

"I never had a glass till I came here. Not even at the convent."

"And did you never get close enough to use somebody's eyes?" said Maulfry, with a sly look.

Isoult had nothing to say to this. Touch her on the concrete of her love, and she was always dumb.

"Well then, I will stay flattering you, and advise," Maulfry pursued. "When that august one chooses to unveil, do you present yourself on knees as you now are. In two minutes you will not be on your own, but on his, if I know mankind."

Isoult changed the talk.

"Do you know, or can you tell me, when my lord will come out, ma'am?" she ventured.

"Come out, child? Out of what? Out of a box?" Maulfry cried in mock rage. "'Tis my belief you know as much as I do. 'Tis my belief you have been at a keyhole."

Mockery gave way; the matter was serious.

"Remember now, Isoult, in doing that you will disobey a greater than I, and as good a friend. And remember what disobedience may mean."

Again she changed her tone in view of Isoult's collapse.

"You look reproaches," she said; "your eyes seem to say, like a wounded hare's, 'Strike me again. I must quiver, but I will never run.' So, child, so, I was but half in earnest. You are an obedient child, and so I will tell Messire, if by any chance I should see him first." And so on, until they went to bed.

When at last that breathing space came, Isoult was nearly choked with the fatigue of her artistic escapades; but there was no time to lose. As soon as she dared she got up in the dark, put her cloak over her night-dress, and crept out into the gallery. The door creaked as she opened it; she stood white and quailing, while her heart beat like a hammer. But nothing stirred. She went first to Maulfry's door and listened. She heard her breathing. All fast there. Then like a hare she fled on to the door she knew so well. There was a light under it: she heard a rustle as of paper or parchment. Whoever was there was turning the leaves of a book. In the silence which seemed to press upon her ears and throb in them, she debated with herself what she should do. She knew that there was indeed no question about it. If he was ill, everything—all her humility and all his tacit authority—must give way. There was but one place for a wife. Maulfry did not know she was his wife. She listened again. Inside the room she now heard some one shift in bed, and—surely that was a low groan. Oh, Lord! Oh, Love! She turned the handle; she stood in the doorway; she saw Galors sitting up in bed with a book on his knees, a lamp by his side. His sick face, bandaged and swathed, glowered at her, with great hollow eyes and a sour mouth dropped at one corner.

She stood unable to move or cry.

"All is well, dear friend," said Galors; "I did but shift and let a little curse. Go to bed, Maulfry."

Isoult had the wit to withdraw. What little she had left after that pointed a shaking finger at one thing only—flight. She had been unutterably betrayed. Her conception of the universe reeled over and was lost in fire. There was no time to think of it, none to be afraid; she did what there was to do swiftly, with a clearer head than she had believed herself capable of. She slipt back to her room without doubt or terror, and put on the clothes in which she had come from the convent, a grey gown with a leather girdle, woollen stockings, thick shoes—over all a long red hooded cloak. This done she stood a moment thinking. No, she dare not try the creaking door again; the window must serve her turn. She opened it and looked out. Through the fretty tracery of the firs she could see a frosty sky, blue-grey fining to green, green to yellow where the moon swam, hard and bright. There was not a breath of air.

She climbed at once on to the window-ledge, and stood, holding to the jamb, looking down at the black below.

A great branch ran up to the wall at a right angle; it seemed made for her intent. Sitting with your legs out of the window it was easy to take hold of a branch. She tried; it was easy, but not in a cloak. So she sat again on the sill, took off her cloak, and tried once more. Soon she was out of the window, swinging by the branch. Then her feet touched another, and very slowly (for she was panic-stricken at the least noise) she worked her way downwards to the trunk of the great tree. Once there it was easy; she was soon on the ground. But she had no notion what to do next, save that she must do it at once—whither to turn, how to get out of the wood the best and safest way. Then another thing struck her. She would be chased, that was of course. She had been chased before, and tracked, and caught. Little as she could dare that, what chance had she, a young girl flying loose in this part of the forest, a young girl decently dressed, looking as she knew now that she looked; what chance had she indeed? Well, what was she to do? She remembered Vincent.

Vincent and Nanno did not sleep in the tower: that would have been inconvenient in Maulfry's view. They had a little outhouse not ten paces from it, and slept there. Thither went Isoult, jumping at every snapt twig; the door yielded easily, but which bed should she try? Nanno, she knew, snored, for Vincent had once made her laugh by recounting his troubles under the spell of it. Well, the left-hand bed was undoubtedly Nanno's at that rate; Isoult went to the right-hand bed and felt delicately with her hand at its head. Vincent's curls!

Then she knelt down and put her face close to the boy's, whispering in his ear.

"Whisper, Vincent, whisper," she said; "whisper back to me. Do you love me, Vincent? Whisper."

"You know that I love you, Isoult," Vincent whispered. "Hush! not too loud," said she again. "Vincent, will you get up and come into the wood with me? I want to tell you something. Will you come very quietly indeed?"

"Yes," said Vincent. The whole breathless intercourse worked into his dreams of her; but he woke and sat up.

"Come," said Isoult. She crept out again to wait for him.

Vincent came out in his night-gown. The moon showed him rather scared, but there was no doubt about his sentiments. Love-blind Isoult herself could have no doubt. She lost no time.

"Vincent, I must tell you everything. I shall be in your hands, at your mercy. I must go away at once, Vincent. If I stay another hour I shall never see the daylight again. They will kill me, Vincent, or do that which no one can speak of. Then I shall kill myself. This is quite true. I have seen something to-night. There is no doubt at all. Will you help me, Vincent?"

Vincent gaped at her. "How—what—why—what shall I do?" he murmured, beginning to tremble. "Oh, Isoult, you know how I—what I whispered—!"

"Yes, yes, I know. That is why I came. You must do exactly what I tell you. You must lend me some of your clothes, any that you have, now, at once. Will you do this?'

"My clothes!" he began to gasp.

"Yes. Go and get them, please. But make no noise, for the love of Christ."

Vincent tip-toed back. He returned, after a time of dreadful rummaging in the dark, with a bundle.

"I have brought what I could find. They are all there. I could not bring what I put on every day, for many reasons. These are the best I have. How will you—can you—? They are not easy to put on, I think, for a girl."

Poor Vincent! Isoult had no time nor heed for the modesty proper to lovers.

"I will manage," she said. "Turn round, please."

Vincent did as he was bid. He even shut his eyes. Presently Isoult spoke again.

"Could you find me a pair of scissors, Vincent?" She had been quick to learn that beauty must be obeyed. She would have asked Vincent for the moon if she had happened to want it, and would have seen him depart on the errand without qualm. Sure enough, he brought the scissors before her held-out hand had grown tired.

"Cut off my hair," she said, "level with my shoulders."

"Your hair!" cried the poor lad. "Oh, Isoult, I dare not."

It reached her knees, was black as night, and straight as rain. It might have echoed Vincent's reproach. But the mistress of both was inexorable.

"Cut it to clear my shoulders, please."

He groaned, but remembered that there would be spoils, that he must even touch this hedged young goddess. So as she stood, doubleted, breeched, and in his long red hose, he hovered round her. Soon she was lightened of her load of glory, and as spruce as a chamber-page.

"Now," she said, "you must tell me the way to the nearest shelter. There is a place called St. Lucy's Precinct, I have heard. Where is that?"

He told her. Keep straight away from the moon. It was just there: he pointed with his hand. As long as the moon held she could not fail to hit it. Beyond the pine-wood there was an open shaw; she could keep through that, then cross a piece of common with bracken cut and stacked. Afterwards came a very deep wood, full of beech-timber. You crossed a brook at Four Mile Bottom,—you could hear the ripples of the ford a half-mile away,—and held straight for the top of Galley Hill. After that the trees began again, oaks mostly. A tall clump of firs would lead you there. Beyond them was the yew-tree wood. The precinct was there. But the moon was her best lamp. He was talking to her in language which she understood better than he. She could never miss the road now.

She thanked him. Then came a pause.

"I must go, Vincent," said she. "You have been my friend this night. I will tell my lord when I see him. He will reward you better than I."

"He can never reward me!" cried Vincent.

She sighed and turned to go, but he started forward and held her with both hands at her waist. She seemed so like a boy of his age, it gave him courage.

"Isoult," he stammered, "Isoult!"

"Yes, Vincent," says she.

"Are you going indeed?"

"I must go at once."

"Shall I see you again?"

"Ah, I cannot tell you that."

"Do you care nothing?"

"I think you have been my friend. Yes, I should like to see you again, some day."

"Oh, Isoult—"

"What?"

"Will you give me something?"

"What have I, Vincent? If I could you know that I would."

He had her yet by the waist. There was no blinking what he wanted. Isoult stood.

"You may kiss me there," she said with the benignity of a princess, and gave him her hand.

The boy's mouth was very near her cheek. Something—who knows what?—

checked him. He let go her waist, dropped on his knees and kissed the hand, turned little prince in his turn. Isoult was as near loving him then as she could ever be. This was no great way, perhaps, but near enough for immediate purposes. When Vincent got up she gave him her hand frankly to hold. They were two children now, and like two children kissed each other without under-thought. Then, as she sped away from the moon, Vincent crept back to his cold bed with an armful of black hair.

CHAPTER XVI

BOY AND GIRL

The woodland Mass in the yew-tree glade was served next morning by an acolyte in cassock and cotta. The way of it was this. Alice of the Hermitage was setting the altar in the light of a cloudy dawn, when she heard a step and the rustling of branches behind her. Looking quickly round, she saw a boy come out of the thicket, who stood echoing her wonder. He was a dark-haired slim lad, in leather jerkin and breeches, had crimson hose on his long legs, on his head a green cap with a pheasant's tail-feather in it. The cap he presently took off in salutation. He said his name was Roy. He had a simple direct way of answering questions, and such untroubled eyes; he was moreover so plainly a Christian, that when he asked Alice if he might serve the Mass she went advocate for him to the priest. So it came about that Isoult, having breakfasted, lay asleep in Alice's bed when a knight came cantering into the precinct followed by a page on a cob. His gilded armour blazed in the sun, a tall blue plume curtesied over his casque. He was so brave a figure—tall and a superb horseman—and so glittering from top to toe, that the old hermit, who came peering out to see, thought him a prince.

"What may your Highness need of Saint Lucy's poor bedesman?" said the hermit, rubbing his hands together.

"My Highness needs the whereabouts of a flitted lady," said the knight in a high clear voice.

Isoult, whom the clatter had awakened, lay like a hare in her form. At this time she feared Maulfry more than Galors.

"Great sir, we have no flitted ladies here. We are very plain folk." So much reproof of gilded armour and its appurtenances the hermit ventured on. But the knight was positive.

"She would have passed this way," he called out. "I know whither she would go. This hold of yours is dead in her road. So advise, hermit."

"I will call Alice," said the hermit.

"Call the devil if he will help you," the other replied.

Isoult heard Alice go out of the cottage.

"Child," said the hermit, "this gentleman seeks a flitted lady who should have passed by here on her way. Have you seen aught of such an one? Your eyes are better than most."

There followed a pause, which to the trembler in the bed seemed time for a death-warrant. Then the quiet voice of Alice told out—

"I have seen no lady. Wait. I will ask."

Isoult heard her returning step. When Alice came into the room she saw Isoult standing ready, all of a tremble.

"Oh, Alice," says she, clinging to her and speaking very fast, "I am the girl they are hunting. I am not a boy. I have deceived you. If they find me they will take me away."

"Will they kill you?"

"Ah, no! There is not enough mercy with them for that."

"Ah, you have done no ill?"

"I served God this morning. I could not have dared."

"True. Who is that knight?"

"I will tell you everything. No man could be so wicked as that knight. It is a woman, desperately wicked. She is in league with a man who would do the worst with me. Save me! save me! save me!" She began to wring her hands, and to blubber, without wits or measure left.

Alice put her hands on her. "Yes, I will save you. Get into bed and lie down. There is a page with the knight. Do you know him?"

"Yes, yes. He will do no harm. He is good."

"Very well. Lie down, and you shall be saved."

Alice went out again into the open.

"Sir knight," she was heard to say, "I have asked Roy, who came hither this morning early to serve our Mass. He has seen no one."

"Who is Roy?" said the knight sharply.

"He was server this morning. He is asleep after a long journey."

"Where?"

"Sir, we have little enough room. He is in my own chamber lying on my bed."

The knight gave a dry laugh.

"You mean that I may not venture into a lady's chamber, shameface? Well, a boy may go where a boy is, I suppose. Vincent, go and explore the acolyte."

"The page may come," said Alice, and watched him go, not without interest, perhaps not without amusement.

The unconscious Vincent was Isoult's next visitant, stepping briskly into the room. He came right up to the bed as in his right and element, a boy dealing with a boy's monkey tricks. One watchful grey eye, the curve of one rosy cheek peering from the blankets, told him a new story.

"Oh, Isoult," says he in a twitter, "is it you indeed?"

"Yes, hush! You will never betray me, Vincent?"

"Betray!" he cried. "Ah, Saints! My tongue would blister if I let the truth on you. But you are quite safe. The damsel won't let her in; she thinks she has a man to deal with. Me she let in!" Vincent chuckled at the irony of the thing. Then he grew anxious over his beloved.

"You had no mishaps? You are not hurt? Tired?"

"All safe. Not tired now. What will she do next?"

"Ah, there! She is for High March. That I know. She means to find you there. She means mischief. You must take great care. You have never seen her in mischief. I have. Oh, Christ!" He winced at the recollection.

"I will go advisedly," said Isoult. "Have no fear for me. I shall be there before she is."

Vincent sighed. "I must go. Good-bye, Isoult. I shall see you again, I am very sure."

"I hope you will. Good-bye."

He did not dare so much as touch the bed, but went out at once to make his report. He had questioned the boy—a dull boy, but he thought honest. Assuredly he had seen no lady on his way. His lies deceived Maulfry, who would have known better but for her proneness to think everybody a fool. Soon Isoult heard the thud of hoofs on the herbage; then Alice came running in to hear the story at large.

The two girls became very friendly. Their heads got close together over Prosper and Galors and Maulfry—the Golden Knight who was a woman! The escape savoured a miracle, was certainly the act of some heavenly power. An Archangel, Alice thought, to which Isoult, convinced that it was Love, assented for courtesy.

"Though for my part," she added, "I lean hardly upon Saint Isidore."

"You do well," said Alice, "he is a great saint. Is he your patron?"

"I think he is," said Isoult.

"Then it is he who has helped you, be sure. No other could know the ins and outs of your story so well, or make such close provision. The Archangels, you see, are few, and their business very great." Isoult agreed.

Of Prosper Alice could not get a clear image. When Isoult was upon that theme her visions blinded her, and sent her for refuge to abstractions. She candidly confessed that he did not love her; but then she did not ask that he should.

"But you pray, 'Give him me all,'" Alice objected.

"Yes, I want to be his servant, and that he should have no other. I cannot bear that any one should do for him what I can do best. That is what I tell the Holy Virgin."

"And Saint Isidore, I hope," said Alice gently; but Isoult thought not.

"It would be useless to tell Saint Isidore," she explained.

"He is a man, and men think differently of these matters. They want more, and do not understand to be contented with much less."

"Forgive me, Isoult. I know nothing of love and lovers. But if you marry this lord—as I suppose you might?"

"He might marry *me*," said Isoult slowly.

"Well, then, is there no more to look for in marriage but the liberty to serve?"

"I look for nothing else."

"But he might?"

"Ah, ah! If he did!"

"Well?"

"Oh, Alice, I love him so!"

"Darling Isoult—I see now. Forgive me."

The two friends cried together and kissed, as girls will. Then they talked of what there was to do. Isoult was resolute to go.

"She will ride straight to High March," she said. "I know her. My lord is there. If she finds not me, she will find him, and endanger his ease. I must be there first. She must follow the paths, however they wind, because she is mounted on a heavy horse. I shall go through the brakes by ways that I know. I shall easily outwit her in the forest."

"But you cannot walk, dearest. It is many days to High March."

"I shall ride."

"What will you ride, goose?"

"A forest pony, of course."

"Will you go as you are—like a boy, Isoult?"

Alice was aghast at the possibility; but Isoult, who had many reasons for it apart from her own safety (forgotten in the sight of Prosper's), was clear that she would. Prosper she knew was the guest of the Countess Isabel, a vaguely great and crowned lady; probably he was one of many guests. "And how shall I, a poor girl, come at him in the midst of such a company?" she asked herself. But if she went with a tale of being his page Roy he might admit her to some service, to hand his cup, or just to lie at his door of a night. The real Roy had done more than this; he would never refuse her so much. So she thought at least; and at the worst she would have space to tell her message.

At noon, the forest pony captured and haltered with a rope, she started. Alice was tearful, but Isoult, high in affairs, had no time to consider Alice. She gave her a kiss, stooping from the saddle, thanked her for what she had done on Prosper's account, and flew. She never looked back to wave a hand or watch a hand-waving; she was in a fever for action. Going, she calculated profoundly. There was a choice of ways. The great road from Wanmouth to High March skirted Marbery Down (where she had watched the stars and heard the sheep-bells many a still night), and then ran east by the forest edge to Worple. It only took in Worple by a wide divagation; after that it curved back to the forest, ran fairly clean to Market Basing, thence over ridges and coombs, but climbing mostly, it fetched up at High March. It was a military road. Well, she might follow Maulfry on this road till within a couple of days of the castle; it would ensure safety for her, and a good footing for her beast. On the other hand, if she rode due north over everything (as she knew she could), she would steal at least one more day. And could she afford to lose a clear day with Prosper? Ah, and it would give a margin against miscarriage of the news by any adverse fate on either of them. Before she framed the question she knew it answered. Her road then was to be dead north across the edge of Spurnt Heath (where her father's cottage was), past Martle Brush, stained with the black blood of Galors, then on to the parting of the ways, and by the right-hand road to High March. Thinking it over, she put her journey at three, and Maulfry's at four days. Maulfry's was actually rather less, as will appear.

If all this prove dull to the reader, I can only tell him that he had better know his way about Morgraunt than lose it, as I have very often done in the course of my hot-head excursions. There are so many trackless regions in it, so many great lakes of green with never an island of a name, that to me, at least, it is salvation to have solid verifiable spots upon which to put a finger and say—"Here is Waisford, here Tortsentier, here is the great river Wan, here by the grace of God and the Countess of Hauterive is Saint Giles of Holy Thorn." Of course to Isoult it was different. She had been a forester all her life. To her there were names (and names of dread) not to be known of any map. Deerleap, One Ash, the Wolves' Valley, the Place of the Withered Elm, the Charcoal-Burners', the Mossy Christ, the Birch-grove, the Brook under the Brow—and a hundred more. She steered by these, with all foresters. What she did not remember, or did not know, was that Maulfry had also lived in Morgraunt and knew the ways by heart. Still, she had a better mount than the Lady of Tortsentier, and Love for a link-boy.

However fast she rode for her mark, her way seemed long enough as she battled through that shadowed land, forded brooks, stole by the edge of wastes or swamps, crossed open rides in fear what either vista might set bare, climbed imperceptibly higher and higher towards the spikes of Hauterive, upon whose woody bluffs stands High March. Not upon one beast could she have done what she did; one took her a day and a night going at the pace she exacted. She knew by her instincts where the herds of ponies ran. It was easy to catch and halter any one she chose; no forest beast went in fear of her who had the wild-wood savour in her hair—but it meant more contriving and another stretch for her tense brain. For herself, she hardly dared stay at all. Prosper's breast under a dagger! If she had stayed she would not have slept. The fever and the fever only kept her up; for a slim and tender girl she went through incredible fatigues. But while the fever lasted so did she, alert, wise, discreet, incessantly active. Part of her journey—for the half of one day—she actually had Maulfry in full view; saw her riding easily on her great white Fleming, saw the glint of the golden armour, and Vincent ambling behind her on his cob, catching at the leaves as he went, for lack of something better. She was never made out by them,—at a time like this her wits were finer than her enemy's,—so she was able to learn how much time she had to spare. That night she slept for three hours. As for her food, we know that she could supply herself with that; and when the deer failed her, she scrupled nothing (she so abject with whom she loved!) to demand it of whomsoever she happened to meet. She grew as bold as a winter robin. One evening she sat by a gipsy fire with as shrewd a set of cut-throats as you would wish to hang. She never turned a hair. Another night she fell in with some shaggy drovers leading cattle from March into Waisford, and shared the cloak and pillow of one of them without a quiver. Having dozed and started half-a-dozen times in a couple of hours, she got up without disturbing her bed-fellow and took to the woods again. So she came to her last day, when she looked to see the High March towers and what they held.

On that day at noon, as she sat resting near a four-went-way, she heard the tramp of horses, the clatter of arms. She hid herself, just in time, in a thicket of wild rose, and waited to see what was threatening. It proved to be a company of soldiers—she counted fifty, but there were more—well armed with spears, whose banneroles were black and white. They rode at a trot to the crossways; there one cried halt. They were within ten yards of her, but happily there were no dogs. Then she heard another horse—that of the captain, as she guessed. She saw him come round the bend of the ride, a burly man, black upon a black horse. There were white feathers in his helmet; on his shield three white wicket-gates. Galors! At this moment her heart did not fail her. It scarcely beat faster. She was able to listen at her ease.

They debated of ways; Galors seemed in doubt, and vexed at doubting. One of them pointed the road to High March.

"No, by the Crucified," said Galors, "that is no road for me just yet, who once showed a shaven crown upon it. I leave High March to the Golden Knight for the hour. He shall make my way straight, bless him for a John Baptist. We are for Wanmeeting, my friends. Wanmeeting, then Goltres."

Said another—"Sir, if that road lead to High March, we must go straight forward to fetch at Wanmeeting."

So they disputed at large. Isoult made out that Galors had raised a company of outlaws (no hard job in Morgraunt at any time, and raised for her ravishment, if she had known it), and was bound for Goltres, where there was a castle, and a lord of it named Spiridion. She could find out little more. Sometimes they spoke of Hauterive town and a castle there, sometimes of Wanmeeting and a high bailiff; but Goltres seemed most in Galors' mind.

Finally they took the road to Wanmeeting. Isoult waited till the sound of the horses died in the swishing of trees, and then sped forward on her feet towards her lord. She knew she was near by, and would not risk time or discovery by catching her pony. By four in the afternoon she had her first view of the great castle rising stately out of the black pines and bright green of the spring foliage, warm grey in the full light of the sun, and solid as the rock it was of. In another hour she was demanding of the porter at the outer bailey Messire Prosper le Gai, in the name of his servant Roy.

CHAPTER XVII

ROY

That clear and mild evening, fluted as April by a thrush in the lilacs, Prosper and the Countess walked together on the terrace. A guard or two, pike in hand, lounged by the balustrade; the deer-hound, with his muzzle between his paws, twitched his ears or woke to snap at a fly: it seemed as if the earth, sure of the sun at last, left her conning tower with a happy sigh. It turned the Countess to a tender mood, where she suffered herself to be played upon by the season—*L'ora del tempo e la dolce stagione.* The spring whimpered in her blood. Prosper felt her sighing as she leaned on his arm, and made stress to amuse her, for sighs always seemed to him unhealthy. He set himself to be humorous, sang, chattered, told anecdotes, and succeeded in infecting himself first and the lady afterwards. She laughed in spite of herself, then with a good will. They both laughed together, so that the guards nudged each other. One prophesied a match of it.

"And no bad thing for High March if it were so," said the other, "and we with a man at the top. I never knew a greater-hearted lord. He is voiced like a peal of bells in a frolic."

"He's a trumpet in a charge home."

"He's first in."

"Fights like a demon."

"Snuffs blood before 'tis out of the skin."

"Ah, a great gentleman!"

"What would his age be?"

"Five-and-twenty, not an ounce more. So ho! What's this on the road?"

The other man looked up, both looked together. The porter came on to the terrace, followed by a dark youth who walked with a limp.

"A boy to speak with Messire," said the porter, and left his convoy.

"Name and business?" asked one of the guards.

"Roy, the page from Starning, to speak with my lord."

"Wait you there, Roy. I will ask for you."

The guard went off whistling. Isoult fixed long looks again on the two at the end of the terrace. She was nearly done.

"You have made a push for it, my shaver," said the second guard, after a study from head to toe.

"My business pushed me."

"Ah, trouble in the forest, eh? Are the roads clear?"

"I met with a company."

"How many pikes?"

"Nearer sixty than fifty."

"Where bound?"

"Goltres, I understood."

"Who led?"

"A black knight."

"Ah. Were you mounted, my lad?"

"Not then. I was in hiding."

"Ah. You know what you're about, it seems."

"Yes," said Isoult.

The messenger returned.

"You are to go and speak to Messire," he said.

Isoult saw Prosper coming towards her. Her heart's trouble began; her knees knocked together, she swayed a little as she walked.

"That boy's had as much as he can stand," said the guard who had questioned.

"What, a'ready?" laughed his mate.

"Not beer, you fool—travel. He's extended—he will hardly reach another yard."

The fact was wholly, the reasoning partly true. Doubt had lain as dregs at the bottom of the draught which had fed her. Now she was at the lees—brought so low that she had to depend upon the worth of her news for assurance of a hearing. True, she had asked no more, nor looked for it—but you cannot tame hopes. A dry patch in her throat burned like fire, but she fought her way. He was close: she could see the keen light in his eyes. Alas! alas! he looked for Roy. A thick tide of despair came surging over her, closing in, beating at her temples for entrance. She lost her sight, fluttered a very rag in the wind, held out her hands for a balance. Prosper saw her feeling about like a blind man. He quickened.

"Danger! danger!" she breathed, and fell at his feet.

He picked her up as if she had been a baby and carried her into the house. As he passed the guards one of them came forward to help.

"The lad's been pushed beyond his strength, my lord," the man ventured.

"So I see," said Prosper, and shook him off. The business must be got through alone.

"A great gentleman," said the man to his mate. "But he fags his servants."

"Bless you, Jack, they like it!" the other assured him, with a laugh at the weakness of his own kind.

Wine on her lips and brows brought her to, but it was a ghost of a boy that lay on the bed and held fixed upon Prosper a pair of haunted eyes. But Prosper stayed at his post. He was very tender to weak things. Here in all conscience was a weak thing! That look of hers, which never wavered for a second, frightened him. He thought she was going to die; reflected that death was not safe without a priest: the thought of death suggested his dream, the dream his old curiosity to see again that which had so stirred him asleep. Well, here she was before him—

part of her at least; for her soul, which he had helped her to win, was fighting to escape. The sounds of the duel, the shuddering reluctance of the indrawn breath, the moan that told of its enlargement, these things, and the motionless open eyes which seemed to say, Look! Body and soul are fighting, and we can only watch! turned him helpless, as we all are in actual audience of death. He sat, therefore, waiting the issue; and if he had any thought at all it was, "God, she was mine once, and now I have let her go!" For we do not pity the dying or dead; but ourselves we pity, who suffer longer and more than they.

Presently Isoult fetched a long sigh, and moved a hand ever so slightly. Prosper took it, leaning over her.

"Isoult," he said, "child, do you not know me?"

He affected more roughness than he felt, as a man's way is. He will always dictate rather than ask. At his words a shiny veil seemed to withdraw from her eyes, whereby he learned that she had heard him. He put the cup to her lips again. Some was spilt, but some was swallowed.

She motioned an answer to his question. "Yes, lord," he made of it.

"Isoult, I ought to be angry with you," said he; and she looked untroubled at him, too far gone to heed the blame of lords or men.

"No, no," her lips framed as she closed her eyes.

She fell asleep holding his hand, and he watched by the bed till midnight, warning off with a lifted finger any who came from the Countess for news of him. Hard thinking sped the vigil: he wondered what could have happened to bring her so near her death or ever he could have word of her. Galors, he was pretty sure, had got to work again; it was good odds that he had been running in couple with the lady of the dead knight. Their connection was proved to his mind. Then Isoult, having escaped by some chance, had naturally headed straight for him—very naturally, very properly. It was his due: he would fight for her; she was his wife. Ah, Heaven, but she was more than that! There were ties, there were ties now. What more precisely she was he could not say; but more, oh, certainly more. Weak things moved him always: here was a weak enough thing, white and shadowy in a bed! He felt the stirring of her hand in his, like a little mouse. Poor frightened creature, flying from all the forest eyes to drop at his feet at last! By God, he would split Galors this time. And as for the woman—pooh, give her a branding and let her go.

At midnight Isoult woke up with a little cry. Her first words were as before —"Danger! danger!"

"You are safe with me, dear," said Prosper.

"Danger to you, my lord!"

"To me, my child? Who can be dangerous to me?"

"Maulfry and Galors. Maulfry most of all."

"Maulfry? Maulfry?" he echoed. Ah, the lady!

She told him everything that had passed from the hour she left Gracedieu, and even Prosper could not but see that she had had one thought throughout and one stay. Maulfry's smiling treachery had shocked her to the soul; but the very shock had only quickened her alarms about his safety. He could not avoid the reflection that this startled creature loved him. Prosper would have been more grateful than he was, and more shrewdly touched, had he not also felt astonishment (tinged, I think, with scorn) that any one should be anxious about his conduct of the war. Women's ways! As if a man-at-arms did not live in danger; and for danger, pardieu. He did not show any of this, nor did he leave the girl's hand. Besides, the affair was very interesting. So he heard her to the end, adding nothing by way of comment beyond an occasional "Good child," or "Brave girl," or the wine cup to her dry lips. Seeing too how deeply her alarms had sunk into her, he had tact enough not to let her guess his intent, which very nakedly was to follow up Galors towards Goltres or Wanmeeting. Upon this matter he contented himself with asking her one question—whether she had ever heard speak of a knight called Salomon de Born? The answer made him start. Isoult shook her head.

"I never heard of him, my lord; but I know that Dom Galors' name is De Born."

"Hum," said Prosper; "he has taken all he can get, it appears. And does he still carry the shield and arms he had before?"

She told him, yes; and that all his company carried his colours, black and white, upon their banneroles and the trappings of their horses.

"In fact our monk sets up for a lord—Messire Galors de Born?"

"So he is named among his men, lord," said Isoult.

"But wait a minute. Do you know the man's name before he entered religion?"

"It was De Born, my lord, as I understood. But I have heard him also called Born."

Prosper thought again, shook his head, made nothing of it, and so kept it for his need.

Next day before dinner he came into the hall leading a black-haired boy by the hand. He went up to the Countess's chair between the ranked assembly.

"My lady Countess," says he, "suffer my page Roy to kiss your hand. He loves me, and I him, if for no better reason than that he does me so much credit. He alone in my father's house has dared it, I may tell you. Take him in then for my sake, madam. The master's master should be the servant's master."

The Countess smiled.

"He is certainly welcome on this showing," she said, "as well as on others. That must be a good servant for whom his master forsakes not only his friends but his supper." Then turning to Isoult, "Well, Roy," she asked, "and art thou whole again?"

"Yes, please my lady," said Isoult.

"Then thou shalt kiss my hand for thy master's sake!" returned the Countess, after looking keenly at the girl.

Isoult knelt and kissed the white hand. The Countess beckoned to one of her pages.

"Go now, Roy, with Balthasar," said she. "He will show thee whatever is needful to be known. Afterwards thou shalt come into hall and serve at thy lord's chair. And so long as he is here thou shalt serve him, and sleep at his chamber door. I am sure that thou art faithful and worthy of so much at my hands. And now, Prosper," she turned to say, as if that business were happily done, "you shall finish your story of the Princess of Tunis and the Neapolitan barber, which you broke off so abruptly yestereven. Then we will go to supper."

The audience was over; Prosper received his wife's reverence with a blush, sighed as he saw her back out of the presence, and sighed still more as he turned to his task of entertaining the great lady his hostess.

Isoult was led away by Balthasar into the pages' quarters, and escaped thence with an examination which was not so searching as it might have been had she not passed for squire to such a redoubtable smiter. She was not long finding out that Prosper was the god of all the youth in High March. His respect won her respect, though it could win him no more from her. She heard their glowing reports, indeed, with a certain scorn—to think that they should inform her of him, forsooth! From the buttery she was taken to run the gauntlet of the women in the servants' hall. Here the fact that she made a very comely boy—a boy agile, dark-eyed, and grave, who looked to have something in reserve—worked her turn where Prosper's prowess might have failed her. The women found her frugality of speech piquant; it laid down for her the lines of a reputation for experienced gallantry—the sort which asks a little wearily, Is this worth my while? It seemed to them that in matters of love Roy might be hard to please. This caused a stir in one or two bosoms. A certain Melot, a black-eyed girl, plump, and an easy giggler, avowed in strict confidence to her room-fellow that night, that her fate had been told her by a Bohemian—a slight and dark-eyed youth was to be her undoing. You will readily understand that this was duly reported by the room-fellow to Balthasar, and by him to Isoult, following the etiquette observed in such matters. Isoult frowned, said little of it, and thought less.

With the other pages she waited behind her master's chair at supper. He still sat at the Countess's right hand as the principal guest (evidently) in her esteem, if not in degree. Isoult had prepared herself for what was to come as best she could. She had expounded, as you have been told, her simple love-lore to Alice of the Hermitage; but it is doubtful if she had known how much like a cow beset by flies in a dry pasture a lover may be made. Every little familiar gesture was a prick. Their talk of things which had happened to them counselled her to despair. When the Countess leaned to Prosper's chair she measured how long this could be borne; but when by chance her hand touched on his arm, to rest there for a moment, Isoult was as near jealousy as a girl, in the main logical by instinct and humble by conviction, could ever be. Then came doubt, and brought fear to drag her last hand from the rock and let her fall. Fear came stealthily to her, like a lurking foe, out of the Countess's unconscious eyes. Isoult had nothing to hope for that she had not already: she knew that now she was blessed beyond all women born; she loved, she was near her beloved; but her heart was crying out at the cold and the dark. There was love in the Countess's looks; Isoult could not doubt it. And Prosper did not take it amiss. Here it was that Isoult was blind, for Prosper had no notions whatever about the Countess's looks.

He was in very high spirits that supper. He liked Isoult to be by him again, liked it for her sake as well as for the sake of the escapade. He had watched her a good deal during the day, and found her worth perusal. She had picked up her good looks again, went bravely dressed in his livery of white and green, with his hooded falcon across her bosom and embroidered slantwise upon the fold of her doublet. Thus she made a very handsome page. She was different though. He thought that there was now about her an allure, a grave richness, a reticence of charm, an air of discretion which he must always have liked without knowing that he liked it. Yet he had never noticed it before. The child was almost a young woman, seemed taller and more filled out. No doubt this was true, and no doubt it braved her for the carrying of her boy's garnish, otherwise a risky fardel for a young woman. He was pleased with her, and with himself for being pleased. So he was very merry, ate well, drank as the drink came, and every time Isoult brought him the cup he looked at her trying to win an answer. Since no answer was to be had he was forced to be satisfied with looking. Once or twice in serving him their hands touched. This also pleased him, but he was shocked to find this rosy girl with the shining eyes had hands as cold as ice. And he so well disposed to her! And she his wife! He pursued his researches in this sort at the cost of more stoups of wine than were needful or his rule. He grew enthusiastic over it, and laid up a fine store of penalties for future settlement. The enthusiast must neglect something; Prosper, being engrossed with his page and his wine, neglected the Countess. This lady, after tapping with her foot in her chamber till the sound maddened her, withdrew early. Immediately she had gone Prosper announced great fatigue. He sent for his page and a torch. Isoult escaped from the noisy herd round the buttery fire, lit her torch at a cresset, disregarded Melot languishing in a dark corner, and met her lord in mid hall.

"Take me to bed, Roy," said he, looking at her strangely.

Isoult led the way; he followed her close.

She went into the dark room with her torch while Prosper stood in the doorway. She lighted the candles: he could see how deliberately she did it, without waver or tremor. His own heart thumping at such a rate, it was astounding to him to watch. Then she beat out the torch on the hearth, and waited. Three strides brought him into the middle of the room, but the look of her stopped him there.

She was rather pale, very grave, looked taller than her height; her eyes seemed like twin lakes of dark water, unruffled and unwinking. Neither of them spoke, though there was fine disorder in two hearts, and one was crying inwardly to Love and the Virgin. Isoult spoke first in a very low voice.

"Lord, now let me go," she said.

The next minute he had her in his arms.

She had been prepared for this, and now suffered what she must, lifeless and pleasureless, with a dull pain in her heart. This was the stabbing pain (as with a muffled knife) with which true love maims itself in its own defence. His aim for her lips was parried; as well he might have embraced a dead woman. Soon his passion burned itself out for lack of fuel; he set her down and looked moodily at her, panting.

"Are you my wife? By the saints, are you not my wife? Why are you here?"

"To serve my lord."

"Serve! serve! And is this the service you do me? Are you not my wife?"

"I am she, lord. I am what you made me. I serve as you taught."

"Does a wife not owe obedience? Hath a lord—hath a husband no right to that?"

"Love is a great lord—"

"By Heaven, do I not love you?"

He could have sworn he did; but Isoult knew better.

"Yesterday my lord loved me not; to-morrow he will not love me. I am his servant—his page."

"Isoult, you know that you are my wife."

"I am your servant, lord," said Isoult. "Listen."

As he stood hiding his face in his hand, this tall and lordly youth, Isoult took up her parable, but so low you could hardly hear it.

"Lord," she said, "when you wed me in the cottage it was for honour and to save my body from hanging. And when you had saved my body you showed me soul's salvation, and taught me how to pray, saying, Deal justly, live cleanly, breathe sweet breath. And when you went away from Gracedieu saying you would come again, I waited for you there, doing all that you had taught me. So I did when I was made a prisoner in the dark tower, and so I would do now that I am blest with sight of you and service. But when I cried for you at Gracedieu you came not, and when I came to warn you of your peril you hoped for Roy, and seeing me your looks fell. And I knew this must be so, and would have gone back to Gracedieu had you told me. For then I should still have been rich with what you had given me once. Now even I will go, asking but one thing of you for a mercy, that you do not send me away beggared of what you gave me before."

"And what did I give you, Isoult?" he whispered.

"'Twas your honour to keep, my lord," said the girl.

He had been looking at her long before she made an end, but not before she had gathered strength from her theme. When he did look he saw that her eyes were large and dark; honesty and clear courage burned steadily there; the candles reflected in them showed no flickering. She had her hands crossed over her bosom as if to hold a treasure close: her treasures were her ring and her faithful heart. He knew now that he could not gain her for this turn, wife or no wife; in this great mood of hers she would have killed herself sooner than let him touch her; and when she had ended her say he knew that she had spoken the truth, a truth which put him to shame. Like a spoilt boy rather than a rogue he began to plead, nevertheless. He went on his knees, unbound her two hands and held them, trying to win his way by protestations of love and desire. The words, emptied of all fact by this time (for the boy was honest enough), rang hollow. She looked down at him sadly, but very gently, denying him against all her love. The fool went on, set on his own way. At last she said—

"Lord, such love as thou hast for me Galors hath also. And shall I let my looks undo me with thee, and thee with me? I will follow thee as a servant, and never leave thee without it be thy will. I beseech of thee deface not thine own image which I carry here. Now let me go."

She touched herself upon the breast. This was how she drove the evil spirit out of him. He got up from his knees and thanked her gruffly. His words came curt and sharp, with the old order in the tone of them; but she knew that he was really ordering himself. She held out her hand, rather shyly—for, the battle won, the conquered had resumed command—he took and kissed it. She turned to go. The evil spirit within him lifted up a bruised head.

"By God!" cried he, "you shall lie in the bed and I at the door."

And so it was, and so remained, while High March held the pair of them. By which it will appear that the evil spirit was disposed in pious uses.

CHAPTER XVIII

BOY'S LOVE

Maulfry did not appear at High March either the next day, or the next. In fact, a week passed without any sign from her, which sufficed Isoult to avoid the tedious attentions of the maids, and to attract those of the Countess of Hauterive. This great lady had been prepared to be gracious to the page for the sake of the master. She had not expected the master to show his appreciation of her act by leaving her alone. The two of them were very much together; Prosper was beginning to court his wife. The Countess grew frankly jealous of Roy; and the more she felt herself slipping in her own esteem, the more irritated with the boy did she grow. She had long admitted to herself that Prosper pleased her as no man had ever done, since Fulk de Bréauté was stabbed on the heath. In pursuance of this she had waived the ten years of age between herself and the youth. It seemed the prerogative of her rank. If she thought him old enough, he was old enough, pardieu. If she went further, as she was prepared to do; if she said, "You are old enough, Prosper, for my throne. Come!" and he did not come, she had a sense that there was *lèse majesté* lurking where there should only be an aching heart. The fact was, that she began to hate Roy very heartily; it would not have been long before she took steps to be rid of him, had not fortune saved her the trouble, as must now be related. Isoult, it is to be owned, saw nothing of all this. Having once settled herself on the old footing with her lord and master, wherein, if there was nothing to gain, there was also nothing to lose, the humble soul set to work to forget her late rebellion, and to be as happy as the shadow of Maulfry and the uncompromising shifts of the enamoured Melot would allow. As for Prosper's courting, it shall be at once admitted that she discerned it as little as the Countess's malevolent eye. He hectored her rather more, expected more of her, and conversed with her less often and less cheerfully than had been his wont. It is probable that he was really courting his wounded susceptibilities.

About a week after the adventure of the bed-chamber, as she was waiting in the hall with the crowd of lacqueys and retainers, some one caught her by the arm. She turned and saw Vincent.

He was hot, excited, and dusty, but very much her servant, poor lad.

"Dame Maulfry is here," he whispered her.

"Where?"

"You will see her soon. She is tricked in the figure of a dancing woman, an Egyptian. She will come telling fortunes and shameful tales. And she means mischief, but not to you."

"Ah! How do you know that, Vincent?"

"She talked very often to herself when we were in the forest. We have been to many places—Wanmeeting, Waisford. There is no doubt at all. `Kill the buck and you have the doe': she said it over and over again. We have seen the sick man. He is quite well now, and very strong. She is to kill your lord and take you alive. She seems to hate him. I can't tell you why. Which is your lord of all those on the dais?"

"Hush. There he sits on the right hand of the Countess. He is talking to her now. Look, she is laughing."

"Oh, he is tall. He looks light and fierce, like a leopard. How high he carries his head! As if we were of another world."

"So we are," said Isoult.

Vincent sighed and went on with his story. "I have run away from Maulfry. She left me to wait for her at the end of the avenue, with three horses, just as I was at Gracedieu—do you remember? But I could never do that again. Now I must hide somewhere."

"Come with me. I will hide you."

She took him to the buttery and gave him over to the cook-maids. She told Melot that this was a fellow of hers who must be tended at all costs. Melot made haste to obey, sighing like a gale of wind. Isoult had rather asked any other, but time pressed. She hurried back to the hall to take her proper place at table, and going thither, made sure that her dagger slid easily in and out. She was highly excited, but not with fear—elated rather.

Supper passed safely over. The Countess withdrew to the gallery, and Prosper followed her as his duty bound him. He was still thoughtful and subdued, but with a passing flash now and again of his old authority, which served to make a blacker sky for the love-sick lady. The sounds of music came gratefully to Isoult; for once she was glad to be rid of him. She sped back to Vincent, enormously relieved that the field of battle was to be narrowed. Maulfry would have been awkward in the open; she knew she could hold her in the passages. There were two things to be prevented, observe. The knife must not discover Prosper, nor Maulfry Isoult. The latter was almost as important on Prosper's account as the former. Isoult knew that. She knew also that it must be risked of the two; but in the passages she could deal with it.

Vincent was sitting by the fire between Melot and Jocosa, another of the maids. Melot bit her lip, and edged away from him as Isoult came in.

"Girls," said the redoubtable Roy, with scant ceremony, "I have to speak to my mate."

Melot bounced out of the room. Jocosa loitered about, hoping for a frolic. A chance look at Master Roy seemed to convince her that she too had better go.

As soon as they were alone Isoult made haste to eat and drink. Between the mouthfuls she said—

"She has not come yet."

"No," said Vincent, "but she will come soon. There is time enough for what she has to do. She had to wait till it was dark. She never works in daylight."

"We are safe now," Isoult said.

"How is that—safe?"

"She will never see my lord except through me. The doorward will bring her to me, or me to her. Then I shall be sent to my lord."

"And will you go, Isoult?"

"Never."

"What will you do?"

Isoult looked down at her belt, whither Vincent's eyes followed hers.

"Ah," he said, "will you dare do that?"

"There is nothing I would not dare for him."

Thereupon Vincent pulls out his dagger as bravely as you please.

"Isoult," says he, "this is man's work. You leave her to me."

"Man's work, Vincent?" But she could not bear to finish the sentence, so changed it. "Man's work to stab a woman?"

"Man's work, Isoult, to shield the lady one loves—honours I should say."

"Yes, that is better."

"No, it is worse. Oh! Isoult, may I not love you?"

"Certainly not."

"But how can I help it? I do love you. What can prevent me?"

Isoult coloured.

"Love itself can prevent you, Vincent."

"Oh! you are right, you are wise, you are very holy. I have never thought of such things as that. And is that true love?"

"Love should kill love, if need were."

"Love shall," said Vincent in a whisper. Whereupon Isoult smiled on him.

They fell to chatting again, discussing possibilities, or facts, which were safer ground. Isoult heard the stroke of ten. Presently after, the page-in-waiting sang out a challenge. A shuffling step stopped, a cracked voice asked for Messire Prosper le Gai.

"Maulfry!" said Vincent with a shiver.

"Hush!"

"It is late to see Messire," said the page.

"He will see me none the less, young gentleman."

"Wait where you stand. I will fetch his squire."

Isoult got up. Vincent was already on his feet.

"Shall we go?" asked the boy.

"Wait," said the girl. "We must get rid of Balthasar."

Balthasar came in with his message to Roy. Isoult affected to know all about it. She sent Balthasar off to find a sealed package, which did not exist, in a turret room where it could not have been. Balthasar went. He was a dull boy.

"Now," said Isoult, and led the way into the passage.

It was pretty dark there and draughty. A flickering cresset threw a flare of light one minute, and was shrivelled to a blue spark the next. It sufficed them to see a tall beribboned shape, a thing of brown skin and loose black hair—a tall woman standing at a distance. Side by side Isoult and Vincent went down towards her. Half-way Isoult suddenly stopped and beckoned Maulfry forward with her hand. The fact was that she had seen how near the woman stood to the guard-room door; she wished to do her business undisturbed. Vincent, however, who knew nothing of the guard-room, had a theory that Isoult was frightened.

Maulfry came bowing forward. Isoult turned and walked slowly away from her, Vincent in company and on the watch; Maulfry followed, gaining. By the buttery door Isoult suddenly stopped and faced round. Maulfry was before her.

"Maulfry," said the girl quietly, "what do you want with my lord?"

Maulfry's eyes shifted like lightning from one to the other. She felt her rage rising, but swallowed it down.

"You little fool," she said, "you little fool, his life is in danger."

"I have warned him, Maulfry. It was in danger."

"Warned him! I can do better than that. Why, your own is as shaky as his. You have brought it about by your own folly, and now you are like to let him be killed. Take me to him, child, for his sake and yours."

"You will never see him, Maulfry."

Maulfry hesitated for a second or two. She was very angry at this trouble.

"You are a great fool for such a little body, Isoult," she said; "more than I had believed. Come now, let me pass." She made to go on: Isoult, to get ready, stepped back a step, but Vincent slipped in between them. He was shaking all over.

"Stay where you are, dame," he said.

Maulfry gave a jump.

"Bastard!" She spat at him, and whipped a knife into his heart. Vincent sobbed, and fell with a thud. In a trice Isoult had struck with her dagger at Maulfry's shoulder. Steel struck steel: the blade broke short off at the haft.

A guard came out with a torch, saw the trouble, and turned shouting to his mates. Half-a-dozen of them came tumbling into the passage with torches and pikes. There was a great smoke, some blinding patches of light, everywhere else a sooty darkness. By the time they were up to the buttery there was nothing to be seen but a boy sitting on the flags with a dead boy on his knees. Maulfry had gone. As for Vincent, Love had killed love sure as fate.

When Prosper heard of it all he was very angry. "Is this how you serve me, child? To fight battles for me? I suppose I should return the compliment by darning your stockings. I had things to say to this woman, many things to learn. You have bungled my plans and vexed me."

Isoult humbled herself to the dust, but he would not be appeased.

"Who was this boy?" he asked her. "What on earth had he to do in my affair?"

"Lord," she said meekly, "he died to save me from death, and once before he risked his life to let me escape from Tortsentier."

Prosper felt the rebuke and got more angry.

"A fool meets with a fool's death. Boys and girls have no business with steel. They should be in the nursery."

"I was in prison, lord."

He remembered then that she might have stayed in prison for all his help. He began to be ashamed of himself.

"Child," he said more gently, "I did wrong to be angry; but you must never thwart my plans. The boy loved you?"

"Few have loved me," said she, "but he loved me."

"Ah! Did he tell you so?"

"Yes, lord."

"And what did you say to that, Isoult?"

"I told him how love should be."

"So, so. And how do you think that love should be?"

"Thus, lord," said Isoult, looking to Vincent's heart.

Prosper turned pale. There were deeps, then, of which he had never dreamed.

"Isoult," he said, "did you love this boy who so loved you?"

She shook her head rather pitifully. "Ah, no!"

"But yet you told him how he should love you?"

"Nay, lord, but I told him how I should love."

"You must have studied much in this science, my child."

"I am Isoult la Desirous, lord."

Prosper turned away. There was much here that he did not understand, and that night before he went to sleep at her door he kissed her forehead—it would have been her hand if his dignity had dared—and then they prayed together as once in the forest.

Afterwards he was glad enough to remember this.

CHAPTER XIX

LADY'S LOVE

For, notwithstanding all that Isoult could urge (which was very little indeed), Prosper started next morning with a dozen men to scour the district for Maulfry. He refused point blank to take the girl with him, and after her rebuke and abasement of the night before, still more after the reconciliation on knees, she dared not plead overmuch. He was a man and a great lord; she could not suppose that she knew all his designs—any of them, if it came to that. He must go his way—which was man's way—and she must stop at High March nursing her heart—which was woman's way—even if High March proved a second Gracedieu and Isabel a more inexorable Maulfry. No act of her own, she resolved, should henceforward lead her to disobey him. Ah! she remembered with a hot flush of pain—ah! her disobedience at Gracedieu had brought all the mischief, Vincent's death all the anguish. Of course it had not; of course Maulfry had tricked her; but she was not the girl to spare herself reproaches. Her loyalty to Prosper took her easily the length of stultification.

So Prosper went; and it may be some consolation to reflect that his going pleased fourteen people at least. First it pleased the men he took with him; for Prosper, that born fighter, was never so humorous as when at long odds with death. Fighting seemed a frolic with him for captain; a frolic, at that, where the only danger was that in being killed outright you would lose a taste of the certain win for your side. For among the High March men there was already a tradition—God knows how these things grow—that Prosper le Gai and the hooded hawk could not be beaten. He was so cheerful, victory so light a thing. Then his cry—*Bide the time*—could anything be more heartening? Rung out in his shrill tones over the open field, during a night attack, say, or called down the darkening alleys of the forest, when the skirmishers were out of each other's sight and every man faced a dim circle of possible hidden foes? Pest! it tied man to man, front to rear. It tied the whole troop to the brain of a young demon, who was never so cool as when the swords were flying, and most wary when seeming mad. Blood was a drink, death your toast, at such a banquet. And that accounts for twelve out of fourteen.

The thirteenth was Countess of Hauterive, Châtelaine of High March, Lady of Morgraunt, etc. A very few days inhabitancy where Master Roy was of the party, had assured this lady that the page must be ridded. She wished him no ill: you do not wish ill to the earwig which you brush out of the window. Certainly if a boy had needs be stabbed by an Egyptian (who incontinent disappears and must be hunted) it were simpler Roy had fallen than the other. But she had no thought of amending the mistakes of Providence. Great ladies who are really great do not go to work to have inconvenient lacqueys stabbed. This at least was not the Countess of Hauterive's way. If Fulk de Bréauté had not been her lover as well as her husband, if he had been (for instance) only her husband, she would have despised Earl Roger fully as much for the affair on Spurnt Heath. No. But she meant Roy to go, and here was her chance.

The fourteenth was Melot, a maid of the kitchen. This young woman, whose love affairs were at least as important in her own eyes as could possibly be those of the Countess her mistress (whom she had hardly ever seen), or of Prosper (whom she conceived as a sexless abstraction, built for the purposes of eating and wearing steel), or of Roy (who, she assumed, had none)—this young woman, I say, was best pleased of them all. She was perhaps pretty; she had a certain exuberant charm, I suppose—round red cheeks, round black eyes, even teeth, and a figure—and was probably apt to give it the fullest credit. Roy's indifference, or reticence, or timidity (whichever it was) provoked her. There was either innocence, or backwardness, or *ennui* to overcome: in any case, victory would be a triumph over a kitchenful of adepts, and here was a chance of victory. So far she owned to failure in all the essays she had made. She had tried comradeship, a bite of her apple—declined. She had put her head on his shoulder more than once—endured once, checked effectively by sudden removal of the shoulder and upsetting of the lady a final time. She leaned over him to see what he was reading—he ceased reading. Comradeship was a mockery; let her next try mischief. For happy mischief the passionist must fume: he had looked at her till she felt a fool. She had tried innuendo—he did not understand it; languishing—he gladly left her to languish; coquetry elsewhere—he asked nothing better. She thought she must be more direct; and she was.

Isoult was in the pantry alone the second day of Prosper's quest. She stood at gaze out of the window, seeing nothing but dun-colour and drab where the sunlight made all the trees golden-green. Melot came in with a great stir over nothing at all, hemmed, coughed, sighed, heighoed. The block of a fellow stood fast, rooted at his window—gaping. Melot was stung. She came to close quarters.

"Oh, Roy," she sighed, "never was such a laggard lad with me before. Where hast thou been to school?"

Thereupon she puts hands upon the dunce, kisses him close, grows sudden red, stammers, holds off, has the wit to make sure—and bundles out, blazing with her news.

In twenty minutes it was all over the castle; Prosper's flag was higher, and Isoult's in the mire. In thirty it had come to my lady's dresser. Isoult, in the meantime, purely unconscious of anything but a sick heart, had wandered up into the ante-chamber, and was poring over a Book of Hours of the Blessed Virgin, leaning on her elbows at a table.

The dresser, having assimilated the news, was only too happy to impart to the Countess. This she did, and with more detail than the truth would warrant. Half hints became whole, backstairs whispers shouted in the corridors; and all went to swell the feast of sound in the lady's chamber. It would be idle to say that the Countess was furious, and moreover untrue, for that implies a scarlet face; the Countess grew as grey as a dead fire. She was, in truth, more shocked than angry, shocked at such a flagrant insult to her mere hospitality. But gradually, as the whole truth seemed to shape itself—the figure she made, standing bare as her love had left her before this satyr of a man; the figure of Prosper, tongue in the cheek, leering at her; the figure of Isoult, a loose-limbed wanton sleepy with vice—before this hideous trinity, when she had shuddered and cringed, she rose up trembling, possessed with a really imperial rage. And if ever a grievously flouted lady had excuse for rage, it was this lady.

Her rages were never storms, always frosts. These are the more deadly, because they give the enraged more time. So she said very little to her dresser. It came to this—"Ah! And where is the woman now?"

The dresser replied that when she had passed by the woman was in the ante-chamber.

"Very well," said the Countess, "you may leave her there. Go." She pointed to a door which led another way. The dresser felt baulked of her just reward. But that was to come.

The Countess, still trembling from head to foot, took two or three swift turns across the room. The few gentle lines about her face were more like furrows; the skin was very tight over the lips and cheek-bones. She opened the door softly.

Isoult was still in the ante-chamber, leaning over the Book of Hours, wherein she had found treated of the 'Seven Sorrowful Mysteries.' Her short hair fell curling over her cheeks; but she was boyish enough, to sight. The Countess went quickly behind her, and before the girl could turn about was satisfied of the amazing truth.

Isoult, blushing to the roots of her hair, stood up. Her troubled eyes tried at first to meet her accuser's stony pair. They failed miserably; almost any plight but this a girl can face. She hung her head, waiting for the storm.

"Why are you here, woman?" came sharp as sleet.

"I came to warn my lord, madam."

"What are you to him?"

Now for it;—no, never! "I am his servant, madam."

"His servant? You would say his—" The Countess spared nothing. Isoult began to rock. She covered her face with her hands and sobbed dry.

"Answer me, if you please," continued the Countess. "What are you to this man?"

Isoult had no voice.

"If you do not answer me I shall treat you for what I know you are. You know the penalty. I give you three minutes."

There was no more then from the Countess for three minutes by the glass. The great lady stood erect, cold and white, seemingly frozen by the frost which burns you. The only sound in the room was the sobbing of the cowed girl, who also stood with hidden face and drooping knees, broken with sobs, but tearless. Ah, what under heaven could she do but as she did? Married to Prosper? How, when he had not declared it; had received her as his servant, and treated her as a servant? How, when she knew that the marriage of such as he to such as she was a disablement far more serious than the relationship thrown at her by the Countess? How, above all, when he had married her for charity, without love and without worship, could she bring scorn upon him who had dragged her out of scorn? Never, never! She must set her teeth hard, bow her head, and endure. The time was up.

"Your answer, woman," said the Countess. There was none—could be none. Only the victim raised a white twitching face to a white stony face, and with desperate eyes searched it for a ray of pity. Again there was none—could be none.

The Countess went quickly up and struck her on the mouth with her open hand. The victim shivered, but stood.

"Go, strumpet!" said the lady. She threw open the door, and thrust Isoult into the crowd of men and maids waiting in the corridor.

Master Jasper Porges, the seneschal, was the man of all the world who loved to have things orderly done. The hall was at his disposition; he arranged his tribunal, the victim in the midst, accuser and witnesses in a body about his stool, spectators to form a handsome ring—to set off, as it were, his jewel.

"Her ladyship gives me a free hand in this affair," he said in a short speech. "You could not have a better man; leave it to me therefore. There must be a judge. By office, by years, by weariness, by experience of all (or most) ways of evil-doing, I am the judge for you. Good; I sit in the seat of judgment. There must be next a jury of matrons, since this is a free and great country where no man or woman (whichever this prisoner may be) can be so much as suspected of sex without a judgment. And since we have not matrons enough, we will make a shift with the maids. A dozen of you to the benches on the table, I beg. So far, good. We need next an accused person. He, or she, is there. Put the person well forward, if you please. Good. Now we are ready for our advocates; we need an *Advocatus Dei*, or accuser, and an *Advocatus Diaboli*, or common enemy, to be defender. Melot, my chicken, you are advocate for God Almighty, and the office is high enough for you, I hope. *Diaboli Advocatus* we have naturally none, since this is a Christian land. Believe me, we are better without such cattle. I proceed, therefore, by the rules of logic which are well known to be irresistible, so much so that had there been a devil's advocate present I must have declined to admit him lest our Christian profession be made a mock. Hence it follows that there is no defence. One might almost foretell the event; but that would be prejudice. We proceed then to interpolate the accused, saying —'Person, you (being a man) are strangely accused of being a woman. The court invites you to declare yourself, adding this plain rider and doom, that if you declare yourself a man, you are condemned in the person of your familiar, the devil, who deceiveth those that say you are a woman; and that if you prove to be a woman, you are condemned by those who dealt with you as a man. Therefore, declare.'"

Master Porges waited, but waited in vain. He was pained. "What, silence?" he whispered awfully. "What, contumacy? Stubborn refusal? Sinking in sin? Can I believe my ears? Very good, prisoner, very good. Melot, my bird of paradise, give your evidence."

This had effect. "I confess," said the accused (speaking for the first time), "I am not a man."

"There now, there now," cried Master Porges in an ecstasy, "the sleeper awakened! The conscience astir! Oh, infallible fount of justice! Oh, crown of the generation of Adam too weighty for the generation of Eve! Observe now, my loving friends, how beautiful the rills of logic flowing from this stricken wretch. Let me deduce them for you. As thus. A woman seeketh naturally a man: but this is a woman; therefore she sought naturally a man. My friends, that is just what she did. For she sought Messire Prosper le Gai, a lord, the friend of ladies. Again. A man should cleave unto his wife: but Messire le Gai is a man, therefore Messire should cleave unto his wife. 'La, la!' one will say, 'but he hath no wife, owl!' and think to lay me flat. Oh, wise fool, I reply, take another syllogism conceived in this manner and double-tongued. It is not good for man to live alone; neither is it good for a lady to live alone, who hath a great estate and the cares of it: but Messire Prosper is that man, and her ladyship is that lady; therefore they should marry; therefore Messire Prosper should cleave unto her ladyship, and what the devil hath this woman to do between a man and his wife now? Aha, I have you clean in a fork. I have purposely omitted a few steps in my ladder of inference to bring it home. Then, look, cometh crawling this accurséd. *O tempora, O Mores! O Pudor! O Saecula Saeculorum!* What incontinency, you will say; and I say, What, indeed! Then cometh fairly your turn. Seneschal, you go on threatening me, this is a Christian castle under a Christian lady, the laws whereof are fixed and stable so that no man may blink them. I say, Aye. You go on to plead, noble seneschal (say you), give us our laws lest we perish. I see the tears; I say, Aye. The penalty of incontinency is well known to you; I say, Aye. It is just. I bow my head. I say, Take your incontinent incontinently, and deal!"

Master Porges got off the table, and, ceasing to be a justice, became a creature of his day. Now, his day was a wild one as his dwelling a barbarous, where the remedy for most offences was a drubbing.

Isoult bowed her head, set her teeth hard, and bent to the storm. The storm burst over her, shrilled, whistled, and swept her down. In her unformulate creed Love was, sure enough, a lord of terrible aspect, gluttonous of blood, in whose service nevertheless the blood-letter should take delight. No flagellant scored his back more deeply nor with braver heart than she her smitten side. It would appear that she was a better Christian than she suspected, since she laid down her life for her friend, and found therein her reward. And her reward was this, that Prosper le Gai, the gallant fighter, remained for Melot and her kind a demi-god in steel, while she, his wife, was adjudged to the black ram. To the black ram she was strapped, face to the tail, and so ran the gauntlet of the yelling host in the courtyard, and of the Countess of Hauterive's chill gaze from the parvise. By this time she had become a mere doll, poor wretch; and as there is no pleasure in a love of justice which is not quickened by a sense of judgment, the pursuers tired after the first mad bout. Some, indeed, found that they had hurt themselves severely by excess of zeal. This was looked upon as clear evidence of the devil's possession of a tail, in spite of the Realists. For if he had not a tail, how could he injure those who drove him out? This is unanswerable.

The end of it all was that no more than three great hearts pursued the black ram with its wagging burden into the forest. Of whom one, feeling the fatuity of slaying the slain, or having, it may be, some lurking seed of nominalism fomenting within, beat off the others and unstrapped the victim's arms and legs.

"Though you are a wanton, God knows," he said, "you are flesh and blood, or were so an hour ago. Be off with you now, and learn honest living."

This was irony of fact, though not of intention. It was prompted by that need which we all have of fortifying ourselves. But it probably saved the girl's life. The men withdrew, and she lay there quiet enough, with a bloody foam on her mouth, for two nights and a day.

It is said, I know not how truly, that the ram stayed by her, was found standing there when she was found. It is like enough; there was a good deal of the animal, beyond the wild-beast savour, about Isoult. She was certainly no formularist; nor had she the reward of those who do well to be angry, which lies, I suppose, in being able to drub with a whole heart.

CHAPTER XX

HOW PROSPER HELD A REVIEW

Messire Prosper le Gai with his dozen men had scoured the forest country from March on the east to Wanmeeting on the west, and from March-Gilbert among the hills of the north to Gracedieu in Mid-Morgraunt, without any sign of the

Egyptian. But at Wanmeeting there had been news of a golden knight, who, unattended, rode into the market-place at sunset asking the whereabouts of Galors de Born and his force. Having learned that they had taken the Goltres road the knight had posted off at a gallop, hot foot. Now Prosper knew what sort of a force Galors might have there, and guessed (from what intelligence Isoult had added to his own) that the golden knight would make at least two brains in it. To follow, to get his dozen men killed, were nothing; but could he be certain Galors would be dropped and Maulfry secured for the appointed branding before the last of them fell? As for his own life, we know that he considered that arranged for. He habitually left it out of the reckoning. On the whole, however, he decided that he could not successfully attack. He must return for reinforcements, taking with him a report which, he relied, would secure them. Waisford had been raided, the fields about it laid waste. There were evidences of burnings and slaughterings on all hands. He put what heart he could into the scared burgesses before he left, and what common-sense. But Galors had gone through like a hot wind.

So Prosper and his men returned to High March. On the morning in which Isoult stirred to open her loaded eyes, and began to moan a little, he and they went by within some forty yards of her—the troopers first, then himself riding alone behind them. He heard the moaning sound and looked up; indeed, he saw the black ram standing, alone as he thought, with drooped head. Prosper was full of affairs. "Some ewe but lately yeaned," he thought as he rode on. The glaze swam again over Isoult's eyes, and the moaning grew faint and near its death. The ram fell to licking her cheek. In this pass she was presently found by a charcoal-burner, who had delivered his loads, and was now journeying back with his asses into the heart of the forest. He also heard the moaning; he too saw the ram. Perhaps he knew more of the habits of ewes or had them readier in mind. He may have had no affairs. The beast, at any rate, was a ram for him, and the licked cheek that of a murdered boy who lay with the other cheek on the sward. The blood about his eyes and hair, the blood on the grass, was dry blood; nevertheless the man turned him over, felt his bones, listened at his heart, and made up his mind that he was not dead. A little wine to his lips brought him to. The charcoal-burner looked into the wounds and washed them, produced black bread, goat's-milk cheese, with a little more wine, finally helped the beaten lad to his feet and to one of his asses. He assumed it was a fight and not a failure to murder: that was safer for him. With the same view he asked no questions. It was a pity to leave the ram, he thought. Butcher's meat was scarce. He killed it then and there, having plenty of asses to hand. In that category, with little doubt, must be placed the ram in question, who, had he had a proper abhorrence of persons who rode him face to the tail, would have kept his skin and lived to found a family.

The charcoal-burner, when all was made fast, set his team in motion. Man, woman, and asses, they ambled off down the green alley towards the middle holds of Morgraunt.

Prosper and his men, lords of those parts, went on their way home to High March. The men disposed in their lodging, Prosper himself rode under the gateway of the castle, crossed the drawbridge, and entered the courtyard amid the mock salutes of the grinning servants. Full of thought as he was, vexed at his check, curiously desiring to see Isoult again (who had such believing eyes!), he took no heed of all this, but dismounting, called for his page. At this there was a hush, as when the play is to begin. Then Master Porges, the seneschal, solemnly awaiting him, solemnly blinked at him, and cleared his throat for a speech.

"Messire," he said, "Messire, to call for a page is an easy matter, but to answer for a page is a difficult matter." He loved periphrasis, the good Porges.

"What do you mean by that, my dear friend?" said Prosper blandly, defying periphrasis.

"Messire," went on Master Porges, hard put to it, "to answer you were to defile the tongue God hath given me for her ladyship's service. To obey is better than sacrifice. Her present obedience is that I should request your presence in the ante-chamber the instant of your appearing before these halls."

"You will do me the honour, seneschal," said Prosper, growing polite, "to answer my question first."

"I will send for the girl Melot, Messire," answered Master Porges.

"You shall send for whom you please, my friend, but you shall answer my question before you move from that step."

The seneschal did not move from the step. He sent a loiterer to fetch Melot from the kitchen, while Prosper waited, the centre of an entranced crowd.

"Ah, the suffering maid!" cried the seneschal as he saw Melot near at hand. "My maid, you must speak to Messire in answer to a question he put me but a few minutes since. Messire, my girl, asked for his page."

Melot's heart began to thump. The steel demigod was before her, she unprepared. The fire was laid, but wanted kindling. Prosper kindled it for his own consuming.

"Pray what has this woman to do here?" he asked.

"Woman indeed!" rounded Melot, breathing again. "Woman! do you call me names, Messire? Keep them for the baggage you fetched in!"

Prosper saw the whole thing in a flash. He grew still more polite.

"Seneschal," he said, "have the goodness to inform your mistress of my coming. Pray that I may wait upon her immediately.... I think," he added after a pause, "I think that you had better go at once."

The seneschal agreed that he had. He went.

Prosper waited in silence, in a crowd equally silent.

The seneschal shortly returned.

"Her ladyship will see Messire at once. I beg Messire to follow me."

He entered the Countess's chamber, and, lifting his head, looked at a white lady on a throne. He had never seen her so before. She was dressed in pure white, with a face near as dead as her clothes. All that was dark about it haunted her masked eyes. She sat with her chin in her hand, looking and waiting for him; when he came, and the seneschal was dismissed with a curt nod, she still sat in the same dead fashion, watchful of her guest, unwinking, pondering. Prosper, for his part, bided the time. He guessed what was coming, but a word from him might have put him in the wrong.

In the end the Countess broke the long silence. He thought he had never heard her voice; it sounded like that of a tired old woman.

"I had thought to find in you, my lord, the son of an old friend, like in spirit as in blood to him whom at first I sought to honour in you. I find I have been mistaken, but for your father's sake I will not tell you how much nor by what degrees. Rather I will beg you go at once from my house."

Said Prosper—

"Madam, for my father's sake, if not for mine, you will tell much more than this to his son. Have your words any hint of reference to the Lady Isoult? Speak of her, madam, as you would speak of my mother, for she is my wife."

The Countess shrank back in her throne as if to avoid a whip. She cowered there. Her eyes dilated, though she seemed incapable of seeing anything at all; her mouth opened gradually—Prosper expected her to scream—till it formed a round O, a pale ring circling black. Prosper, having delivered his blow, waited in his turn; though his breath whistled through his nostrils his lips were shut, his head still very high. The blow was a shrewd one for the lady. You might have counted twenty before she began to talk to herself in a whisper. Prosper thought she was mad.

"I should have known—I should have known—I should have known," she whispered, very fast, as people whisper on a death-bed.

"Madam," he broke in, "certainly you should have known had it seemed possible to tell you. Even now I can tell you no more than the bare fact, which is as I have stated it. And so it must be for the moment, until I have completed an adventure begun. But so much as I tell you now I might have told you before. It is shame to me that I did not. Marriage to me is a new thing, love still a strange thing. Had I thought then as I now do, be sure you would never have seen me here without my wife, whom now, madam, I will pray leave to present to you, the Lady Isoult le Gai."

During this narration the Countess had risen slowly to her feet. She was labouring under some stress which Prosper could not fathom. For a little she stood, working her torture before him. Then she suddenly smote herself on the breast and cried at him—"You have done more misery than you can dream." And again she struck herself, and then, coming down from her throne like a wild thing, she shrieked at him as if possessed—"You fool, you fool! Look at me!"

He could not help himself; look he must. She came creeping up to him. She caught at his two hands and peered into his face with her blind eyes.

"Do you love Isoult, Prosper?"

He could hardly hear her. But he raised his head.

"By God and His Christ, I believe that I do," said he.

The Countess took a dagger from her girdle, unsheathed it, and put it in his hand. She knelt down before him as a woman kneels to a saint in a church. With a sudden frenzy she tore open the front of her gown so that all her bosom was bare, and then as suddenly whipt her hands behind her back.

"Now kill me, Prosper," she whined; "for I love thee, and I have killed thy love Isoult."

So she bowed her head and waited.

But Prosper gave a terrible cry, and turned and left her kneeling. He ran down the corridor blindly, not knowing how or whither he fared. At the end of it was a door which gave on to the Minstrel Gallery over the great hall. Into this trap he ran and fetched up against the parapet. Below him in the hall were countless faces—as it seemed, a sea of white faces, mouthing, jeering, and cursing. He stood glaring blankly at them, fetching his breath. Words flew about—horrible! Out of all he caught here and there a scrap, each tainted with hate and unspeakable disgrace.

"Come down, thou polluter." Again, "Serve him like his wench."—"Trounce him with his woman."—"Send the pair to hell!"

The dawning attention he began to pay sobered his panic, quenched it. What he learned by listening struck him cold. He took pains; he could hear every word now, surely. He was really very attentive. The chartered rascals packed in the hall took this for irresolution, and howled at him to their hearts' content. Once more Prosper held to his motto—bided the time. The time came with the coming of Master Porges—that smug and solemn man—into the assembly. The seneschal looked round him with a benignant air, as who should say, "My children all!" The listening man in the gallery watched all this.

Suddenly his sword flashed out. Prosper vaulted over the gallery, dropped down into the thick of them, and began to kill. Kill indeed he did. Right and left, like a man with a scythe, he sliced a way for himself. There were soldiers, pikemen, and guards in the press: there was none there so tall as he, nor with such a reach, above all, there was none whose rage made him cold and his anger merry. However they were, they could scarcely have faced the hard glitter of his blue eyes, the smile of his fixed lips. He could have carved with a dagger, with a bludgeon, a flail, or a whip. As it was, to a long arm was added a long sword, which whistled through the air, but through flesh went quiet. There had been blows at first from behind and at the side of him. The long mowing arms stayed them. It became a butchery of sheep before he was midway of the hall, thence the rest of his passage to the door was between two huddled heaps, with not a flick in either.

He reached his goal, shot the bolt, and turned, leaning against the door. The heaped walls of that human sea had by this flowed over his lane; now they stood eyeing him who faced them and wiped his blade with a piece cut from the arras —eyeing him askance with silly, shocked faces. Behind them a few grunted or sobbed; but for the most part he had done his work only too well.

Having wiped exquisitely his sword and sheathed it, Prosper took a step forward. The heap of men huddled again.

"Let one go to fetch Melot," he said softly.

No one stirred.

"Let one go to fetch Melot."

No motion, no breath.

"Ah," said he as if to himself, and laid hand to pommel. The heap shuddered and turned on itself. It swarmed. Finally, like a drop from a sponge, Master Porges exuded and stood out, a sweating monument.

"Seneschal," said Prosper, with a bow, "I am for the moment about to ask a favour of you. Have the goodness to oblige me." He unbolted the door and held it open for the man.

Master Porges gasped, looked once to heaven, thought to pray.

"*In manus teas, Domine!*" he sighed.

"Exactly," said Prosper, and kicked him out. The breathless audience was resumed.

A timid knocking—a mere flutter—at the door ushered in as tip-toe a couple as you might easily see. Master Porges fell to his knees and prayers; Melot was too far gone for that. She simply did everything she was told.

"Melot," said Prosper, "you will tell me the whole tale from the beginning. It was you who first knew the Lady Isoult?"

"Yes, Messire."

"It was you who told the others?"

"Yes, Messire."

"Your mistress then saw the Lady Isoult?"

"Yes, Messire."

"What happened next?"

"My lady struck her, and pushed her into the corridor, Messire."

"Ah! And then?"

"And we were all there, Messire."

"Ah, yes. Waiting?"

"Yes, Messire."

"And then?"

"Then we had a procession, Messire."

"Who ordered it?"

"The seneschal had the ordering, Messire."

"*O Pudor!* O afflicted liar!" prayed Master Porges.

But the tale went on. The afflicted liar forgot nothing except Master Porges' syllogisms. These she took for granted. At the end Prosper said to her—

"Melot, you may go. I do not punish women, and you have only done after your kind. Go to the others."

The pack opened and swallowed her up. Prosper turned to Master Porges, who was gabbling prayers for his enemies.

"Master Seneschal," he said, "since it is you who have driven this herd of hogs to do your work, now I shall drive them to do mine. And in teaching you through them what it is to do villainy to ladies, I teach them through you. They could not have a better guide than their headman; and as for you, I will take care that you are well grounded in what you have to teach."

"Ah, Messire," babbled the shiny rogue, "have I not done after my kind also?"

"You have indeed, my friend," Prosper replied. "Now I will do after mine."

To be short, he had Master Porges stripped, horsed, and stoutly flogged then and there. This he did by the simple device of calling up his agents by name, having the general's knack of judging men. Master Porges was a pursy man, but there were burlier than he; a couple of lean stablemen made good practice with the stirrup-leathers. At the end the entire herd were his slaves. One fetched his horse, another his shield and spear, three fought for the stirrup. A dozen would have shown him the way to the last scene of the martyrdom (for so, by vivid comparison, the common enthusiasm conceived it); but for this he chose the man who had unstrapped the girl. This worthy had not failed to recommend himself to notice on that score. He received his reward. Prosper addressed him two requests. The first was, "Lead," and the man led him. The second was, "Go," and the man fled back. Prosper was left alone before a form of bruised bracken to make what he could of it.

He was a man of action, not given to reflections, not imaginative, essentially simple in what he thought and did. What he did was to dismount and doff his helmet. Next, with the butt of his spear, he battered out the cognizance on his shield till no *fesse dancettée* rippled there. "I will bear you next when I have won you," said he to the maimed arm. Bare-headed then he knelt before the form in the fern and prayed.

"Lord God of heaven and earth, now at last I know what the love of woman is. Let my wife learn of me the love of an honest man. And to that end, Father of heaven, suffer me to be made a man. *Per Christum Dominum*," etc.

At the end of his prayer he knelt on, and what drove in his brain I know not at all. The unutterable devotion of that meek and humble creature who called him master and lord, who had lain by his side, walked at his heels, sat at his knee, served at his table, put his foot to her neck (she so high in grace, he so shameless in brute strength!), bowed to a yoke, endured scorn, shame, bleeding, stripes, blindness, and the swoon like death—all this was something beyond thought: it was piercingly sweet, but it beat him down as a breath of flame. He fell flat on his face upon the black fern and blood, and so stayed crying like a boy.

When he got up he buckled on his helm, mounted, and rode straight for Goltres.

Master Porges knew an image-maker at March, and paid him a visit. He caused to be made a little stone figure of a lady, very beautiful, with a brass aureole round her victorious head. She was depicted trampling on a grinning knight— evidently the devil in one of his many disguises, though as like Prosper as description could provide. Underneath, on the pedestal, ran the legend—*Sancta Isolda Dei Genetricis Ancilla Ora Pro Nobis*. He set this up in his chamber over a faldstool, and said three *Paters* and nine *Aves* before it daily. He reported that he derived unspeakable comfort from the practice, and for my part I believe that he did.

CHAPTER XXI

HOW THE NARRATIVE SMACKS AGAIN OF THE SOIL

The charcoal-burner's convoy, bearing at once the evidence and the reward of his humanity, a battered lady on one ass and her flayed friend on another, jogged leisurely through the forest glades. The time was the very top of spring, the morning soft and fair, but none of the party took any heed: the charcoal-burner because he was by habit too close to these things, Isoult because she was in a faint, the black ram because he had been skinned. When Isoult did finally lift her head and begin to look timidly about her, she found herself in a country unfamiliar, which, for all she knew, might be an hour's or a week's journey from High March, where Prosper was. Prosper! She knew that every mincing step of the donkey took her further from him, but she was powerless to protest or to pray; life scarce whispered in her yet. And what span of miles or hours, after all, could set her wider from him than discovery, the shame, the yelling of her foes, had hounded her?

In this new blank discomfiture of hers, she was like one who has been taught patiently to climb by a gentle hand. The hand trusts her and lets go—down, down she falls, and from the mire at the bottom can see the sunny slopes above her, and the waiting guide stretched at rest until she come. The utter abasement of her state numbed her spirit; any other spirit would have been killed outright. But to her one thing remained, that dull and endless patience of the earth-born, poor clods without hope or memory, who from dwelling so hidden in the lap of the earth seem to win a share of its eternal sufferance. Your peasant will bow his

144

back as soon as he can stand upright, and every year draws him nearer to the earth. The rheumatics at last grip him unawares, and clinch him in a gesture which is a figure of his lot. The scarred hills, the burnt plains, the trees which the wind cows and lays down, the flowers and corn, meek or glad at the bidding of the hour—the earth-born is kin to these, more plant than man. I have done ill if I have not thus expounded Isoult la Desirous, for without such knowledge of her you will hardly understand her apathy. She had been lapped so long on the knees of earth; her flights in the upper air had been so short, and her tumble with a broken wing so sharp, that she resumed the crouch, the bent knees, the folded arms, the face in hands of the earth-born, with hardly a struggle. If she had been meant for the air, she would be in the air; if she was meant to die a serf as she had lived, why, at the rate she was spending, death would be quick—*ecco*! The word comes pat when you talk of such lives as hers, for the Italian peasant is the last of the earth-born, invincibly patient.

So Isoult, it seems, had the grace to know how far she had fallen, but not the wit to try for redemption once more. In accepting her tumble for a fate, I think it is clear that she was so far earthy as to be meek as a woodflower. Says she, If the rain fall, the dew rise, the sun shine, or wind blow mild, each in their due season —well, I will look up, laugh and be glad. You shall see how lovely I can be, and how loving. If the frost bind the ground in May, if you parch me with frozen wind, or shrivel me with heat, or let me rot in the soak of a wet June—well, I will bend my neck; you will see me a dead weed; I shall love you, but you shall hardly know it. If you are God, you should know; but if you are a man—ah, that is my misfortune, to love you in spite of common-sense.

Isoult believed she was abandoned by Prosper; she believed that she deserved it. She must be graceless, would die disgraced, having served her turn, she supposed. If, nevertheless, she persisted in loving, who was hurt? Besides, she could not help it any more than she could help being a scorn and a shame. Fatalist! So it was with her.

The charcoal burner had no curiosity. She hadn't been quite murdered; she was a boy; boys do not readily die. On the other side, they are handy to climb woodstacks, labour saving appliances—with the aid of an ash plant. And he was a clear fat sheep to the good. So he asked no questions, and made no remarks beyond an occasional oath. They slept one night in the thicket, rose early, travelled steadily the next day, and in course reached a clearing, where there were three or four black tents, some hobbled beasts, a couple of lean dogs, and a steady column of smoke, which fanned out into a cloud overhead. Here were the coal stacks; here also she found the colliers, half-a-dozen begrimed ruffians with a fortnight's beard apiece. No greetings passed, nor any introduction of the white-faced boy shot into their midst. One of them, it is true, a red-haired, bandy-legged fellow, called Falve, looked over the newcomer, and swore that it was hard luck their rations should be shortened to fatten such a weed; but that was all for the hour.

At dusk, suppertime, there was a cross examination, held by Falve.

"What's your name, boy?"

"Roy."

"To hell with your echoes. Where do you come from?"

"I don't know."

"What can you do?"

"As I am bid."

"Can you climb?"

"Yes."

"Cook?"

"Yes."

"Wink at a woman?"

"I see none."

"Fight?"

"At need."

"Take a licking?"

"I have learnt that."

"By God he has, I'll warrant," chuckled the man who had found her.

"Hum," said Falve. "Are you hungry, Roy?"

"No."

"Then do you cook the supper and I'll eat it. Do you see this little belt o' mine?"

"Yes."

"It's a terror, this belt. Don't seek to be nearer acquaint. Go and cook."

The ram proved excellent eating—tender and full of blood. Humane, even liberal, counsels prevailed over the sated assembly. The boy seemed docile enough, and likely; just a Jack of the build needful to climb the stacks of smouldering boughs, see to the fires, cord the cut wood and the burnt wood, lead the asses, cook the dinner, call the men—to be, in fact, what Jack should be. Jack he was, and Jack he should be called. Falve held out for a thrashing as a set-off; it seemed unnatural, he said, to have a belt and a boy at arms'-length. It was outvoted on account of the lateness of the hour, but only delayed. The beds were made ready, and Jack and his masters went to sleep.

The argument, which, holding as I do steadfastly with Socrates, I must follow whithersoever it runs, assures me that charcoal-burning is a grimy trade, and the charcoal-burners' Jack the blackest of the party; for if he be not black with coal-smoke, he will be black and blue with his drubbings. Isoult, in the shreds of Roy, grew, you may judge, as black and uncombed as any of the crew. She had not a three-weeks' beard, but her hair began to grow faster; the roses in her cheek were in flower under the soot. Her hair curled and waved about her neck, her eyes shone and were limpid, her roses bloomed unawares; she grew sinewy and healthy in the kind forest airs. She worked very hard, ate very little, was as often beaten as not. All this made for health; in addition, she nursed a gentle thought in her heart, which probably accounted for as much as the open air. This was the news of Prosper's return to High March, and of the fine works he performed there in the hall. It came to her in a roundabout way through some pony drovers, who had it from Market Basing. The pietist at March, who made the image of Saint Isolda, may have spread the news. At any rate it came, it seeded in her heart, and as she felt the creeping of the little flower she blushed. It told her that Prosper had avenged her—more, had owned her for his. This last grain of news it was which held her seed. If he owned her abroad—amazing thought!—it must be that he loved her. As she so concluded, a delicate, throbbing fire fluttered in her side, and stole up to burn unreproved and undetected in her cheeks. Her reasoning was no reasoning, of course; but she knew nothing of knightly honour or the dramatic sense, so it seemed incontrovertible. At this discovery she was as full of shame as if she had done a sin. A sin indeed it seemed almost to be in her, that one so high should stoop to one so low, and she not die at once. Sacrilege—should not one die rather than suffer a sacrilege to be thrust upon one? So Clytie may have felt, and Oreithyia, when they discerned the God in the sun, or wild embraces of the wind.

Yet the certainty—for that it was—coincided with her lurking suspicion of the virtue lying in her own strong love. It made that suspicion hardy; it budded, as I have said, and bore a flower. She could feel and fondle her ring again, and talk to it at night. "Lie snug," she would say, "lie close. He will come again and put thee in place, for such love as mine, which endureth all things, is not to be gainsaid." Thus she grew healthy as she grew full of heart, and gained sleek looks for any who had had eyes to see them.

Luckily for her, at present there was none. It is providence for the earth-born that their mother's lap soon takes furrows in which they may run. The charcoal-burners' life was no exception: hard work from dawn to dusk, food your only recreation, sleep your only solace. The weather is no new thing to you, to gape at and talk about. As well might the gentry talk about the joys of their daily bath. You have no quarrels, do no sins, for you have neither women nor strong waters in your forest tents. And if you knew how, you would thank God that you are incapable of thought, since a thinking vegetable were a lost vegetable. To think is to hope, and to hope is to sin against religion, which says, God saw that it was good. More than any reflecting man your earth-born believes in God, or the devil. It comes to much the same, if you will but work it out. He is a deist, his God an autocrat.

Isoult, the demure little freethinker, had another secret god—him of the iris wings. She loved, she was loved; she dared hope to be happy. So far of the earth as to be humble, so far from it as to hope, she grew in the image of her god and was lovely; she remembered the precepts of her mother earth and was patient. Whenever she could she washed herself in the forest brooks; so woods and running water saw in her the blossoming rod. At these times she could have hymned her god had she known how; but Prosper had only taught her what his priests had taught him, that this was a world where every one is for himself, and to him that asks shall be given. To him that asks twice should be twice given. The consequence is that life is a great hunting, with no time for thanksgiving unalloyed. You must end your *Gloria* in a whining petition. Having, however, nothing to ask, she sat at these times in ecstasy inarticulate, her rags laid by for a season, looking long and far through the green lattice towards the blue, bent upon exploration of the joyful mysteries. A beam of the sun would fall upon her to warm her pale beauty and make it glow, the wind of mid-June play softly in her hair, and fold her in a child's embrace. Then again she would toy with her ring. "Ring, ring, he will come again, and put thee where thou shouldest be. Meantime lie still until he lie there instead of thee."

July heats stilled the forest leaves; the coal-stacks grew apace. The charcoal-burners' Jack had hair to his waist and had to hide it in his cap; the charcoal-burners' beards were six weeks old. There was talk of nights of a market in Hauterive, where Falve's mother kept a huckster's shop.

CHAPTER XXII

GALORS CONQUAESTOR

Prosper's aim on leaving High March after his gests of arms had been Goltres, for there he had believed to find Galors. But Galors was a man of affairs just now who had gone far since Isoult overheard his plans. His troop of some sixty spears had grown like the avalanche it resembled. For what the avalanche does not crush it turns to crushing. Galors harrying had won harriers. In fact, he headed within a fortnight of his coming into North Morgraunt a force which was the largest known since Earl Roger of Bellesme had made a quietness like death over those parts. By the time of Prosper's exodus, that is by mid-May, his tactical situation was this—it is as well to be precise. He had Hauterive and Waisford. Goltres was in the hollow of his hand. If he could get Wanmeeting he would be master of the whole of the north forest, west of Wan. Here would be enormous advantage. By a forced march and a night surprise he might get Market Basing, on the east side of the river; and if he did that he would cut the Countess of Hauterive practically off the whole of Morgraunt. Going further, so far as to cut her off March, whence she drew her supplies, she would be at his mercy. He could pen her in High March like a sheep, and make such terms as a sheep and a butcher were likely to arrange.

For, strategically, North Morgraunt would be his; with that to the good South Morgraunt could await his leisure. The key will show how the Hauterive saltire stood with the Galors pale.

Now the whole of this pretty scheming was based upon one simple supposed fact, that the Countess's daughter was then actually in her mother's castle. Galors knew quite well that he could not hold Morgraunt indefinitely without the lady. Even Morgraunt was part of the kingdom; and though rumour of the King's troubles came down, with wild talk of Aquardente from the north and Bottetort from the south-west combining to slaughter their sovereign, the King's writ would continue to run though the king that writ it were under the earth: it was unlikely that a shire would be let fall to a nameless outlaw when five hundred men out of Kings-hold could keep it where it was. But a name would come by marriage as well as by birth. All his terms with his penned Countess would have been, amnesty and the heiress.

At first he prospered in everything he undertook. Waisford and Hauterive were under-garrisoned, and fell. Goltres, very remote, was unimportant except as a base. The Countess at this time, if not engaged philandering with Prosper, was troubled on the northern borders. As a matter of fact Galors had been able to secure that no messengers to High March should cross Wan, and that none from it, having once crossed, should ever re-cross. This was the state of affairs when Prosper passed the edge of the High March demesnes and took the road for Wanmeeting and Goltres.

He had not gone far out of the Countess's borders before he saw what had happened. The country had been wasted by fire and sword: cottages burnt out, trampled gardens, green cornlands black and bruised—desolation everywhere, but no life. Death he did come upon. In one cottage he saw two children dead and bound together in the doorway; at a four-went way a man and woman hung from an ash-tree; of a farmstead the four walls stood, with a fire yet burning in the rick-yard; in the duck-pond before the house the bodies of the owners were floating amid the scum of green weed. That night he slept by a roadside shrine, and next morning betimes took the lonely track again. Considering all this as he rode, he reached a sign-post which told him that here the ways of Wanmeeting and Waisford parted company. "Wanmeeting is my plain road," thought he, "but plainer still it is that of Galors—and not of Galors alone. I think the longer going is like to be my shorter. I will go to Waisford." He did so. After a patch of woodland was a sandy stretch of road fringed with heather and a few pines. A man was sitting here, by whose side lay his dead young wife with a handkerchief over her face. Prosper asked him what all this misery meant; for at High March, he added, they had no conception of it.

The man turned his gaunt eyes upon him. "We call it the hand of God, sir."

"Do you though? I see only the hand of man or the devil," said Prosper.

"May be you are in the right, Messire. Only we think that if God is Almighty He might stay all this havoc if He would. And since He stays it not we say He winks at it, which is as good as a nod any day."

"You are out, sir," said Prosper. "As I read, God hath given men wits, and suffers the devil in order that they may prove them. If they fail in the test, and of two ways choose the wrong, is God to be blamed?"

"Some of us have no such choice. It is hard that the battle of the wits should be over our acres, and that our skulls should be cracked to prove which of them be the tougher."

"God is mighty enough to make laws and too mighty to break them, as I understand the matter," said Prosper. "But who, under God or devil, hath done this wrong?"

"Sir," said the man, "it is the Lord of Hauterive (so styled), who hath taken Waisford and destroyed it with the country for ten miles round about it, and killed all the women who could not run fast enough, and such of the men as did not run to him. And this he did upon the admirable conceit that the men, having no women of their own, would take pains that they should not be singular in the country, but full of lessons in butchery, would become butchers themselves. It seems that there was ground for the opinion. As for me, I should certainly have been killed had he found me, for butchering is not to my taste—or was not then. But I was on a journey, and came back to find my house in ashes and my new wife, what you see."

"But who," cried Prosper, "in the name of the true Lord, is your lord of Hauterive? And how dare he take upon himself the style and fee of the Countess of Hauterive, Bellesme, and March? I have no reason to love that lady, but I thought all Morgraunt was hers."

"Morgraunt is hers, and Hauterive, and all the country from March unto Wanmouth," said the countryman. "But this lord is an outlaw who was once a monk down at Malbank in the south; and hath renounced his flock and gathered together a crew as unholy as himself. And the story goes that he did it all for the sake of a girl who scorned him. Now then he holdeth Hauterive as his tower of strength, has harried Waisford, and threatens Wanmeeting town, giving out that he will edge in the lady, besiege High March itself, wed the Countess, and have the girl (when he finds her) as his concubine. So he will be lord of all, and God of no account so far as I can see. And the name of this almighty scamp, Messire-"

"Is Galors de Born," put in Prosper.

The countryman got up and faced him.

"Are you a fellow of his?" he asked. "For, look you, though I must die for it, I will die killing."

"Friend," Prosper said gently, "the man is my enemy whom I had thought disabled longer by a split throat which he got of me. I see I have yet to deal with him. Tell me now where he is."

"I can tell you no more," said the fellow, "than that his tower is in Hauterive. He hath guards along the river and a post at Waisford. We shall have trouble to cross the water. He is said to be for Wanmeeting; but I know he has High March in his eye, because the girl he wants is believed to be there. He has been here also, as you see, God damn him."

"God hath damned him," said Prosper, "but the work is in my hands."

"You will need more than your hands for the business, my gentleman. He hath five hundred spears."

"The battle is between his and mine nevertheless."

"Then there is the Golden Knight, as they call him, come from hell knows where; not a fighter but a schemer; and swift, my word! And cruel as the cold. Will you tackle him?"

"I shall indeed," said Prosper. "Farewell, I am for my luck at Waisford."

"I would come with you if I might," said the man slowly.

"Come then. Two go better than one against five hundred."

"Let me bury my pretty dead and I am yours, Messire."

"Ah, I will help you there if I may," Prosper replied.

They dug a shallow grave and laid in it the body of the young girl. Prosper never saw her face, nor did her husband dare to look again on what he had covered up. Prosper said the prayers; but the other lay on his face on the grass, and got up tearless. Then they set off.

Five miles below Waisford they swam the river without any trouble from Galors' outposts: a wary canter over turf brought them to the flank of the hill; they climbed it, and from the top could see the Wan valley and what should be the town. It was a heap of stones, scorched and shapeless. The church tower still stood for a mockery, its conical cap of shingles had fallen in, its vane stuck out at an angle. Prosper, whose eyes were good, made out a flag-staff pointing the perpendicular. It had a flag, *Party per pale argent and sable.* A dun smoke hung over the litter.

"We shall do little good there," said he; "we are some days too late. We will try Wanmeeting."

Agreed. They fetched a wide detour to the north-west, climbed the long ridge of rock which binds Hauterive to the place of their election, and made way along the overside of it, taking to cover as much as they could. By six o'clock in the evening they were as near as they dared to be until nightfall. As they stood they could see the ridge rear its ragged head to watch over the cleft where-through the two Wans race to be free. Upon the slope of this bluff was the town itself, a walled town the colour of the bare rock, with towers and belfries. The westering sun threw the whole into warmth and mellow light.

"The saltire still floats," cried Prosper; "we are not too late for this time."

They were let in at dusk by the Martin Gate, not without some parley. The only word Prosper would give had been, "Death to Galors de Born." This did not happen to be the right word. Matters were not to be adjusted either by "Life to the Countess," for Prosper did not happen to wish it her.

The High Bailiff and the Jurats argued at some length whether what he had said did not imply the other of necessity.

"If you talk of necessity, gentlemen," finally said the High Bailiff, "in my advice it is written that our necessity is too fine for dialectic. Our present need is to kill the common enemy. Here is a gentleman who asks for no other pleasure. Let him in." And they did.

Prosper was in love at last; but he did not lose his head on that account. It was not his way. The girl he had first pitied, next desired, then respected, then learned, finally adored, was gone. Well, he would find her no doubt. She had but two enemies, Galors and Maulfry; who hunted in couple just now. She might be anywhere in the world, but it was most likely that where she was they were also. If he found them he should find her. That was why, without having any desire to befriend the Countess, who had in his judgment made a fool of herself first and an enemy of him afterwards, he undertook the defences of Wanmeeting.

For it came to that. He found a thin garrison, a pompous bailiff, wordy and precise, headboroughs without heads, and a panic-stricken horde of shopkeepers with things to lose, who spent the day in crying "Danger," and the night in drinking beer. Outside, somewhere, was an enemy who might be a rascal, but was certainly a man. Professional honour was touched on a raw. Since he was in, in God's name let him do something. After a day spent in observing the manners and customs of Wanmeeting in a state of semi-siege, he got very precise ideas of what they were likely to be in a whole one. He called on the High Bailiff and spoke his mind.

"Bailiff," he said very quietly, "your defences are not good, but they are too good to defend nothing. I am sorry I cannot put your citizens at a higher figure. There does not seem to me to be a man among them. They chatter like pies, they drink like fishes, they herd like sheep, they scream like gulls. They love their wives and children, but so do rabbits; they are snug at home, but so are pigs in a stye; they say many prayers, they give alms to the poor. But no prayers will ever stay Galors, and the alms your people want I spell with an 'r.' I know Master Galors, and he me. If he comes here the town will be carried, the men hanged, the women ravished, and I shall be killed like a rat in a drain. Now I set little store by my life, but I and the man I have brought with me intend to die in the open. Do what you choose, but understand that unless things alter to my liking, I take myself, my sword, and my head for affairs into the country."

"And who are you, Messire, and what do I know of your head for affairs?" cried the High Bailiff, on his dignity.

"My name is Prosper le Gai, at your service," the youth replied; "and as for my head, it becomes me not to speak."

"If you will not speak of it, why are you here?" asked the High Bailiff, at the mercy of his logic.

"I am here, sir, for the purpose of killing Dom Galors de Born."

"You speak very confidently, young gentleman."

"There is no boasting where there is no doubt."

"Is there no doubt, pray, whether he might kill you?"

"I intend to remove that doubt," said Prosper.

"Pray how, sir?"

"By killing him first."

The end of it all was that the High Bailiff, in the presence of the Jurats and citizens, solemnly girt on Prosper the sword of the borough, and declared Messire Prosper le Gai of Starning to be generalissimo of its forces. Prosper at once paraded the garrison.

He rated the men roundly, flogged two of them with his own hand for some small insubordination, and made fast friends in all ranks. Having established a pleasant relationship by these simple means, he spoke to them as follows.

"Gentlemen," he said, "have the goodness to remark that I have taught you how to parade. In time I doubt not you will follow me with as good a will as you have hitherto followed your own devices. These, I take leave to tell you, were very foolish. If you follow me I shall lead you in the thick of the fighting, should there be any. If you leave me, or if I have the honour to be killed, you will all have your throats cut. I do not mean to be killed, gentlemen, and rely upon you in the alternative which remains."

He took a guard and went the round of the defences. Wherever he went he brought heart with him. As for the burgesses and the burgesses' wives, they thought him a god. The result was, that in six weeks he had half the place under arms, a fighting force of one thousand pikes and five hundred archers, an outer wall of defence ten feet by six, and provision to stand a two months' siege. This brought the time to July.

On July 14 one of his scouts brought home the news that Galors had concentrated on Hauterive, while keeping close watch along Wan. He himself was no one knew where, scouring the country for traces of the girl Isoult la Desirous, who had escaped from High March. Meantime a detached force under the Golden Knight had surprised Goltres, and put the inhabitants to the sword. They held that stronghold, and were said still to be there.

Prosper sent for his horse, and rode down to the council house to see the High Bailiff.

"Bailiff," he said, "Galors will not be here yet awhile. If he comes you will know what to do. But I do not think he will come just yet."

"Ah, Messire, will you desert us?" cried the good soul.

"If you put it so, yes."

"You are tired of warfare, Messire?"

"Warfare, pardieu! I am tired of no warfare. I am going to make some for default of it."

"And leave us all here?"

"And leave you all here."

"Would you have us assume the offensive, sir?"

"By no means, Bailiff. I would have you mind your walls. But forgive me, I must be off."

"Where are you going, Messire?"

"I am going to find Galors, or at least those who will save me the trouble. Adieu, Bailiff."

Prosper galloped away as if the devil were in him. The High Bailiff assumed command.

CHAPTER XXIII

FALVE THE CHARCOAL-BURNER

While Prosper is galloping after Dom Galors, and Dom Galors is galloping after Isoult, let us turn to that unconscious lady who hides her limbs in a pair of ragged breeches, and her bloom under the grime of coal-dust. Her cloud of hair, long now and lustrous, out of all measure to her pretence, she was accustomed to shorten by doubling it under her cap. An odd fancy had taken her which prevented a second shearing. If Prosper loved her she dared not go unlovely any

156

more. Her hair curtained her when she bathed in the brook and the sun. Beyond doubt it was beautiful; it was Prosper's; she must keep it untouched. This gave her an infinity of bother, but at the same time an infinity of delight. She took pride in it, observed its rate of growth very minutely; another fancy was, that before it reached her knees she should give it with all herself to its master. It is so easy to confuse desires with gratifications, and hopes with accomplishments, that you will not be surprised if I go on to say, that she soon made the growth of her hair *data* by which to calculate her restoration to his side. She was to have a rude awakening, as you shall judge.

The July heats lay over the forest like a pall, stilled all the leaves and beat upon the parched ground. Isoult, seduced by the water and her joy to be alone with her ring, audacious too by use, took longer leave. So long leave she took one day that it became a question of dinner. The one solemn hour of the twenty-four was in peril. Falve was sent to find her, and took his stick. But he never used it; for he found, not Roy indeed, but Roy's rags on the brookside, and over the brook on the high bank a lady, veiled only in her hair, singing to herself. He stood transported, Actaeon in his own despite, then softly withdrew. Roy got back in his time, cooked the dinner, and had no drubbing. Then came the meal, with an ominous innovation.

They sat in a ring on the grass round an iron pot. Each had a fork with which he fished for himself. Down came Falve smirking, and sat himself by Isoult. He had a flower in his hand.

"I plucked this for my mistress," says he, "but failing her I give it to my master."

She had to take it, with a sick smile. She had a sicker heart.

The horrid play went on. Falve grinned and shrugged like a Frenchman. He fed her with his fork—"Eat of this, my minion;" forced his cup to her lips—"Drink, honey, where I have drunk." He drank deep and, blinking like a night-bird, said solemnly—

"We have called you Jack, to our shame. Your name shall properly be called Roy, for you should be a king."

The men made merry over this comedy, finding appetite for it; but to the girl came back that elfin look she had almost lost since she had known Prosper. She had worn it the night she came plump on Galors, but never since. Now again hers were a hare's eyes, wide and quaking.

From that hour her peace left her, for Falve never did. Escape was impossible; the man eyed her as a cat a mouse, and seemed to play upon her nerve as if she had been a fine instrument. He became astonishingly subtle, dealt in images like a modern poet, had the same art of meaning more than he said to those who had the misfortune to understand him. He never declared what he knew, though she could not but guess it; did not betray her to the others; seemed to enjoy the equivoque, content to wait. So he kept her on tenterhooks; she felt a cheat, and what is worse, a detected cheat. This filled her deep with shame. It made her more coy and more a prude than she had ever need to be had she gone among them kirtled and coifed. At last came the day when that happened which she had darkly dreaded. A load of coals went off to Market Basing; to dinner came herself only, and Falve.

She trembled, and could neither eat nor drink. Falve made amends, ate for three and drank for a dozen. He grew sportive anon. He sang tavern songs, ventured on heavy play, would pinch her ear or her cheek, must have her sit on his knee. But at this her fortitude gave way; she jumped up to shake herself free. There was a short tussle. Her cap fell off, and all the dusky curtain of her hair about her shoulders ran rippling to her middle. No concealment could avail between them now. She stood a maid confessed, by her looks confessing, who watched him guardedly with lips a-quiver.

Falve did not hesitate to take her hand. "Come and see," he said, and led her away. Across the brook he showed her a but newly made, covered with green boughs—his work, it appeared, under the cover of a week of sweating nights. He led her in, she saw all his simple preparations: the new-stamped floor, the new-joisted roof, a great bed in the corner. Then he turned to her and said—

"Your name is not Roy, but Royne. And you shall be queen of me, and of the green wood, and of this bed."

Isoult began to shake so violently that she could hardly stand.

"How! does not the prospect please you?" said Falve. She could only plead for time.

"Time?" asked he, "time for what? There is time for all in the forest. Moreover, you have had time."

"Would you have me wed you, Falve?" she faltered.

"Why, I set no store by your church-music, myself," rejoined Falve.

"But I set great store by Holy Church. You would never dishonour me, Falve?"

"My dear," said Falve, "you will have guessed by now that I am a lady's man. I am wax in their pretty hands—red wax or white wax. According as you squeeze me, my dear, you make me a Golias or a bishop, as you wish. You would have me a bishop, eh?"

"I do not understand, Falve."

"The husband of one wife, my lass, as the Scripture saith. Is that your fancy?"

"I would like to be a wife."

"Then a wife you shall be, my honey, though a friend or a bondmaid is equally good Scripture, to say nothing of simplicity. Now that being settled, and a bargain a bargain, let us seal."

She escaped with his tarnish on her hand; but he respected her promise, and troubled her no more by contact. Nevertheless she had to pay. His dwarfish propensity to wit led him the wildest lengths. The rogue began to sigh and gesture and slap his ribs. He affected the lover preposterously; he was over weary of his rough life, he would say; he must marry and settle down in the hut by the brook.

"And then," he ran on, "thou, Roy, shalt come and live there, serving me and my wife. For I love thee, boy, and will not leave thee. And I warrant that she will not be jealous when I play with thee; nor shall I grudge thy love of her—nay, not if thou shouldst love her as myself. For thus Moses bade us in the Commandments." And so on. "By Saint Christopher, that long man of God," he swore at another bout, "thou and my wife shall sleep in one bed, and I not be dishonoured!"

The other men began to prick up their ears at these speeches, and looked shrewdly at their boy more than once. As for Isoult, she knew not where to turn. She seemed to be quavering over an abyss.

Meantime the hour of her wedding, as Falve had appointed it, drew near. In middle July the whole gang were to go to Hauterive with coal for the Castle.

Falve's mother, I have told you, lived there in a little huckster's shop she had. Falve's plan was to harbour Isoult there for the night, and wed her on the morrow as early as might be. But he told the girl nothing of all this.

They set out, then, betimes in the morning, and by travelling late and early reached Hauterive in two days. And this in spite of the weather, which was cold and stormy. The town stands high on the hither shoulder of that ridge which ends at Wanmeeting, but by reason of the dense growth of timber in that walk of the forest you do not get a view of it from below until you are actually under the walls. Isoult, who had no reason to be interested in any but her own affairs just then, and was, moreover, wet through and shivering, did not notice the flag flying over the Castle—*Party per pale argent and sable.* It was not till the whole caravan stood within the drawbridge that she saw over the portcullis an escutcheon whereon were the redoubtable three white wicket-gates, with the legend, *Entra per me.* She realized then that she was being drawn into the trap-teeth of her grim enemy, and went rather grey. There was nothing for it, she must trust to her disguise. It had deceived the colliers, it might deceive Galors. Ah! but there was Maulfry. It would never deceive her. All the comfort she could take was that Galors was lord of the town, and she collier's knave. Now colliers' knaves do not see much of their lords paramount, nor rulers of cities look into the love-affairs of colliers or seek for such among them. If Maulfry were there, Heaven help her! But she began to think she might cope with Galors.

When the asses were unloaded in the inn-yard, and the coal stacked under cover, Falve took his prisoner by the hand and led her by many winding lanes to his mother's shop. This was in Litany Row, a crazy dark entry over against the Dominican convent. The streets and alleys were empty, the rain coursed down all the gutters of the steep little town; its music and their own plashy steps were all they could hear. Knocking at a little barred door in Litany Row, they were admitted by a wrinkled old woman with wet eyes.

"Mother," said the fellow, "this boy is no boy, but a maid with whom I intend to marry at cockcrow. Let her sleep with thee this night, and in the morning dress her in a good gown against I come to fetch her."

The old woman looked her up and down in a way that made the girl blush.

"Well," she said, "thou art a proper boy enough, I see, and I will make thee a proper girl, if God hath done His part."

"That He hath done, mother," says Falve with a grin. "See here, then."

With that he pulls off Isoult's green cap. All her hair tumbled about her shoulders in a fan.

"Mother of God," cried the old woman, "this is a proper girl indeed, if other things are as they should be, to accord with these tresses."

"Never fear for that, mother," said Falve. "Trust me, she will be a good wife out and in. For, let alone the good looks of the girl, she is very meek and doeth all things well, even to speaking little."

"And what is she named, this pretty miss?" asked the crone.

"Tell her your fancy name, wife," said Falve, giving her a nudge; "show her that you have a tongue in your round head."

"I am called Isoult la Desirous, ma'am," said the girl.

"La, la, la!" cried the old dame, "say you so? The name hath promise of plenty; but for whose good I say not. And who gave you such a name as that, pray?"

"I have never known any other, ma'am."

"Hum, hum," mumbled the dame. "I've heard more Christian names and names less Christian, but never one that went better on a bride."

"Mother, a word in your ear," said Falve.

The couple drew apart and the man whispered—

"Keep her close; let her never out of your sight, that I may marry her to-morrow, for since I set eyes on her as a maiden whom I first took to be a boy, I have had no peace for longing after her."

"Have no fear, my son Falve," said his mother, "she shall be as safe with me as the stone in a peach. I'll get her dry and her natural shape to begin with, and come morning light, if you have not the comeliest bride in the Nor'-West Walk, 'twill be the Church's doing or yours, but none o' mine. Have ye feed a priest, boy?"

"Why, no," said the fellow.

"Seek out Father Bonaccord of the new Grey Friars. 'Tis the happiest-go-lucky, ruddiest rogue of a priest that ever hand-fasted a couple. He'll wed ye and housel ye for a couple of roses. [Footnote: Silver coins of those parts, worth about three shillings a-piece.] The Black Friars 'ull take three off ye and tie ye with a sour face at that. Bonaccord's the man, Brother Bonaccord of the Grey Brothers, hard by Botchergate."

"Bonaccord for ever!" roared Falve. He blew a kiss to his wife and went off on his errand.

CHAPTER XXIV

SECRET THINGS AT HAUTERIVE

The first thing the old lady did was to go to an oak chest which was in the room, and rummage there. With many grunts and wheezes (for she was eaten with rheumatism) she drew out a bundle done up in an old shawl. This she opened upon the floor.

"I belonged to a great lady once," said she, "though I don't look like it, my dear. These fal-lals have been over as dainty a body as your own in their day; and that was fifteen years ago to a tick. She gave 'em all to me when she took to the black, and now they shall go to my son's wife. Think of that, you who come from who knows who or where. If they fit you not like a glove, let me eat 'em."

There were silks and damasks and brocades; webbed tissues of the East, Coän gauzes blue and green, Damascus purples, shot gold from Samarcand, crimson stuffs dipped in Syrian vats, rose-coloured silk from Trebizond, and embroidered jackets which smelt of Cairo or Bagdad, and glowed with the hues of Byzantium itself. Out of these she made choice. The girl shed her rags, and stood up at last in a gown of thin red silk, which from throat to ankle clung close about her shape. The dark beauty went imperially robed.

"Wait a bit," said her dresser; "we'll look at you presently when you are shod and coifed to fit."

She gave her a pair of red stockings and Moorish slippers for her feet; she massed up her black hair into a tower upon her head, and roped it about with a chain of sequins which had served their last chaffer at Venice; she girt a belt of filigree gold and turquoise about her waist, gave her a finishing pat, and stood out to spy at her.

"Eh, eh! there you go for a jolly gentlewoman," she chuckled, and kissed her. "Give you a pair of sloe-black eyes for your violets, tip your nails with henna red, and you'd be a mate for the Soldan of Babylon in his glory. As you stand you're my bonny Countess Bel warmed in the blood—as she might have been if Bartlemy had had no vigil that one year."

They sat to table and ate together. The old dame grew very friendly, and, as usual with her class, showed a spice of malice.

"There is one here, let me tell you," she said as she munched her bacon, "even the lord of this town, who would be glad to know his way to Litany Row before morning." Isoult paled and watched her unconscious host; she knew that much already. "Yes, yes," she went on, the old ruminant, "he hath a rare twist for women, if they speak the truth who know him. There is one he hath hunted high and low, in forest and out, they say, and hath made himself a lord for her sake, whereas he was but a stalled ox in Malbank cloister. He hath made himself a lord, and killed his hundreds of honest men, and now he hath lost her. He—he!"

The good woman chuckled at her thoughts over all this irony of events.

"I might do son Falve a sorry turn," she pursued, "if I would. I should get paid for it in minted money, and Saint Mary knows how little of that has come my way of late. And I dare say that you would not take the exchange for a robbery. A lord for a smutty collier." She looked slyly at Isoult as she spoke. The girl's eyes wide with fear made her change her tune. If the daughter-elect were loyal, loyalty beseemed the mother.

"What!" she quavered, "you are all for love and the man of your heart then? Well, well! I like you for it, child."

Isoult's heart began to knock at her ribs. "Can I trust her? Can I trust her?" she thought; and her heart beat back, "Trust her, trust her, trust her."

With bed-time came her chance. The old woman, whose geniality never endangered her shrewdness, bid the girl undress and get into bed first. The meek beauty obeyed. She was undressed, but not in bed, when there came a rain of knocks at the door.

"Slip into bed, child, slip into bed," cried the other; "that's a man at the door."

Isoult, half-dead with fright, once more obeyed. The knocking continued till the door was opened.

"Who are you, in the name of Jesus?" said the woman, trembling.

"Jesus be my witness, I come in His name. I am Brother Bonaccord," said a man without.

"Save you, father," the woman replied, "but you cannot come in this night. There's a naked maid in the room."

Isoult's plight was pitiable. She could do absolutely nothing but stay where she was. She dared not so much as cry out.

"If she is a maid, it is very well," said Brother Bonaccord; "but I am quite sure she is not."

"Heyday, what is this?" cried Falve's mother, highly scandalized.

"Listen to me, Dame Ursula," the friar went on with a wagging finger. "Your son came with gossip of a marriage he was to make with a certain Isoult—"

"'Tis so, 'tis so, indeed, father. Isoult la Desirous is her name—a most sweet maid."

"No maiden at all, good woman, but a wife of my own making."

"Ah, joys of Mary, what is this?"

"Ask her, mistress, ask her."

"I shall ask her, never you fear. Stay you there, father, for your life."

"Trust me, ma'am."

Dame Ursula went straight up to the bed and whipped off the blankets. There cowered the girl.

"Tell me the sober truth by all the pains of *Dies Irae*," whispered her hostess. "Are you a maiden or none?"

It was a shrewd torment that, double-forked. To deny was infamy, to affirm ruin.

However, there was no escape from it: Isoult had never been a learned liar.

"I am a maid, ma'am," she said in a whisper.

"Cover yourself warm, my lamb, I'll twist him," said the delighted mother. She went quickly to the door.

"May our lord the holy Pope of Rome find you mercy, father," she vowed, "but you'll find none here. The girl has testified against you. Now will you marry 'em?"

"That I will not, by our Lord," replied the friar.

"There's infamy abroad, and I'll leave it, for it's none of my making. I wish you good-night, mistress. Bid your son to the Black Brothers. Saint Dominic may deal with him. Saint Francis was a clean man, and so must we be clean."

"Then get ye clean tongues lest ye lick others foul, ye brown viper," screamed Mrs. Ursula, as he splashed down the kennel.

Isoult was desperate; but luck pointed her one road yet. You will remember the trinkets round her neck: Prosper's ring was one, the other was that which old Mald had felt for and found safe in her bosom on her wedding night. When, therefore, Mrs. Ursula came bridling into the light full of her recent victory, she saw the girl before her trembling, and holding out a gold chain at a stretch.

"Lord's name, child, you'll catch your death," cried she. "Slip on your night-gown and into the bed."

"Trust her now, trust her now," went Isoult's wild heart. "Not yet, mother," said she, "you must hear me now."

Ursula dropped into a chair. Isoult knelt before her and put the ring in her old hand.

"Mother, look at this ring," she began, out of breath already, "and look at me, and then let me go. For with this ring I was wed a year ago to a certain lord whom I love dearly, and to whom I have never yet come as a wife. So what I told you was true, and what the Grey Friar told you was true also, when he said that I was a wife of his wedding. He wed me to my lord sure and fast to save me from a hanging; but not for love of me was I taken by my husband, and not for desire of his to mate his soul to mine. But for love of the love I bore him I dared not let him come, even when he would have come. We have been a year wedded, and many days and nights we have wandered the forest and dwelt together here and there, until now by some fate we are put apart. But I know we shall come together again, and he whom I love so bitterly shall set the ring in its place again where he first put it, and himself lie where now it lies. And so the wound and the pain I have shall be at last assuaged, and, Love, who had struck me so deep, shall crown me."

So said Isoult, kneeling and crying. Whatever else she may have touched in her who listened, she touched her curiosity. The old woman dropped the ring to look at the girl. True enough, below her left breast there was a small red wound, and upon it a drop of fresh blood.

Mrs. Ursula took the wet face between her two chapped hands and laughed at it, not unkindly.

"My bonny lass," said she, "if this be all thou hast to tell me it will not stay my son Falve. Here in this forest we think little of the giving of rings, but much of what should follow it. But thy wedding stopped at the ringing, from what I can learn. That is no wedding at all. Doubt not this knight of thine will never return; they never do return, my lassie. Neither doubt but that Falve will wed thee faster than any ring can do. And as for thy scratch and crying heart, my child, trust Falve again to stanch the one and still the other. For that is a man's way. And now get into bed, child; it grows late."

There was nothing for it but to obey. Her game had been played and had failed. She got into bed and Ursula followed.

Then as she lay there quaking, crying quietly to herself, her heart's message went on that bid her trust. Trust! What could she trust? The thought shaped itself and grew clearer every minute; the answer pealed in her brain. The token! she recalled her mother's words, the only words she had spoken on her marriage night. "It shall not fail thee to whomsoever thou shalt show it."

"Help, Saint Isidore!" she breathed, and sat up in the bed.

This made the old woman very cross.

"Drat the girl," she muttered, "why don't she sleep while she can?"

Isoult leaned over her and put the token in her hand. "Look also at this token, mother, before we sleep," she said.

Mrs. Ursula, grumbling and only half awake, took the thing in one hand and hoisted herself with the other. She sat up, peered at it in the light of the cresset, dropped it to rub her eyes, fumbled for it again, and peered again; she whispered prayers to herself and adjurations, called on Christ and Christ's mother, vehemently crossed herself many times, scrambled out of bed, and plumped down beside it on her two knees.

"Mild Mary," she quavered, "mild Mary, that is enough! That I should live to see this day. Oh, saints in glory! Let us look at it again."

Isoult drooped over the edge of the bed; Ursula looked and was astounded, she wondered and prayed, she laughed and cried. Isoult grew frightened.

"Wed her!" cried the old dame in ecstasy. "Wed the Queen of Sheba next!" Then she grew mighty serious. She got up and dropped a curtesy.

"It is enough, Princess. He dare not look at you again. At dawn you shall leave this place. Now sleep easy, for if I hurt a hair of your head I might never hope for heaven's gate."

She made the girl sleep alone.

"This is my proper station before you, madam," said she, and lay down on the floor at the foot of the bed.

It was no dream. In the morning she was up before the light. Isoult found a bath prepared, and in her gaoler of over-night a dresser who was as brisk as a bee and as humble as a spaniel.

"Old servants are the best," said the crone in her defence; "they're not so slippery, but they know how things should go on and off. Ah, and give me a young mistress and a beauty," she went on to sigh, "such as God Almighty hath sent me this night."

Either Saint Isidore had entered the token, or the token had been swallowed by Saint Isidore.

When the girl was dressed in her red silk gown of the night before, with a hood of the same for her head, her red stockings and her red shoes, she was set at table, and waited upon hand and foot. No questions were asked, but very much was taken for granted. Ursula had her finger to her lip every sentence; she wallowed in mystery.

"You are not safe here, Princess," she whispered, "but I will put you where only safety is for the moment—in Mid-Morgraunt. Affairs, as you know, are not well where they should be; but as soon as you are bestowed, I will go forth with that which will make them as bright as day. I will see one I never thought to face again; I shall win honour which God knows I am late a-winning. Leave everything to me."

Isoult asked nothing better, for the very sufficient reason that she knew nothing. Her earth-born habit of taking all things as they came in order stood her in good part; she had no temptation to ask what all this meant. But she did not forget to thank the great Saint Isidore latent in the crystal.

Everything being ready, the old woman threw a long brown cloak over her charge before they ventured out into the still twilight streets. The wet was steaming off the ground, but the day promised fair. Hauterive was nearly empty: they were not challenged at the gate, met nobody terrific. Once outside the walls they descended a sharp incline, struck almost immediately a forest path, and in half-an-hour from that were deep in the dewy woods. Old Ursula held on briskly for a mile or so in and out of fern and brake. Then she stopped, out of breath, but beaming benevolence and humility.

"We are safe enough now, madam," she said, and went on to explain, "Hold you by that path, Princess, until beech and holly end and oaks begin. Follow the dip of the land, you will come to Thornyhold Brush; with those you find there you may stay until you know who shall send for you. That may be likely a week or more, for I am not so young as I would be, and the roads are thick with Galordians. Now kiss me quickly if you will stoop so low: it is the last time I shall ask it of you."

Isoult thanked her with sparkling eyes and warm red lips; then she stood alone in the wood watching her old friend go. Afterwards she herself took to the path, wondering, but light-hearted and minded to run.

The spruce Falve, curled and anointed for the bridal, found no wife, but his mother, who called him a fool, a knave, a notorious evil-liver and contemner of holy persons. This was hard to bear, for part of it at least he knew to be quite true. What was harder was, that hitherto he had always believed his mother of his party. But there is no pietist like your reformed rake; so Falve left the huckster's shop vowing vengeance. The day was July 18, and all the town astir, for Galors de Born and his riders were just in from a raid.

CHAPTER XXV

THE ROAD TO GOLTRES

On July 14 Prosper left Wanmeeting at a gallop, in the driving rain. There had been thunder and a change in the weather; the roads were heavy and the brooks brimming; but by noon he was in the plain, and by night at One Ash, a lonely dead tree as often gallows as not. There he slept in his cloak. Next morning he was early in the saddle, and had reached the fringe of Goltres Heath by breakfast time—if the hour without the thing can be called by such a comfortable name.

He knew there was a cross-road somewhere near by from Goltres to Hauterive Town. He should go warily, for if the first were invested there must needs be communications with the base, which was Hauterive. Sure enough, he had not seen the finger-post before he saw the pikes. There were three mounted men there, one of whom had his face to the north and was shading his eyes to spy over the heath. In a dozen more strides (for he was at no pains to skulk from three troopers) a man saw him, gave a shout and spurred over the heather. Prosper pulled his horse into a gallop, resolved to bring things to a quick conclusion. Spear in rest he came down on his fellow like a gale of wind.

The man swerved at the onset; Prosper rocketed into him; horse and man went over in a heap. "Bungler," cried Prosper, and went on. The other two faced him together standing. Prosper drove in between them, and had one of them off at the cost of a snapt spear. He turned on the other with his sword whirling round his head.

"Quarter, Messire!" cried the trooper, "here comes one of my betters for you."

In effect, a knight on a chestnut horse was coming from Goltres, a most resplendent knight in golden armour, with yellow trappings slashed and fluttering about him.

"The Gold Knight!" said Prosper, drawing a sharpish breath; "this is better than I looked for. My man," he went on, turning, "I have measured you with my eye. I think the sign-post will bear you."

"I have no doubt of it, Messire," said the man ruefully. "You shall put it to the proof so sure as I live," continued Prosper, "if you stir from where you stand. I have to speak with your master."

"Oh, make yourself quite easy, Messire, and trust me," said the man; "I see with whom I have to deal."

"Then deal not with him, my friend," said Prosper, and went to meet the Golden Knight.

The Golden Knight set spear in rest and came cantering down the track. Prosper let him come. When he was within hail, "Put up your spear, dame," said he, "and listen."

The Golden Knight pulled up short, but held his spear couched against the worst. Prosper spoke again quite cheerfully.

"You and I have met, Dame Maulfry."

"You are speaking foolishness and wasting my time, Messire. I neither know you nor your dame."

"You may have known my shield in more gaudy trim. Did I not turn grave-digger for you some years ago?"

"Oh, oh! you are Prosper le Gai?"

"That is my name, Madam Maulfry. You know me at last."

"Yes, I know you. Take care. You are in no friendly country."

"I am a very friendly soul, but I will take care. You, I think, have many friends in these parts—one in special, a holy person, a man of religion. Is it so?"

"He is a man of many parts, Prosper. He hath an arm."

"He hath a gullet, I know," said Prosper cheerfully. "It is of him I would speak, dame, at this moment. I shall meet him before long, I hope, and should like to be advised by an old acquaintance. Will you tell me why he chose out the arms of the man you and I put into the ground?"

"Why would you know that, Prosper?"

"It seems to me an odd choice. There is a story about them. I am curious."

"What is your story, Prosper? I will tell you this, that I tried to dissuade him."

"Ah!"

"Well, sir, your story?"

"You told me they were the arms of De Genlis. Surely you were mistaken in that?"

"I will be frank with you, Prosper. I was mistaken. They are the arms of Salomon de Montguichet."

"Pardon me, dame," said Prosper, "they are the arms of Salomon de Born."

He never dealt cleaner blow with a spear. The Golden Knight stood up rocking in his stirrups. Then he dropped his weapon and began to wail like a woman.

"Oh no, no, no! Oh, Prosper, be merciful! Oh, God, kill me, kill me, kill me! Tell me you have lied, Prosper, or I must die."

"I have not lied, madam. You have lied," said Prosper, watching with a bleak smile.

On a sudden the Golden Knight spurred his horse violently. The beast lunged forward and shot off at a mad gallop with his flanks streaming blood. Prosper watched him go.

"Follow! follow!" cried the Golden Knight to the man by the sign-post.

"I cannot, my lord," the man shouted as his master flew, "I am a man of my word."

"Be off with you, you rascal," cheered Prosper; "I have said my say."

The man did not hesitate. Prosper watched the flying pair, a quiet smile hovering about his mouth. "My shot told it seems," he said to himself. "If Salomon de Born were not what I believe him to have been, what is the grief of Madam Maulfry? Well, we will see next what Galors de Born has to say to it."

He turned his face towards the north and rode on. If he had followed the two-out of sight by now—he would have got nearer his heart's desire; but he could not do that. He had formed a judgment calmly. If he wanted Isoult he must find Galors. Galors had Hauterive but had not Goltres. Therefore Galors was at Goltres. Prosper always accredited his enemies with his own quality. So he rode away from Isoult as proud as a pope.

We will follow the Golden Knight while our breath endures. We can track him to Hauterive. He never stayed rein till he reached it, and there at the gates dropped his chestnut dead of a broken heart. In the hall of the citadel it was no Golden Knight but a grey-faced old woman who knelt before Galors in his chair. Her voice was dry as bare branches.

"If ever you owe me thanks for what I have done and will yet do for you, Galors, my lover, you shall pay them now. Prosper is at Goltres. He and Spiridion will be there alone. I give you back Spiridion. Give me the life of Prosper, give me his head and his tongue, give me his heart, and I will be your slave who was once your world. Will you do it, Galors? Will you do it this night?"

"By God I will," said Galors.

"There is one other thing"—the woman was gasping for breath—"one little thing. Give me back the arms you bear. You must never wear them again. I always hated them; no good can ensue them. Give them to me, Galors, and wear them no more."

"By God again," said Galors, "that is impossible! I will never do it. What! when the whole forest rings with *Entra per me*, and wicket-gates dazzle every eye on this side Wan? My friend, where are your wits? That droll of a Montguichet did me a turn there before you had him, mistress."

"Ah, Galors," was all she could say, "he has found me again. I am sick of the work, Galors; let me go home."

"Speed me first, my delight," cried Galors, jumping up. He shouted through the door, "Ho, there! My horse and arms! Turn the guard out! In three minutes we are off."

The woman crept away. She had worked her hardest for him, but he wanted nothing of her.

"Dirty weather, by the Rood," said Galors, looking out at the rain. "Dirty weather and a smell of worse. Hearken to the wind in the turrets. Gentlemen, we are for Goltres. Spare no horseflesh. Forward!" and he was gone through the dripping streets at the falling in of a wild day. It was the day Falve had brought in his bride-expectant to Litany Row.

Half-an-hour later Maulfry rode out of the east gate alone, and never held or looked back till she was safe in Tortsentier.

CHAPTER XXVI

GUESS-WORK AT GOLTRES

A scud of wind and rain hampered Prosper on his ride over Goltres Heath. The steady increase of both in volume and force kept him at work all day; but towards dusk the wind dropped a little, the clouds split and drifted in black shreds over a clear sky full of the yellow evening light. Just at the twilight he came to a shallow mere edged with reeds, with wild fowl swimming upon it, and others flying swiftly over on their way to the nest. At the far end of the lake, but yet in the water, was a dim castle settling down into the murk. A gaunt shell it was, rather than a habitable place; its windows were sightless black; only in the towers you could see through them the pale sky behind. The wind ruffled the mere, little cold waves lapped in the reeds; there was no other house in sight whichever way you turned. In all the dun waste of raw and cold it was Goltres or nothing for a night's lodging.

"Galors has been before me again," thought Prosper. "The place is a skeleton, the husk of a house. Well, there must be a corner left which will keep the rain out. We shall have more before day, if I am anything of a prophet."

There was a huge bank of cloud to windward; the wind came uneasily, in puffs, with a smell of rain. Prosper's horse shivered and shook himself from head to heels.

"As I live," cried Prosper suddenly, "there is a light in the house." In a high window there was certainly a flickering light. "Where there's a light there's a man or a woman. Where there's one there is room for two. I am for Goltres if I can win a passage."

Riding up the shore of the lake he found an old punt.

"Saracen," said he to his horse, "I shall take to the water. Thou shalt go thy will this night, and may heaven send thee the luck of thy master." So saying he unbridled him, took off his saddle and let him go, himself got into the punt and pushed out over the mere.

The great hulk of Goltres rose threatening above him, fretted by little waves, staring down from a hundred empty eyes. He made out a water-gate and drove his punt towards it. It was open. He pushed in, found a rotting stair, above it a door which was broken away and hanging by one hinge.

"The welcome, withal free, is cold," quoth Prosper, "but we cannot stand on ceremony. It might be well to make sure of my punt." He manoeuvred it under the stair with some trouble, lashed it fore and aft, and entered Goltres by the slippery ascent, addressing himself as he went to God and Saint Mary the Virgin.

The wooden stair led him into a flagged passage which smelt strongly of fungus. He went down this as far as it would go, found a flight of stone steps with a swing door a-top, pushed up here, and burst into a vast hall. It was waste and empty, echoing like a vault, crying desolation with all its tongues. There seemed to have been wild work; benches, tables, tressles, chairs, torn up, dismembered and scattered abroad. There were the ashes of a fire in the midst, some broken weapons and head-pieces, and many dark patches which looked uncommonly like blood. Prosper made what haste he could out of this haunted place; the rats scuttled and squeaked as he traversed it from end to end.

Beyond its great folding doors he found another corridor hung with the ribbons of arras; in the midst of it a broad stone staircase. Up he went three steps at a time, and stood in the counter-part of the lower passage—a corridor equally flagged, equally gloomy, and smelling equally of damp and death. There were, so far as he could see, open doors on either side which stretched for what seemed an interminable distance. But at the far end was the light he was after; he cared little how many empty chambers there might be so that there was one tenanted. He started off accordingly in pursuit of the light. The passage ran the whole length of the house; the empty doors as he passed them gave on to bare walls and broken windows. Over many of them hung thick curtains of cobwebs and dust; white fungus cropped in the cracks; the rats seemed everywhere. Now and then he caught sight of a shredded arras on the walls; in one room a disordered bed; on the floor of another a woman's glove. Never a sight of life but rats, and never a sound but his own steps, the shrieking of the wind, the rattle of crazy windows.

The door of the lighted chamber was set open. Prosper stood on the threshold and looked in.

It was a narrow dusty place heaped with books on tables, chairs, and floor. The lamp which had beaconed him from over the water was of brass, and hung from the ceiling by a chain. At the window end sat a young man with long yellow hair, which was streaked over his bowed back; he was reading in a Hebrew book. The book was on a reading-stand, and the young man kept his place in it with his thin finger. He seemed short-sighted to judge by the space betwixt his nose and his book. By his side on a little lacquered table was a deepish bowl of dull red porphyry filled with water. Every now and again the young man, having secured his place firmly with his finger, would gaze into the bowl through a little crystal mace which he kept in his other hand. Then he would fetch a deep sigh and return to his book.

Beyond the man, his bowl, and his books, Prosper could see little else in the room. There was, it is true, a shelf full of bottles, and another full of images; but that was all.

Prosper stepped lightly into the room and laid a hand upon the reader's shoulder. The young man did not start; he carefully recorded his place before he lifted a thin face from his work to his visitor. You were conscious of an extravagantly peaked nose, like the beak of some water-fowl, of the wandering glance of two pale eyes, and of little else except a mild annoyance.

"What is your pleasure, fair sir?" asked the young man.

"Sir," began Prosper, "I fear I have intruded upon your labours."

"You have," said the young man.

It was an uncompromising beginning. The young man beamed upon him, waiting.

"Nevertheless, sir," Prosper went on, "I am driven to force myself upon your hospitality for the night. Your house is large and apparently roomy. It is dark and wild weather, with a prospect of tempest. I must sleep here or on the moors."

"Sir," said the other, "you shall be welcome to my poor house, and that notwithstanding the last guests I harboured murdered everybody in it but myself.

175

If it had not been for the intercession of a very charming lady, who has but now left me, I had been dead ere this and unable to play the host either to her or you. This I say not as casting any imputation upon you, of whom I am willing to believe as much as, nay, more than, our limited acquaintance may warrant. Regard it rather as my excuse for affording you little more than a roof."

"By my faith," said Prosper, "I had believed the castle to be deserted or sacked. But I am sorry enough to hear that my foreboding was so near the truth."

"It was a certain lord calling himself Galors de Born, he and his company, who did these harms upon my house," the young man explained. "Me too he will assuredly murder before many days. Unless indeed the lady of whom I spoke just now should return."

"I think I may say that she will not return, and that it will be better for you if she do not. Galors, too, has other fish to fry. But if he should happen to come, I pray God that I may be by with a company to fight at your back." So Prosper.

"If God hear your prayer, which I should have thought more than dubious," returned his host, "I only hope He may see fit to help you to a company as well, for I have none. And as to fighting at my back, I promise you I am a most indifferent leader, being, as you see, somewhat immersed in other affairs."

Prosper had really very little to say in answer to this. By way of changing the talk, he asked if the castle were not Goltres.

"You are quite right, sir," replied the other, "it is Goltres; and I am Spiridion, the lord of Goltres, of a most ancient stock—yet much at your service."

Prosper bowed to his host, who at once resumed his prying and gazing. This did not suit the other's temper at all, for he was above all things a sociable soul. So after a minute he cut in again on another tack.

"You are a great student, fair sir," said he.

"Yes, I am," said the young man.

"Then may I know what it is you search out so diligently, first in the book, and then in your bowl of water?"

"Most certainly you may," replied his host. "I seek to find out what

God may be."

Prosper grew grave. "I had thought you a student of fishes," said he, "but I find you dive deeper. Yet indeed, sir, for my part I think we had best be content to love and serve God as best we may, discerning Him chiefly in the voice of honour and in His fair works. Moreover, Holy Church biddeth us nourish a lively faith. Therefore, as I think, the harder our understanding of God is to come at, the more abundant our merit who nevertheless believe."

"That may be so," said the other. "But I can hardly be expected to love that which I know not, or to believe that which I cannot express. And as for Holy Church, what Holy Church may consider I know not; but when you speak of discerning God in honour and fair works, I understand you, and take up your argument in this manner. For what you think most eloquent of God may be a beautiful lady."

"God is truly there for me," said Prosper, and thought of Isoult's good eyes.

"And for me, fair sir," cried his host kindling, "if all women were as lovely and wise as my friend of late. There indeed was a woman redolent of God."

"Ah, you are out there, sir," said Prosper; "you are terribly out."

The young man smiled. "Look now, my friend, where we are with our definitions," said he. "We divide at the onset. Now, say that instead of a woman, I found a turnip-field the most adorable thing in the world. Can we both be right? No, indeed. Now my reading tells me of all the gods whom men have worshipped—of Klepht and Put and Ra; of Melkarth also, and Bel; of Moloch, Thammuz, and Astarte (a Phoenician deity). I learn next of the gods of Olympus, of those of Rome and Etruria; of the Scandinavians, and of many modern gods. Now either these peoples have made their own gods, in which case I too can make one; or God hath revealed Himself to some one alone—and then He would seem to have dealt ungenerously with the others, equally His creatures, and left blind; or He hath never revealed Himself, which is against Nature; or He is not. These are the questions I would solve, if Galors give me time."

"Sir, sir," cried Prosper, "you do but fog yourself to little purpose! But you should live honestly and sanely, going much abroad, and you would have no doubts."

"My author," said Spiridion calmly, indicating his Hebrew text, "tells me that there are one-and-thirty different ways of finding God out. Of which crystal-gazing, says he in a famous passage, is the readiest. But as yet I have not found it so. Maybe I shall try yours another day—if I have another day."

Whereupon, as if reminded of his delaying, he would have turned again to his work; but Prosper clapped a hand to his shoulder.

"Have done with groping in books, Spiridion," cried he, "and tell me if you think this a time for such folly, when your life is threatened by Galors and his riders?"

"It is the time of all times," returned Spiridion; "for if I know not who is really God of all the host with claims to His rank, how shall I pray when my visitation comes, or how pray that it come not? It was for lack of this knowledge that my people were murdered the other day. So you see that the affair is urgent."

"I think the defence of the house and a long sword would fit your case better," said Prosper dryly. "Meanwhile, you must forgive me if I remind you that I have ridden all day without food or rest, and beg of you to afford me one or the other."

"Ten thousand pardons!" said Spiridion, getting up at once, "that my little griefs should make me forget your serious claims upon my hospitality. Come, sir, here are bread and olives, here is a flask of a very passable wine—all at your service. Afterwards we will share a bed."

They sat on books, and ate what there was. Outside the wind had freshened; it buffeted fitfully but fiercely at the window, and came with dashes of rain. Down the corridor they could hear the casements swinging and banging, and over all the wind itself roaring through the great bare passages as if they had been tunnels.

"A wild night, Spiridion," said Prosper. "And what a night," thought he, "for a surprise."

"Wild enough," replied Spiridion, "but I am indifferent to weather, being seldom abroad. How do you find this wine?"

"Excellent," said Prosper, and drained his glass.

"Of this Galors, whom I think you know," Spiridion continued, "I hear bad reports. Not only has he cut the throats of my household, but from the account given me by my fair friend (concerning whom," he said with a bow, "we are agreed to differ), I fear he is otherwise of a wild and irregular conversation."

"You are right there, my friend," laughed Prosper.

"If he murders me," the other went on, sipping his wine, "it will be on some such night as this."

"I have just said as much to myself," Prosper replied; "but I will do my best to prevent him, I assure you."

"You are so courteous a defender, fair sir," said Spiridion, "I could wish you a more worthy client."

Prosper inwardly agreed with him. Shortly afterwards Spiridion bowed him to bed. For himself he carefully undressed and put on his night-shirt; then, lying down, he was asleep in a moment. The storm was by this time a gale, the noise of it continuous out doors and in. Prosper judged it expedient to have his arms within reach; the more so as he could not help fancying he had heard the sound of rowlocks on the mere. He stripped himself therefore to his doublet and breeches, heaped his armour by the bedside, slung his shield and sword over the foot, and then lay down by his peaceful companion. He had not forgotten either to look to the trimming and feeding of the lamp.

Sleep, however, was miles from him in such a pandemonium of noise. The wind wailed and screamed, the windows volleyed, wainscots creaked, doors rattled on their locks. Sometimes with a shock like a thunder-clap the body of the storm hurled against the walls; the great house seemed to shudder and groan; then there would be a lull as if the spirits of riot had spent themselves. In one of these pauses Prosper was pretty sure he heard a step on the stairs. Not at all surprised, for it was just such a night as he would have chosen, he listened painfully; but the noise drowned all. Came another moment of recoil, he heard it again, nearer. He got out of bed, went to the door, opened it silently, and listened. There were certainly movements in the house, feet coming up the stairs; he thought to catch hoarse whisperings, and once the clang of metal. There was no time to lose, He shut, bolted, and locked the door; then turned to his armour. A swift step undisguised in the corridor put all beyond question; there was an attack preparing. He had no time to do any more than snatch up shield and sword, before he saw the flame of a torch under the door and heard the voices of men.

Prosper stood sword in hand, waiting.

"Spiridion," he said, "wake up!"

Spiridion moaned, stirred a little, and sank again. A high voice called out—

"Spiridion, thou thin traitor, open the door and deliver up him thou harbourest."

The wind shrieked and mocked; then Spiridion woke up with a shiver.

"The hour is come before my God is ready. Now I must die unknowing," said he, and sat up in bed with his yellow hair all about his face.

"It is me they seek," said Prosper. "Now then if it will save thee I will open and go out to them." He went straight to the door, put his face against the key-hole, and cried out—"If I come out, will ye save Spiridion alive?"

There followed a babble of voices speaking all at once; afterwards the same shrill voice took up his challenge, wailing like the wind—"Spiridion, open the door before we break it in."

Prosper said again—"Will you have me for Spiridion?"

"We will have both, by God," rang a deep note, the voice of Galors.

As if at a signal swords began to batter at the door, pommels and blades. One pierced the panel and struck through on the inside. Prosper snapped it off short. "One less," he said; "but they will soon be done with it."

"My friend," said Spiridion, who was shivering with cold (his night-shirt being over short for the season), "my friend, I must die. What can I do for thee? The time is short."

"Brother," answered Prosper, "get a sword and harness, and I will keep the door till thou art ready. Then we will open it suddenly, and do what becomes us."

"Dear friend," Spiridion said mildly, "I have no sword. And since I am to die, I will die as well in my shirt as in a suit of mail."

"Certainly you are a great fool," said Prosper. "Yet I will defend you as well as I can. Get behind me now, for the door is shaking, and cannot hold out much longer."

Their assailants, without any further speech among themselves, beat at the door furiously, or with short runs hurtled against it with their shoulders. It seemed impossible it should stand, yet stand it did. Then one, Galors, cried suddenly out, "Fetch a hatchet!" and another ran helter-skelter down the corridor. The rest seemed to be waiting for him; the battering ceased.

"Here," said Spiridion, standing in his night-shirt before the shelf of images, "here are images of Christ on the Cross, of Mahound (made by a Maltese Jew), of Diana of the Ephesians, and Jupiter Ammon. Here too, are a Thammuz wrought in jade, and a cat-faced woman sitting naked in a chair. All are gods, and any one of them may be very God. Before which should I kneel? For to one I will as surely kneel as I shall surely die."

Prosper flushed red with annoyance. "Brother," said he, "thou art a greater fool than I thought possible. Die how you will. God knows how little of a god am I; but I will do what I can. Hey, now! look about!" he called out the next minute, and leapt back into the room. The door split in the midst and fell apart. Two men fully armed, with their vizors down, burst into the light; they were upon him in a flash. Prosper up with his shield and drove at them. They were no match for him with swords, as they very soon found when he penned them back in the entry. One of the pair, indeed, lost his arm in the first passes of the game, but the press of men behind forced them suddenly and violently forward whether they would or no. Prosper skewered one of them like a capon, against his own will, for he knew what must happen of that. Precisely; before he could disengage his weapon two more were at him in front, and one dodging round behind him with the hatchet slogged at his head with the back of it. Prosper tottered; it was all up with him. Another assailant slipped in under his guard with a pike, which he drove into his ribs. A second stinging blow from the hatchet dropped him. Prone on his face he fell, and never knew of the trampling he had from the freed pass.

They cut down and slew Spiridion as he was kneeling in his shirt before the crucifix; and then Galors came into the room to see that the work was done.

Prosper was lying on his face as he had fallen, with a great hole in his head. Galors suffered a contempt which he could not afford to such an enemy. He kicked the body. "Rot there, carrion," he said; then, with an after-thought, "No— rot in the water. Throw the pair of them by the window," he ordered his men, "and wait outside the gates for, me. I have things to do here." This was done.

When he was alone he stripped off all his armour, and put on instead Prosper's equipment. The defaced shield vexed him. Nothing was left of the blazon;

nothing was left at all but the legend, "*I bide my time.*"

"That, is what I will do no longer," said Galors with a heavy oath. "I have bided long enough; now, friend Prosper, do you bide yours. As for the cognizance, I know it very well by this; it shall be on again by the morning. Then we will see if I can do as Prosper what I have failed to do as Galors."

He headed his troop for Hauterive, reached it before daylight, and ended (as he thought) a signal chapter in his progress. As for Prosper, he bided his time with a broken head in Peering Pool.

CHAPTER XXVII

GALORS RIDES HUNTING

On the morning after the storm at Goltres, July 18, Galors sat in the hall of his stronghold habited as he had ridden in but a few hours before. In came a red-haired peasant, asking to be made his man.

"Why so, fellow?" asked Galors.

"Lording," said Falve, "because my mother hath done me a wrong."

"Why, thou dog?" cried Galors. "Would'st thou cut thy mother's throat under my flag?"

"Lording," Falve answered, "I would not cut my mother's throat under the Pope's flag. But I know thee to be a great lord, master of all these walks of Morgraunt. If I were made free of thy company I could ask thee a mercy; and if I asked thee a mercy it would be that thou should'st order my mother to give me back my wife."

"How, thy wife, rogue?" said Galors, who was weary of the man.

"Lording, she was to have been my wife this day. But she lay last night with my mother, and by the show of a certain token, which unknown to me she wore about her, prevailed upon my mother to let her go. So now she has escaped into the forest, and I am beggared of her without thy help."

By this Galors was awake. He leaned forward in his chair, put chin to hand, and asked quietly—"How was she called, this wife of thine, my knave?"

"Lording," replied the poor eager rogue, "she was a boy at first, called Roy; then she revealed herself a maiden."

"I asked her maiden name, red fool."

"Her name, my lording, was Isoult la Desirous."

"Ah! At last!"

He got up from his chair, saying shortly, "Take me this instant to thy mother."

"But lord—"

"Silence, lout, or I swing you sky-high. To your mother without a word."

Poor Falve, in a cold sweat, obeyed. They found the old lady making breathless preparations for departure.

"Mother," began Falve, "my Lord Galors—"

"Peace, fool!" broke in Galors. "Dame," he said civilly, "I must thank you for the great charge you have been at with a certain lady much in both our hearts. No doubt she has spoken to you of Messire Prosper le Gai. Madam, I am he."

"As God is great," Falve cried, "I could have sworn the lord of this town was Messire Galors de Born."

"And so he was but yesterday," said Galors. "But now I hold it for the Countess Isabel."

The old woman was convinced at this name. She caught Galors by the arm.

"And will you take back the lamb to the dam?" she bleated.

"That is all I ask," replied Galors, speaking the truth.

"You may catch her, Messire—you may catch her. Ah, if I could only have known of you yester-e'en! She's had but seven hours' start of you. Take the path for Thornyhold Brush, and you'll find her. Jesu Christ! when I saw the bleeding bird again I could have died, had there not been better work before me."

"The bleeding bird? Ah! the token, you would say."

"Yes, Messire, yes! The pelican in piety—the torn breast! The I and F. Ah! blood enough shed, blood enough. Go quickly, Sir Prosper, and testify for your name; 'tis of good omen and better report. And have you killed that sick wolf Galors, Messire? There, there, God will bless you for that, and prosper you as you have prospered us!"

Galors swallowed the pill and went out with no more ceremony. Falve ran after him.

"Eh, eh, Messire!" he spluttered. Galors let him splutter till they were within the courtyard. Then he called to a trooper.

"Take this man and flog him well," said he. Falve was seized.

"Ah, my lording," cried he, "what do you there? Must I be flogged because I have lost my wife?"

"No, dog. But because you have married mine."

"Nay, nay, mercy, my lording! I have not yet married her."

"Ha!" said Galors, "then you shall be flogged for jilting her."

And flogged he was. And the flogging cost Galors his prize.

Galors now bestirred himself. First he sat down and wrote a letter to the Countess, thus conceived.

"To the high lady, the Lady Isabel de Forz, Countess of Hauterive, Countess Dowager of March and Bellesme, Lady of Morgraunt—Galors de Born, Lord of Hauterive, Goltres, and West Wan, sendeth greeting in the Lord everlasting.

"That which your Serenity lost early is not too late found, and by us. The crystal locket, having the pelican in the Crown of Thorns, when we bring it upon the bosom where it hath ever slept waiting for the day which shall reveal it to you, will testify whether we lie or lie not. Know, however, that she shall assuredly come, and not unattended; but as, befits her condition, under the hand of him who, having found her, will provide that she be not lost again. It is not unknown to you, High Mightiness, how our power and estate have grown in these days to the threatening of your own. So it is, indeed, that now, in blood, in fees, in renown, in power of life and member, we are near enough to you to seek alliance still more close. And this is the last word of Galors; let the wearer of the crystal locket come home as the betrothed of the Lord Galors de Born, and heiress of High March and Morgraunt, Countess of Hauterive in time to be, and she shall come indeed. Otherwise she comes not; but Hauterive wears the crown which High March looks to put on. Thus we commend you to the holy keeping of God. From our tower of Hauterive, on the feast of Saint Arnulphus, bishop and martyr, the 15th calends of August, in the first year of our principality West of Wan."

This letter, sealed with the three wicket-gates and the circumscript, *Entra per me*, he sent forward at once by a party of six riders, one of whom carried a flag of truce. Then with but three to follow him, he rode out of the town, taking the path for Thornyhold Brush.

CHAPTER XXVIII

MERCY WITH THE BEASTS

Isoult, so soon as she had seen the last of old Ursula, turned her face to the south and the sun. She walked a mile through bush and bramble with picked-up skirts; then she sat down and took off her scarlet shoes and stockings, threw them aside, and went on with a lighter tread. Not that she was above the glory of silk robes and red slippers, or unconscious that they heightened the charm of her person—the old woman's glass, the old woman's face had told her better than that. Indeed, if she could have believed she would meet with Prosper at the end of that day, she would have borne with them, hindrance or none. But this was not to be. Her hair was yet a good six inches from her knees. So now, bare-legged and bare-footed, her skirts pulled back and pinned behind her, she felt the glad tune of the woods singing in her veins, and ran against the stream of cool air deeper into the fountain-heart whence it flowed, the great silence and shade of the forest. The path showed barer, the stems more sparse, the roof above her denser. Soon there was no more grass, neither any moss; nothing but mast and the leaves of many autumns. Keeping always down the slope, and a little in advance of the sun, by mid-day she had run clear of the beech forest into places where there grew hornbeams, with one or two sapling oaks. There was tall bracken here, and dewy grass again for her feet. She rested herself, sat deep in shade listening to the murmur of bees in the sunlight and the gentle complaining of wood-pigeons in the tree-tops far toward the blue. She lay down luxuriously in the fern, pillowed her cheek on her folded hands, closed her eyes, and let all the forest peace fan her to happy dreaming. It was impossible to be ill at ease in such a harbour. The alien faces and brawl of the town, the grime, the sweat, the blows of the charcoal-burners, her secret life there in the midst of them, the shame, the hooting and the stunning of her last day at distant High March, Maulfry, Galors, leering Falve—all these grim apparitions sank back into the green woodland vistas; all the shocks and alarums of her timid little soul were subdued by the rustling boughs and the crooning voices of the doves. She saw bright country in her dreams. Prosper was abroad on a spurred horse; his helmet gleamed in the sun; his enemies fell at his onset. The deer browsed about her, from the branches a squirrel peeped down, the woodbirds with kindly peering eyes hopped within reach of her cradled arms. Soon, soon, soon, she should see him! She would be sitting at his knees; her cheek would be on his breast, his arm hold her close, his kind eyes read all her love story. What a reward for what a little aching! She fell asleep in the fern and smiled at her own dreams. When she awoke two girls sat sentinel beside her.

They were ruddy, handsome, cheerful girls, with scarcely a pin's point of difference between them. They had brown eyes, brown loose hair, the bloom of healthy blood on their skin. One was more fully formed, more assured; perhaps she laughed rather less than the other; it was not noticeable. Isoult, with sleepy eyes, regarded them languidly, half awake. They sat on either side of her; each clasped a knee with her two hands; both watched her. Then the elder with a little laugh shook her hair back from her shoulders, stooped quickly forward, and kissed her. Isoult sat up.

"Oh, who are you?" she wondered.

"I am Belvisée," said the kissing girl.

"I am Mellifont," said the laugher.

"Do you live here?"

"Yes."

"Is this Thornyhold?"

"Thornyhold Brush is very near."

"Will you take me? I am to wait there."

"Come, sister."

Belvisée helped her up by the hand. When she was afoot Mellifont caught her other hand and kissed her in her turn—a glad and friendly little embrace. Friends indeed they looked as they stood hand-linked in the fern. All three were of a height, Isoult a shade shorter than the sisters.

She contrasted her attire with theirs; her own so ceremonious, theirs, what there was of it, simple in the extreme. A smock of coarse green flax, cut at a slant, which left one shoulder and breast bare, was looped on to the other shoulder, and caught at the waist by a leather strap. It bagged over the belt, and below it fell to brush the knees. Arms, legs, and feet were bare and brown. Visibly they wore nothing else. Mellifont laughed to see the scrutiny.

"We must undress you," she said.

"Why?"

"You cannot run like that."

"No, that is quite true. But——"

"Oh," said Belvisée, "you are quite safe. No men come where the king is."

"The king!"

"King of the herd."

"Ah, the deer are near by."

"All Thornhold is theirs. The great herd is here."

"Do you live with them?"

"Yes."

"And they feed you?"

"Yes."

"Ah," said Isoult, "then I shall be at peace till my lord comes, if there are no men."

"Have you a lord, a lover?"

"Yes, he is my lord, and I love him dearly."

"We have none. What is your name?"

"I am called Isoult la Desirous."

"Because you are a lover?"

"Yes. I am a lover."

"I will never love a man," said Belvisée rather gravely. "All men are cruel."

"I will never have a lover, nor be a lover, until men know what love is," said Mellifont in her turn.

"And what is love, do you think?" Isoult asked her thrilling.

"Love! Love! It is service," said Belvisée.

"Service and giving," said Mellifont.

Isoult turned aside and kissed Mellifont's cheek.

They had reached the low ground, for they had been walking during this colloquy. Oaks stood all about them, with bracken shoulder high. Into this the three girls plunged, and held on till they were stopped by a shallow brook. The sisters waded in, so did Isoult when she had picked up her skirts and petticoats. After a little course up stream through water joyfully cool they reached a place where the brook made a bend round the roots of an enormous oak; turning this they opened on a pool broad and deep.

"We will robe you here," said Belvisée, meaning rather to unrobe her.

The great gnarly roots of the oak were as pillars to a chamber which ran far into the bank. Here the two girls undressed Isoult, and here they folded and laid by her red silk gown. She became a pearly copy of themselves in all but her hair. Her hair! They had never seen such hair. Measuring it they found it almost to her knees.

"You cannot go with it loose," said they. "We must knot it up again; but we will go first to the herd."

"Let us go now," added Mellifont on an impulse, and took Isoult by the hand.

Crossing the brook below the pool, they climbed the bank and found themselves in a sunny broad place. The light glanced in and out of the slim grey trees. The bracken was thinner, the grass rich and dewy. Here Isoult saw the great herd of red deer—hundreds of hundreds—hinds and calves with some brockets and harts, busy feeding. Over all that spacious glade the herd was spread out till there seemed no end to it.

A sentinel stag left feeding as they came on. He looked up for a moment, stamped his foot, and went back to grass. One or two others copied him; but mostly the three girls could go among them without notice. Imperceptibly, however, the herd followed them feeding on their way to the king, so that by the time they reached him there was a line of deer behind them, and deer at either flank.

The great hart also stamped his foot and stood at gaze, with towering antlers and dewy nostrils very wide. Before him Belvisée and Mellifont let go of Isoult's hand: she was to make her entry alone. She put them behind her back, hardly knowing what was expected of her, shrank a little into herself and waited timidly. Slowly then the great hart advanced before his peering courtiers, pacing on with nodding head and horns. Exactly in front of Isoult he planted his forefeet, thence he looked down from his height upon her. She had always loved the deer, and was not now afraid; but she covered herself with her hair.

The king stag smelt her over, beginning at her feet. He snuffed for a long time at the nape of her neck, blew in her hair so as to spray it out like a fountain scattered to the wind; then he fell to licking her cheek. She, made bold, put a hand and laid it on his mane. Shyly she stood thus, waiting events. The great beast lifted his head high and gave a loud bellow; all the deer chorused him; the forest rang. So Isoult was made free of the herd.

Belvisée and Mellifont lay beside her on the grass. Isoult lay on her face, while Mellifont coiled and knotted up her hair.

"If love is giving, and you are a lover, Isoult," said she, "you would give your hair."

"I have given it," said Isoult, and told them her story as they all lay there together.

"And to think that you have endured all this from men, and yet love a man!" cried flushed Mellifont, when she had made an end.

But Isoult smiled wisely at her.

"Ah, Mellifont," she said, "the more you saw of men, the more you would find to love in him."

"Indeed, I should do no such thing," said Mellifont, firing up again.

"You could not help it. Everyone must love him."

"That might not suit you, Isoult," said Belvisée.

"Why should it not? Would it prevent my love to know him loved? I should love him all the more."

"Hark!" cried Mellifont on a sudden. She laid her ear to the ground, then jumped to her feet.

"Come to the herd, come to the herd," she whispered.

Belvisée was on her feet also in a trice. Both girls were hot and bright.

"What disturbs you?" asked Isoult, who had heard nothing.

"Horsemen! quick, quick." They all ran between the trees to regain the deer. Isoult could hear no horses; but the sisters had, and now she saw that the deer had. Every head was up, every ear still, every nostril on the stretch. Listening now intently, faint and far she did hear a muffled knocking—it was like a beating heart, she thought. Whatever it was, the deer guessed an enemy. Upon a sudden stamp, the whole herd was in motion. Led by the hart-royal, they trotted noiselessly down the wood, till in the thick fern they lay still. The girls lay down with them.

The sound gained rapidly upon them. Soon they heard the crackling of twigs, then the swish of swept brushwood, then the creaking of girths. Isoult hid her face, lying prone on her breast.

Galors and his men came thundering through the wood. Their horses were reeking, dripping from the flanks. The riders, four of them, looking neither right nor left, past over the open ground, where a few minutes before she whom they desperately sought had been lying at their mercy. But Galors, fled by all things living in Morgraunt, scourged on like a destroying wind and was gone. Isoult little knew how near she had been to the unclean thing. If she had seen him she would have run straight to him without a thought, for he bore the red feathers in his helmet, and behind him, on the shield, danced in the glory of new gilt the *fesse dancettée*.

It may be doubted if the instincts of the earth-born can ever pierce the trappings of a knight-at-arms. They trust in emotions which such gear is designed to hide or transfigure. Isoult, observe, had caught Prosper out of his harness, when before the face of the sky she had thrilled him to pity. But when once he had stooped to her, for the very fact, she made haste to set him up on high in her heart, and in more seemly guise. There and thenceforward he stood on his pedestal figured, not as a pitiful saviour (whom a girl must be taught to worship), but as an armed god who suffered her homage. She was no better (or no worse, if you will) than the rest of her sex in this, that she loved to love, and was bewildered to be loved. So she would never get him out of armour again. Her god might not stoop.

CHAPTER XXIX

WANMEETING CRIES, 'HA! SAINT JAMES!'

The story returns to Prosper le Gai and his broken head. The blow had been sharp, but Peering Pool was sharper. It brought him to consciousness, of a sort sufficient to give him a disrelish for drowning. Lucky for him he was unarmed. He found himself swimming, paddling, rolling at random; he swallowed quantities of water, and liked drowning none the better. By the little light there was he could make out the line of the dark hull of Goltres, by the little wit he had he remembered that the water-gate was midway the building or thereabouts. He turned his face to the wall and, half clinging, half swimming, edged along it till he reached port. The last ebb of his strength sufficed to drag him up the stair; then he floated off into blankness again.

When he stirred he was stiff, and near blind with fever. A cold light silvered the pool; it was not yet dawn. His plight was pitiable. He ached and shivered and burned, he drowsed and muttered, dreamed horribly, sweated and was cold, shuddered and was hot. One of his arms he could not lift at all; at one of his sides, there was a great stiff cake of cloth and blood and water. He became light-headed, sang, shouted, raved, swore, prayed.

"To me, to me, Isoult! Ah, dogs of the devil, this to a young maid! Yes, madam, the Lady Isoult, and my wife. Love her! O God, I love her at last. Hounded, hounded, hounded out! Love of Christ, how I love her! Bailiff, Galors will come —a white-faced, sullen dog. Cut him down, bailiff, without mercy, for he hath shown no mercy. The man in the wood—ha! dead—Salomon de Born. Green froth on his lips—fie, poison! She has killed Galors' only son. Galors, she has poisoned him—oh, mercy, mercy, Lord, must I die?" And then with tears, and the whining of a child—"Isoult, Isoult, Isoult!"

In tears his delirium spent itself, and again he was still, in a broken sleep. The sun rose, the sky warmed itself and glowed, the crispy waves of Peering Pool glittered, the white burden it bore floated face upwards, an object of interest and suspicion for the coots; soon a ray of generous heat shot obliquely down upon the sleeper on the stairs. Prosper woke again, stretched, and yawned. Most of his pains seemed now to centre in the pit of his stomach, a familiar grief. Prosper was hungry.

"Pest!" said the youth, "how hungry I am. I can do nothing till I have eaten."

He tried to get up, and did succeed in raising himself on all fours. But for the life of him he could do no more. He sat down again and thought about eating. He remembered the bread and olives, the not unkindly red wine of the night before. Then he remembered Spiridion, dispenser of meat and many questions.

"That poor doubting rogue!" he laughed. But he sobered himself. "I do ill to laugh, God knows! The man must be dead by now, and all his doubts with him. I must go find him. But I must eat some of his bread and olives first."

Once more he got on all fours, and this time he crawled to the stop of the stairway. Clinging to the lintel and hoisting himself by degrees, he at last stood fairly on his feet—but with a spinning head, and a sickness as unto death. He tottered and flickered; but he stuck to his door-post.

"Bread and olives!" he cried. "I am to die, it seems, but by the Lord I will eat first."

He made a rush for it, gained so the great hall, dizzied through it somehow, and out into the corridor. He flung himself at the stone stairs with the desperation of his last agony, half crawled, half swarmed up to the top (dragging his legs after him at the end, like a hare shot in the back), and finished his course to Spiridion's chamber on hands and knees. He had probably never in his life before worked so hard for a breakfast. He was dripping with sweat, shaking like gossamer; but his fever had left him. Bread and a bottle of wine did wonders for him. He felt very drunk when he had done, and was conscious that pot-valiancy only gave him the heart to tear off his clothes. A flask of sweet oil from Spiridion's shelf helped him here. Next he probed the rents. He found a deepish wound in the groin, a sword-cut in the fleshy part of his left arm; then there was his head! He assured himself that the skull was whole.

"I never respected my ancestors before," he cried. "Such a headpiece is worthy of a Crusader."

He kindled a fire, heated water, washed out his hurts, oiled them and bound them up with one of Spiridion's bed-sheets.

"Now," he reflected, "by rights I should go and hunt for my poor host. But I am still drunk unfortunately. Let me consider. Spiridion must pass for a man. If he is dead he will wait for me. If he is not dead he is no worse off than I am. Good. I will sleep." And he slept round the clock.

Next morning when he awoke he was stiff and sore, but himself. He finished the bread, drank another bottle of wine, and looked about for his armour. It was not there. Instead, the white wicket-gates gleamed at him from a black shield, white plumes from a black headpiece, and the rest of a concatenation.

"*Entra per me*," he read. "Enter I will," said Prosper, "and by you. This device," he went on, as he fitted the *cuisses*, "this device is not very worthy of Dom Galors. It speaks of hurry. It speaks, even, of precipitation, for if he must needs wear my harness, at least he might have carried his own. Galors was flurried. If he was flurried he must have had news. If, having news, he took my arms, it must have been news of Isoult. He intended to deceive her by passing for me. Good; I will deceive his allies by passing for himself. But first I must find Spiridion."

He had too much respect for his enemy, as you will observe if I have made anything of Galors. Galors was no refiner, not subtle; he was direct. When he had to think he held his tongue, so that you should believe him profound. When he got a thought he made haste to act upon it, because it really embarrassed him. None of Prosper's imaginings were correct. If the monk had been capable of harbouring two thoughts at a time, there would not have been a shred of mail in the room.

That sodden thing lipped by the restless water was Spiridion. He lay on his back, thinner and more peaked than ever in life; his yellow hair made him an aureole. He looked like some martyred ascetic, with his tightened smile and the gash half-way through his neck.

Prosper leaned upon his punt-pole looking sorrowfully at him.

"Alas, my brother," he said half whimsically, "do you smile? Even so I think God should smile that He had let such a thing be made. And if, as I believe, you know the truth at last, that is why you also smile. But shut your eyes, my brother," he added, stooping to do the office, "shut your eyes, for you wore them thin with searching and now can see without them. Let them rest."

Very tenderly he pulled him out of the water, very reverently took him to land. He buried him before his own gates, and over him set the crucifix, which in the end he had found grace to see. He was too good a Christian not to pray over the grave, and not sufficient of a hero to be frank about his tears. At the end of all this business he found his horse. Then he rode off at a canter for Hauterive.

* * * * *

It is one thing to kindle military fires in the breast of a High Bailiff, quite another to bid them out. Prosper had overstepped his authority. The High Bailiff of Wanmeeting held himself in check for the better part of a week after his generalissimo's departure; at the end of five days he could endure it no more. His harness clamoured, his sword tarnished for blood; he had fifteen hundred men in steel. That would mean fifteen hundred and one tarnishing blades, and the unvoiced reproaches of fifteen hundred and one suits of mail. In a word, the High Bailiff itched to try a fall with the redoubtable Galors de Born.

He sent, therefore, a man to ring the great bell of the parish church. This assembled the citizens pell-mell, for the times were stirring. The High Bailiff, being assured of his auditory, summoned the garrison, put himself at the head of them on a black stallion, sounded trumpets, and marched into the Market-place. The cheers clipped him like heady wine; but it was the eloquence of the women's handkerchiefs that really gave him heart. Standing in his stirrups, hat in hand, he made a short speech.

"Men of Wanmeeting and brothers," he said, "to-day you shall prove yourselves worthy of your Lady Paramount, of your late master, and of me. Galors de Born, the arch-enemy, is skulking in his strong tower, not daring to attack us. Men of

Wanmeeting, we will go and bait him. Hauterive is ours. Follow me, crying, Ha! Saint James!"

"Ha! Saint James!" shouted the men, with their caps pike-high.

The Bailiff glowed in his skin. He drew his sword.

"Forward!" He gave the word.

The entire ardent garrison marched out of the town, and Wanmeeting was left with its women and elders, anybody's capture.

The consequence of these heroical attitudes was, that Prosper, riding hard to Hauterive, came in sight of a besieging army round about it—a tented field, a pavilion, wherefrom drooped the saltire of De Forz, a long line of attack, in fine, a notable scheme of offence. He saw a sortie from the gates driven back by as mettlesome a cavalry charge as he could have wished to lead.

"The Bailiff of Wanmeeting, as I live by bread!" he cried out.

He stayed for some time watching the fray from a little rising ground. The cavalry, having beaten in the defenders, retired in good order; the archers advanced to cover a party of pikemen with scaling-ladders.

"Now is my time to board the Bailiff," said Prosper, and rode coolly across the field.

The High Bailiff saw, as he thought, Galors himself riding unattended towards him.

"Ha! negotiations," said he; "and in person! I have hit a mark it seems. I may take a high tone. Unconditional surrender and all arms, hey?"

Prosper rode up, saluting.

"Messire de Born," said the Bailiff.

"Prosper le Gai," said the other.

"Madam Virgin! I thought you had perished, Messire."

"Not at all, Bailiff. Was that why you took over my command?"

The Bailiff bowed. "I gladly relinquish it, Messire."

Prosper nodded pleasantly.

"That last charge of yours could hardly have been bettered, though I think you might have got in. How many men did you drop?"

"Ten, Messire. We brought off the wounded."

"Ten is enough. You shall lose no more. Call off that scaling party."

The Bailiff repeated the order.

"Your men know their work," said Prosper; "but why do they cry for Saint James?"

The High Bailiff coloured.

"Well, Messire," he said, "there is undoubtedly a Saint James, an Apostle and a great Saint."

"Of the greatest," said Prosper. "But, pardon. I thought your burgh was devoted to Saint Crispin?"

"Messire, it is so. But there were reasons. First, your battle-cry should be familiar——"

"As Saint Crispin to Wanmeeting?"

"As the name of James, Messire. For it is my own poor name."

"Ah," said Prosper, "I begin to see."

"Then," said the Bailiff, pursuing his reasons, "a battle-cry should be short, of one syllable——"

"Like Saint Dennis?" Prosper asked.

"Like Saint George, Messire."

"Or Saint Andrew?" said Prosper sweetly.

"Or—"

"Or Montjoy, or Bide the Time, eh, Bailiff?"

"Messire, you have me at a disadvantage for the moment. The name is, however, that of a Saint."

"Say no more, Bailiff, but listen. There need be no more bloodshed over this place. Get your men together, to advance at a signal from within. I will go alone into the town. Now, do you notice that little square window in the citadel? When you see the Saltire hang there you will march in and meet me at the Bishop's Gate."

"Oh, Messire, what will you do?"

"Leave that to me," Prosper said, as he rode off.

He rode close to the moat and kept by it, making a half circuit of the walls. He had calculated on Galors' armour, and calculated well, for nobody molested him from the defenders' side. At the Bishop's Gate he reined up, and stood with his spear erect at the length of his arm.

"Who comes?" cried the sentry.

"*Entra per me*," growled Prosper, with a shot for Galors' sulky note.

The gate swung apart, the bridge fell, the portcullis was drawn up. Prosper rode through the streets of Hauterive amid the silence of the inhabitants and the cheers of the garrison—two very different sets of persons. He went into the citadel, displayed the appointed signal, then returned on horseback to the Bishop's Gate. He had not a word to say, but this was quite in character. So he stood waiting.

There was presently a fine commotion at the gate; a man came running up to him.

"Messire, they are going to attack the gate!"

"Open it," said Prosper.

"Messire?"

"Open it, hound!"

The man reeled, but carried the order. Prosper rode stately out; and when he returned a second time it was at the head of the Countess Isabel's troops.

"Bailiff," said he, when they were in the citadel and all the news out, "I am no friend of your mistress, as you know; but I am not a thief. Hauterive is hers. To-morrow morning I shall declare it so; until then Galors, if you please, is Lord. Let me now say this," he continued. "I admire you because you have a high heart. But you lack one requisite of generalship, as it appears to me. You have no head. Get back at once to Wanmeeting with one thousand of your men, and leave me five hundred of them to work with. You may think yourself lucky if you find one stone on another or one man's wife as she should be. By the time you are there you will no doubt have orders from High March. You may send news thither that this place is quiet and restored, as from to-morrow morning, to its allegiance. Good morning, Bailiff."

The Bailiff was very much struck with Prosper's sagacity, and went at once. Prosper and his five hundred men held the citadel.

He confided his secret to those whom he could trust; the remainder fraternized in the wine shops and dealt liberally in surmise. The general opinion seemed to be that Galors had married the Countess Isabel.

* * * * *

Having thus ridded him of all his charges, Prosper could steer the ship of his mind whither his soul had long looked—to Isoult and marriage. Marriage was become a holy thing, a holy sepulchre of peace to be won at all costs. No crusader was he, mind you, fighting for honour, but a pitiful beaten wayfarer longing for ease from his aching. He did not seek, he did not know, to account for the change in him. It had come slowly. Slowly the girl had transfigured before him, slowly risen from below him to the level of his eyes; and now she was above him. He shrined her high as she had shrined him, but for different reasons as became a man. What a woman loves in man is strength, what a man loves in women is also strength, the strength of weak things. The strength of the weak thing Isoult had been that, she had known how to hold him off because of her love's sake. There is always pity (which should become reverence) in a man's love. He had never pitied her till she fought so hard for the holiness of her lover.

Oddly enough, Isoult loved him the more for the very attack which she had foiled. Odd as it may be, that is where the truth lies. As for him, gratitude for what she had endured for his sake might go for nothing. Men do not feel gratitude—they accept tribute. But if they pity, and their pity is quickened by knowledge of the pitiful, then they love. Her pleading lips, her dear startled eyes stung him out of himself. And then he found out why her eyes were startled and why her lips were mute. She was lovely. Yes, for she loved. This beseeching child, then, loved him. He knew himself homeless now until she took him in.

CHAPTER XXX

THE CHAINED VIRGIN OF SAINT THORN

The Abbot Richard of Malbank Saint Thorn went hunting the deer in Morgraunt with a good company of prickers and dogs. In Spenshaw he unharboured a stag, and he followed him hard. The hart made straight for Thornyhold Brush where the great herd lay; there Mellifont, who was sentry for the time, heard him and gave the alarm. Fern brakes will hide man from man, but here were dogs. The hunted hart drove sheer into the thicket on his way to the water; a dog was at his heels, half-a-dozen more were hard on him. The herd had scattered on all hands long before this. Mellifont saved herself with them, but Belvisée tarrying to help Isoult was caught. A great hound snapped at her as he passed; she limped away with a wounded side. Isoult, too much of a woman and too little of a hind, stood still. She had closed with Fate before.

Up came the Abbot's men with horns and shouting voices for the baying of the deer. He, brave beast, was knifed in the brook and broken up, the dogs called off and leashed. Then one of the huntsmen saw Isoult. She had let down her hair for a curtain and stood watching them intently, neither defiant nor fearful, but with a long, steady, unwinking gaze. Her bosom rose quick and short, there was no other stressful sign; she was flushed rather than white. One of the men thought she was a wood-girl—they all knew of such beings; he crossed himself. Another knew better. Her mother Mald was a noted witch; he whistled.

A third thought she was uncommonly handsome; he could only look. The dogs whimpered and tugged at the leash; they doubtless knew that there was blood in her. So all waited till the Abbot came up much out of breath.

Isoult, cloaked in her panoply of silence, saw him first. In fact the Abbot had eyes only for the dead hart which had led him such a race. One of the prickers ran forward and caught at his stirrup-leather.

"Lord Abbot, here is the strangest thing my eyes have ever seen in Morgraunt. As we followed the chase we drove into a great herd which ran this way and that way. And in the thick of the deer were three young women scantily attired, as the one you see yonder, going with the beasts. Of whom two have got clear (one bitten by the mouse-coloured hound), and this one remains speechless. And who the others were, whether flesh and blood or wind and breath, I cannot tell you; but if this laggard is not Isoult, whom we call La Desirous, Matt-o'-the-Moor's daughter, I am no fit servant for your Holiness' diversions."

The Abbot had pricked up his ears; now he looked sharply at Isoult.

"You are right, Sweyn," he said; "leave her to me. Girl," he turned to her, "this time it shall likely go hard with thee. Trees are plenty and ropes easy to come by. I warned thee before. I shall not warn thee now."

Isoult bowed her head.

"What dost thou do here, herding in the wood with wild beasts?" he went on.

"Lord, none but the beasts will give me food or rest or any kindness at all. There is no pity in man nor woman that I have seen, save in two, and one is dead. Prosper le Gai, my lord, and husband, hath pity, and will come to me at last. And whether he shall come to my body alone or my spirit alone, he will come. And now, lord, hang me to a tree."

"Dost thou want to be hanged?" he asked.

"Nay, lord, I am too young to be hanged," she said. "Moreover, though I am wedded to my lord, I am not a wife. For only lately he hath loved me, and that since we were put apart."

"Wed, and a virgin, girl? Where is thy husband?"

"Lord, he is searching for me."

"Where hath he been, what hath he done—or thou, what hast thou done, for such a droll fate as this?"

Isoult very simply told him everything. Of Galors he already had some news— enough to dread more. But when he heard that the girl had actually been in High March Castle, had been expelled from it, he crossed himself and thanked God for all His mercies. He became a devout Christian at this critical point in Isoult's career, whereby her neck was saved a second time from the rope. He felt a certain pity—she a handsome girl, too, though his type for choice was blonde—for her simplicity, and, as he certainly wished to obtain mercy, reflected upon the possible blessings of the merciful. Besides, Galors was at large, Galors who knew the story, to say nothing of Prosper, also at large, who did not know the story, but did know, on the other hand, the Countess Isabel. Difficult treading! But so the habits of a lifetime for once chimed in with its professions. Even as he stood pitying he roughed out another set of shifts. Prosper and his unconsummated marriage might be set aside—the fool, he thought with a chuckle, deserved it. There remained Galors. He would get the girl married to a mesne of the abbey, or stay! he would marry her elsewhere and get a dowry. She had filled out astonishingly, every line of her spoke of blood: there would be no trouble about a dowry. Then he might supplant Galors by being beforehand with him at the Countess's ear. Gratitude of the mother, gratitude of the daughter, gratitude of the son-in-law! Thus Charity walked hand in hand with Policy. The girl was a beauty. What a picture she made there, short-frocked, flushed and loose-haired, like an Amazon—but, by Mars, not maimed liked an Amazon. The Abbot was a connoisseur of women, as became a confessor and man of the world.

"If I do not hang thee, Isoult, wilt thou come with me to Saint Thom?"

"Yes, lord, I will come."

"Up with you then before me," said the Abbot, and stooped to lift her. Her hair fell back as she was swung into the saddle. "My lady," thought the Abbot, "it is clear you are no Amazon; but I should like to know what you wear round that fine little neck of yours."

He bided his time, and sent the men and dogs on ahead. Then at starting he spurred his horse so that the beast plunged both his riders forward. The burden of the chain slipt its harbourage, and the next minute the Abbot had ring and locket in the palm of his hand.

"What is this ring, my girl?" he asked.

"My lord, it is my wedding-ring, wherewith I was wed in the cottage."

"Ah, is that it? Well, I will keep it until there is need."

Isoult began to cry at this, which cut her deeper than all the severances she had known. She could confess to the ring.

"Don't cry, child," said the Abbot, whom women's tears troubled; "believe me when I say that you shall have it for your next wedding."

"Oh, my ring! my ring! What shall I do? It is all I have. Oh, my lord, my lord!"

This pained the Abbot extremely. He got what satisfaction there was from the thought that, having dropt it behind him, he could not give it back for all the tears in the world. He was busy now examining the other token—a crystal locket whereon were a pelican in piety circled with a crown of thorns, and on the other side the letters I and F interlaced. He knew it better than most people.

"Isoult, stop crying," he said. "Take off this chain and locket and give them to me."

So she did.

"Ah, my lord," she pleaded as she tendered, "I ask only for the ring."

"Plague take the ring," cried the Abbot very much annoyed. "I will throw it away if you say another word about it."

The threat chilled her. She dried her eyes, hoping against hope, for even hope needs a sign.

When he had his prize safe in Holy Thorn, the Abbot Richard, who had a fantastic twist in him, and loved to do his very rogueries in the mode, set himself to embroider his projects when he should have been executing them. His lure was a good lure, but she would be none the worse for a little gilding; there must be a pretty cage, with a spice of malice in its devising, to excite the tenderer feelings. It should be polite malice, however—a mere hint at a possible tragedy behind a smirk.

He dressed her in green silk because she was fresh-coloured and had black hair. If she had been pale, as when he first knew her, and as she was to be again before he knew her no more, the dress would have been red, depend upon it. He put a gold ring on her finger, a jewel on her forehead, a silver mirror and a Book of Hours bound in silver leaves to swing at her girdle. Her chamber was hung with silk arras,—the loving history of Aristotle and a princess of Cyprus;—she had two women to wait upon her, to tire her hair in new ways and set new crowns upon it; she had a close garden of her own, with roses and a fountain, grass lawns, peacocks. She had pages to serve her kneeling, musical instruments, singing boys and girls. He gave her a lap-dog. Finally he kissed her and said—

"You are to be queen of this place, Isoult the Much-Desired."

All this the Abbot did. This also he did—his crowning piece. He caused her to wear round her waist a girdle made of bright steel in which was a staple. To the staple he fixed a fine steel chain—a toy, a mimicry of prisons, but in fact a chain —and the other end of a chain was fixed to a monk's wrist. The chain was fine and flexible, it was long, it could go through the keyhole—and did—but it was a chain. Wherever the girl went, to the garden, to table, to music, to bed, abroad, or to Mass, she was chained to a monk and a monk to her. The Abbot Richard rested on the seventh day, contemplating his labours with infinite relish. It seemed to him that this was to be politic with an air. So far as he might he did everything in that manner.

Isoult bore the burden much as she had borne the thwackings of the charcoal-burners, with ingrained patience. Seriously, one only cross fretted her—the loss of her ring. This indeed cried desertion upon her. Prosper had never seemed so far, nor his love so faint and ill-assured. It would seem that kindness really killed her by drugging her spirit as with anodyne. As she had fallen at Gracedieu, so she fell now into a languid habit where tears swam in flood about the lids of her eyes, where the eyes were too heavy for clear sight and the very blood sluggish with sorrow. She grew pale again, hollow-eyed, diaphanous—a prism for an unearthly ray. Her beauty took on its elfin guise; she walked a ghost. Night and day she felt for the ring; though she knew it was not there, her hand was always in her vest, her bosom always numb and cold. Sometimes her urgent need was more than she could bear. A trembling took her, an access of trembling which she could not check. At such times, if others were about her, she would sit vacant and speechless, smiling faintly for courtesy; her eyes would brim over, the great drops fall unchecked. There would be no sobbing, very little catching of the breath. The well of misery would fill and overflow, gently and smoothly irresistible. Then the shaking would cease and the fount be dry for a season. So she grew more a spirit and less a maid; her eyes waxed larger, and the pupils whelmed the grey in jet.

The people of Malbank frankly took her for a saint. Martyrs, virgins, and such rare birds do not hop in every cage; but what more reasonable than that the famous Abbot of Saint Thorn should catch one in his own springes? Those who maintained that the chained white creature, who knelt folded at the Mass, or on a white palfrey rode out on the heath guarded by two monks, was the stormy girl who had kept swine about the middens, Matt's bad daughter Isoult la Desirous, those were leagued with the devil and his imps, who would not see a saint if all heaven walked the earth.

The report fell in excellently with the Abbot's calculation. No one believed in the Isoult fable save Mald, whom the girl had seen once or twice, and himself; every one talked rather of the Chained Virgin of Saint Thorn. She became an object of pilgrimage. The Abbot grew to call her chamber the feretory; the faithful gave alms, particularly the seamen from Wanmouth. Then others came to behold, more to his liking, proposing barter. She was observed of the Lord of Hartlepe, the young Lord of Brokenbridge, the Lord of Courthope Saint James; of the Baron of Starning and Parrox, also, from the East Demesne. This Baron Malise, thin and stooping, having Prosper's quick eyes without his easy lordship over all who met them, and Prosper's high voice twisted querulous, came to view his young brother's wife. She pleased, but the price did not please. He and the Abbot haggled over the dowry; Malise, as obstinate as Prosper, would not budge. So they haggled. Finally came Galors de Born, Lord of Hauterive and many other places in the north, not to be denied.

CHAPTER XXXI

'ENTRA PER ME'

When Galors overshot his mark in Thornyhold he flew very wide. It is well known there are no roads. Thornyhold is but the beginning of the densest patch of timber in all the forest. Malbank is your nearest habitation; Spenshaw, Heckaby, Dunsholt Thicket, Hartshold, Deerleap are forest names, not names of the necessities of men. You may wander a month if you choose, telling one green hollow from another; or you may go to Holy Thorn at Malbank, or endure unto Wanmouth and the sea. If you were Galors and needed counsel you would not choose the wood; naturally you would avoid Malbank. There would remain to you Wanmouth.

Galors went to Wanmouth. It was the Countess's country of course; but his disguise was good enough. People read the arms and hailed a le Gai or one of that house. It was at Wanmouth that he learned what he wanted. Malise, after one of his interminable chafferings with the Abbot Richard, took it on his way to the east.

"My Lord Baron of Starning," said the Vice-Admiral of the port, "we have had a friend of your house here a week or more."

"Eh, eh!" said Malise, feeling his pocket, "what does the rogue want with his friendship? I'm as poor as a rat. Who is he?"

"Oh, for that," replied the other, "he seems a great lord in his way, wears your blazon, is free with his money, and he swears like a Fleming."

"Bring him to me, Admiral, bring him to me. I shall like this man."

So Galors was brought in, to be graciously received by the head of the house of Gai. His blunt manner deceived Malise at once. In his experience people who wanted to borrow dealt differently. Here was a lofty soul, who might, on the other hand, be guided to lend! In the course of a long conversation Melise unbosomed. He was newly a lover and liked the part. The Baron ended his confession thus—

"So, my dear friend, you see how it is with me. I have never met you before— the more's the pity. I accept your civilities, but I make no promises—you know our legend? Well, I bide my time—he—he! No boasting, but upon my honour, my reputation does not make me out ungrateful. I say to you, go to Malbank; observe, watch, judge, then report to me. The detail I leave to you. I should recommend a disguise. The place has become one of pilgrimage—go as a pilgrim! You will see whether the prize is worth my while. I am sure you have taste—I know it. Observe, report. Then we will act."

"Ravishment of ward?" asked Galors dryly.

"Ward! She is not his ward. How can she be? Who is she? Nobody knows. The thing is a crying scandal, my dear friend. A woman in an abbey parlour! An alcove at Holy Thorn! Are we Mohammedans, infidels, Jews of the Old Law? Fie!"

"You do not know her name, Baron?"

"She is the Chained Virgin of Saint Thorn, I tell you. She has no other name. She sits in a throne in choir, pale as milk, with burning grey eyes as big as passion-flowers! She is a chained Andromeda on the rock of Peter. Be my Perseus!"

"Hum," said Galors, half to himself, "hum! Yes, I will go at once."

"My dear friend——"

"Not a word more, Baron. Go home to Starning, go where you like, and wait. If you see me again the lady will be with me."

"You shall not find me ungrateful, I promise," cried Malise, going out.

"Damn your gratitude," said Galors, when the door was shut.

A mortified Perseus in drab cloak and slouch hat, he went to Malbank next day and verified his prognosis. The Abbot sang Mass, his old colleagues huddled in choir; the place echoed with the chastened snuffling he knew so well. Galors had no sentiment to pour over them. Standing, bowing, genuflecting, signing himself at the bidding of the bell, he had no eyes for any but the frail apparition whose crown of black seemed to weigh her toward the pavement. The change wrought in her by a year's traffic might have shocked, as the eyes might have haunted him; but she was nothing but a symbol by now. A frayed ensign, she stood for an earldom and a fee. The time had been when her beauty had bewitched him; that was when she went flesh and blood, sun-browned, full of the sap of untamed desires. Now she was a ghost with a dowry; stricken, but holding a fief.

He judged the chain, the time, the place, the chances. He had three men. It was enough. Next Sunday he would act. Then for the forest roads and High March!

That next Sunday was Lammas Day and a solemn feast. All Malbank was in the nave, a beaten and weather-scarred bundle of drabs packed in one corner under the great vaulting ribs. Within the dark aisles the chapels gloomed, here and there a red lamp made darkness darker; but the high altar was a blaze of lights. The faces, scared or sharp-set, of the worshippers fronted the glory open-mouthed, but all dull. Hunger makes a bad altar-flame; when it burns not sootily it fires the fabric.

Afterwards came something which they understood—Isoult between her two women, the monk behind. A girl chained by the middle to a monk—Oh, miracle! She sat very still in her carved chair, folding her patient hands. So thin, so frail, so transparent she was, they thought her pure spirit, a whisp of gossamered breath, or one of those gauzy sublimations which the winter will make of a dead leaf. The cowed audience watched her wonderfully; some of the women snivelled. The white monks, the singing boys, the banners and tapers,

Ceremoniar, Deacon, Subdeacon, the vested Abbot himself, passed like a shining cloud through the nave. All their light came from the Chained Virgin of Saint Thorn. And then the Mass began.

There was a ring of hoofs outside, but no one looked round, and none came in. A shadow fell across the open door. At a *Dominus Vobiscum* you might have seen the ministrant falter; there might have been a second or two of check in his chant, but he mastered it without effort, and turned again with displayed hands to his affair. The choir of white hoods, however, watched the shadow at the west door. Isoult saw nothing and heard nothing; she was kneeling at prayer. It may be doubted if any prayed but the girl and the priest.

The holy office proceeded; the Sanctus bell shrilled for the first time. Hoofs shattered scandalously on the flags, and Galors, with an armed man on either hand of him, rode into the nave. The choir rose in a body, the nave huddled; Isoult, as she believed, saw Prosper, spear, crest, and shield. Her heart gave a great leap, then stood still. Perhaps there was a flicker in the Abbot's undertone; his lips may have been dry; but his courage was beyond proof. He held on.

Isoult was blanched as a cloth; lips, fingers and ears, the tongue in her open mouth—all creeks for the blood were ebbed dry. Her awful eyes, fixed and sombre stars, threatened to gulf her in their dark. Love was drowned in such horror as this.

Galors swung out of the saddle. In the breathless place the din of that act came like a thunder-peal, crackling and crashing, like to wreck the church. He drew his sword, with none to stay him, and strode forward. If the Abbot Richard heard his step up the choir the man is worthy of all memory, for he went on with his manual acts, and his murmur of prayer never ceased. He may have heard nothing—who knows what his motions were? He was a brave man.

The bell rang—rang again—God beamed in the Host. The people wavered, but use held. They bowed prone before God in His flake of new flesh.

"*Deus in adjutorium*," muttered the Abbot to himself.

"*Entra per me!*" thundered Galors, and ran him through the body.

After the first shudder had swept through the church there was no sound at all, until some woman hidden began a low moan, and keened the Abbot Richard. No one dared to stir while those grim horsemen in the nave sat like rocks.

Galors turned to Isoult where she froze rigid in her throne, severed the chain at a blow, and went to take her. Some sudden thought struck him; he turned her quickly round to the light and without ceremony fumbled at her neck. She grew sick to feel him touch her.

"The Abbot hath it." Her lips formed the words. Galors went back to the dead priest and pulled off chain and locket.

"Oh, my ring, my ring!" whined the girl as he slipt the chain over her. He did not seem to hear her, but snatched her up in his arms as if she had been a doll and set her on his horse. He swung himself into the saddle behind her as he had swung himself out of it, reined up short and turned. The three men rode out with their burden. When they had gone the Deacon (who got a mitre for it) solemnly laid the fallen host between his lord's lips. The act, at once pious and sensible, brought up the congregation from hell to earth again. At such times routine is the only saving thing.

Once free of the Abbey precincts the three horsemen forded Wan. At a signal pre-arranged one of them fell back to keep watch over the river. Galors went forward with one in his company on to the heath, dropped him after three or four hours' steady going, and rode on still. His third man was to meet him at the edge of Martle Brush. Never a word had he spoken since his great "*Entra per me!*" but without that the act had been enough to tell his prize, that whatever her chains had been before, the sword-stroke had riveted them closer. There had been no chain like his mailed arm round her body.

Nothing could be done. Indeed she was as yet paralyzed; for wild work as had been done in her sight, this was savagery undreamed. She could get no comfort, she never thought of Prosper. Even Prosper, her lord, could not stand before such a force as this. As for good Saint Isidore, the pious man became a shade, and vanished with his Creator into the dark.

Night came on, but a low yellow moon burnt the fringe of the rising woods. They were retracing almost the very stones of the track she and Prosper had followed a year before.

Matt's intake they passed, she saw a light in the window. The heath loomed ghostly before them, with the dark bank of trees rising steadily as they neared. Athwart them rose also the moon; there was promise of a fine still night. They entered the trees, heading for Martle Brush.

Suddenly Galors pulled up, listening intently. There was no sound save that strange murmur the night has (as if the whole concave of heaven were the hollow of a shell), and the secret rustling of the trees. Still Galors listened. It was so quiet you might almost have heard two hearts beating.

As an underchant, sinister accompaniment to the voices of the night, there came to them the muffled pulsing of a horse's hoofs; a quick and regular sound—a horse galloping evenly with plenty in hand.

Both heard it. Galors drove in the spurs, and the chase began. They were yet a mile away from Martle Brush. If they could cross the brook and gain the ridgeway, it was long odds on their being overtaken that night.

CHAPTER XXXII

'BIDE THE TIME'

Walking the rounds at Hauterive the night of his coming there, a man sprang out at Prosper from a black entry and stabbed at him between the shoulders. "For the ravisher of Isoult!" was all the message that did not miscarry, for Galors' mail of proof stopped the rest. Prosper whipt round in an instant, but the assassin had made up the passage-way. There was a quick chase through the break-neck lanes of the steep little town, then blood told. Prosper ran his man to earth in a churchyard. He proved to be a red-haired country lout, whose bandy legs had been against him in this work. He asked for no quarter, seemed beside himself with rage.

"Friend," said Prosper, "you struck me from behind. You must have wished to make very sure. Why?"

Said Falve, "Thou ravisher, Galors."

"I cannot be called Galors to my face; politics may go to the devil. Keep my secret, countryman; I am in Galors' shell, but I will be Galors no more."

Falve dropped on his knees. "Oh, my lord, my lord—" he began to cry out.

"Enough of lords," said Prosper. "Some of them do not very lordly, I grant you. Your words touched me nearly. Be so good as to make yourself plain. Who is Isoult?"

"Isoult la Desirous, my wife, Messire."

"Your wife!" cried Prosper, grinding his teeth.

"As good as that, my lord. I should have married her in the morning if my mother hadn't played the Turk on me."

So he had the whole story out of him. Prosper learnt that Isoult had been put in her way to safety by the old woman, who immediately after had made that way the most perilous of all—with the best intentions always.

"Master Falve, I am your debtor," said Prosper at the end; "I wish you good evening."

"Messire, will you not find my wife?"

"Your wife again, sirrah!" cried he, turning sharply.

"Ah, my lord, if you have any ill-will to that——"

"I have the greatest possible ill-will, my man, because she is already my own."

"Heaven round about us, was there ever such a married woman!" cried poor Falve, tearing his hair.

The politics of a lady to whom, so far as he then knew, he owed no service held Prosper till the morning. The rest of the night he spent walking the ramparts. At the first flutter of light he beat up the garrison, assembled the men of both parties, and declared himself.

"Hauterive returns to its allegiance," said he. "Conradin de Lamport is commandant. The former garrison will deliver up all arms and take the oath of fealty. A declaration of hue-and-cry is posted for Galors, with a reward for his head. In three days' time the Countess will send her Viceroy to claim the keys. Gentlemen, I bid you good morning."

Conradin de Lamport was the name of the man who had accompanied him into Wanmeeting. Prosper knew he was to be trusted. Then with conscience cleared he mounted his horse and left Hauterive.

Keeping a sharp look-out as he went, he was rewarded by the find of a shoe, glowing like a crimson toadstool in the moss. Not far off were its fellow, and a pair of drenched silk stockings. He kissed the vestiges of the feet of Isoult, hung them to the peak of the saddle, and forward again like a westerly gale. After this came a fault which delayed him the best part of three days. The deer were dumb animals for him, whose business had hitherto been to bleed not milk them. There were deer feeding in the glades of Thornyhold; but Belvisée was nursing her wound under the oak by the pool, and Mellifont was beside her. The deer snuffed an enemy in the friend of their friend; they gave him a lead astray, which unconsciously he took. Thus he found himself, after two days' aimless wandering and two nights' dreamless sleep, on the high ground by Deerleap, with the forest behind and the rolling purple fells stretched out before him, and at last a blue gauzy ribbon which he knew for the sea. Out of heart he turned and beat back to Thornyhold, this time to better purpose.

A rustle in the fern, a start, a glint of the sun on a side not furry, a flash of flying green and russet, a streamer of hair like a litten cloud—by Heavens, how the brown girl ran! Prosper, laughing but keen, gave chase. She led him far, in and out of the oak stems, doubling like a hare; but he rode her down by cutting off the corners: flushed, panting and wild, defiant she stood, ready to flinch at the blow.

Prosper's horse was properly breathed; as for him he burst into a laugh.

"My child, you bolted like a rabbit. But own that I gave you a good run."

"You beat me," said Mellifont.

"Well, and now I am going to do what I like with you."

"Of course."

"You must be obedient. Answer my question now. Why did you run?"

"Because you came."

"Why did you run?"

"Because you are a man."

"Madam Virgin, what a prude! Did you think I should hurt you?"

"Yes."

"Well, have I?"

"Not yet."

"Look at me now. Do I look like hurting you?" He put up his visor. The softest brown eyes a girl can have trembled over him.

"No—o. Oh!" The negative was drowned in discovery. Prosper followed her gaze. He held up the red stockings.

"Do you know them, child?"

"I know to whom they belong. Are you going to hunt her?"

"Hunt her! I am going to find her. I think she has had hunting enough, God bless her."

"Yes, she has," said Mellifont gravely.

Prosper stooped in his saddle and laid a hand on her head.

"My dear," said he, "I love that hunted lady beyond everything in the world; I never knew how much until I had lost her. But no wrong will happen to her till she hears me tell her the truth. If you know anything you must not hide it from me."

Mellifont peered up at him through her hair.

"Are you Prosper?" she asked.

"Yes, I am indeed. Did she speak to you about me?"

"Often."

"Is she—ah, Lord of Hosts! she is not here?"

"No, not now. She was here. Come with me. But you must leave your horse and sword behind you."

Prosper obeyed her without a thought. Mellifont took his hand and led him to the hollow under the oak. Belvisée was there, dumbly nursing her side, which a stooping hind was licking when the pair came up. Prosper received the red robe and the sequins from her hands, and in time pieced the story together. It cut him to the soul.

"Take me to the place where the dogs got her," he said in a whisper. Belvisée and Mellifont led him there. Once more, then, he wasted his eyes on crushed herbage, black fern, and stained earth; again loathed himself very heartily for what he had not done; but in time understood what he had done. He turned deliberately to the sisters. "Belvisée and Mellifont, listen to what I shall tell you. There is no strength like a woman's, and no blindness like that of a man. For the woman is strong because she is blind and cannot see the man she loves as he is; therefore she makes him in her own glorious image. But the man is blind because he is strong, and because he seeth himself so glorious that he can abide no other near him save as a servant. In that he doth deadly sin to Love, because the food of Love is service, and he that serves not Love starves him. But the woman feedeth him with her own milk; so Love is with her till she dies. I, by the mercy of God, have learned what Love is, and can feed him with service. And Isoult la Desirous has taught me, who is now Isoult la Desirée."

Prosper ceased. Mellifont was crying on Belvisée's shoulder. The latter said—

"Prosper, if all men were like thee, we might leave the forest and dwell with them."

"Come with me," he said, "and I will see you safely bestowed."

"No, no; we will stay where we are known and with whom we know. All men are not like you."

"As you must, it must needs be," replied Prosper. He kissed each on the cheek, and watched them go hand-in-hand down the glade. The herd closed in upon them, so neither he nor the Argument knows them any more.

Prosper knelt down to pray; but what he found set him to better work. He found Isoult's wedding-ring.

"By God," he cried, "who made men to labour, I will pray with my hands this turn!"

He ran for his horse and sword. Courage came with his gallop, courage and self-esteem, without which no man ever did anything yet. With self-esteem returned sober thought.

"I can do Malbank in three or four hours. There is light enough for what I have to settle there. I will spare my horse and save time in the end. Meantime I will think this affair out." So said Prosper galloping to Prosper on his feet, the late moralist. His plan was very simply to confront the Abbot with his ring. If that failed he would scour his own country, raise a troop, and lay leaguer on Saint Thorn. He had forgotten Galors. He was soon to have a reminder of that grim fighter.

The doors of the great church stood open, so Prosper rode in. It was cold and dark, and smelt of death and candle-fumes. The pilasters of the nave were already swathed in black velvet; in the choir were great lights set on the floor, in the midst of them a bier. A priest was at a little altar by the bier's head, other cowled figures crouched about it. There was a low murmur of praying, even, whining, and mechanical. On the bier Prosper saw the comely Abbot Richard Dieudonné, in cope and mitre, holding in his hand the staff of his high office. This pastor of the Church was at peace; the man of the world was sober with access of wisdom; the man of modes smiled pleasantly at his secret thoughts. Very handsome, very remote, very pure he looked; for so death purges off the dross which we work into the good clay.

Prosper, meditative always at the sight of death, stood and pondered upon it. Everything was well, no doubt; such things should be! but the indifference of the defunct seemed almost shocking. Do they not care for decent interment? Then he turned to a bystander.

"You mourn for your father?" he asked.

"Master, we do indeed. What! a great lord, a throned and pompous priest, to be felled like a calf; his body spitted like a lark's! No leave asked! You may well judge whether we mourn. I suppose there never was such a mournful affair since a king died in this country."

"Murdered?" cried Prosper, highly scandalized.

"Murdered by Prosper le Gai for the sake of the Chained Virgin."

"By Prosper le Gai?"

"'Tis so indeed. And well he did his work, if there's anything in wrist play. For first he spits the Abbot, and then he sunders the chain, and next he overhauls the girl, and next the Abbot. And he puts her under his arm like a marketable hen, and away he gallops over the heath. Hot work!"

"Galors' work," said Prosper to himself as he turned away.

He prayed at three altars for the man's soul, turned, mounted, and galloped. He forded Wan. A horseman met him on the further bank, shouting. Prosper lowered his head and shot at him as from a catapult. The spear drove deep, the man threw his arms out, sobbed, and dropped like a stone. Prosper went on his race.

It was growing dusk when he stood on the threshold of Matt's intake, battering at the door. The hag-ridden face of old Mald stared out. She parted her tattered hair from her eyes and pointed a shaky finger at him.

"Galors," she wailed, "Galors, thou monk forsworn, thinkest thou to have the Much-Desired? No, but her husband has her at last, and shall have her with all that is hers—ah, though he have done murder to get her. Swear back, Galors, and pray for thy dead master."

Prosper held up his hand to stay the tide.

"Mother, I am Prosper, the husband of the Much-Desired. No murder have I done, though I have seen murder. And I have not my wife; but I believe she is with Galors."

Old Mald came fawning out to him at this, and took his hands in her own trembling hands.

"He passed an hour agone," said she. "He will do her no wrong till he hath her at High March, trust him for that. And by now he should be near Martle, and she before him on the saddle-bow."

She began to weep and wag her silly head. Prosper made to go, having no time to waste; but, "Stop," she quavered, "and hear me out. Though the Abbot Richard was murdered at his prayers, yet withal he got his deserts, for he hatched a worse wrong than ever Galors did. The child was chained by the middle, and came to me chained riding a white palfrey. In green and white she came, and round her middle was a chain, long and supple, and a monk on horseback held the end thereof. She came to me to the hearth at the length of her chain, and held me in her dear arms, and kissed me, cheeks and forehead. Down I sat on my stool and she on the knees of me, and she hid her face on my leanness while she spoke of you, my lord—called you her dear heart, and told of all the bitter longings she had. Ah, now! Ah, now! If you but knew."

"God forgive me," cried the lacerated wretch, "but I know it all! Yet tell me what else she said."

"There was little more," said Mald, "for the monk pulled at her, and she went as she came."

"Have they passed an hour gone?" said Prosper in a dry whisper.

"Ah, and more."

"God be with you," said he; "pray for her."

"Pray!" mocked the crone in a rage; "and pray what will that do?"

"No more than I, mother, just now. God is all about us. Farewell!"

And he was gone amid flying peats.

Midway of the heath a second knight met him, challenged him, and charged. Prosper was not for small game that night. His head grew cooler, as always, for his haste, his arm steady as a rock. Thereupon he ran his man through the breastbone. He broke his spear, but took the other's, and away. At the edge of the wood the moon-rays gleamed a third time upon mail. It was Galors' last sentry, who hallooed to stay him. Prosper was on him before he was ready, and hurled him from the saddle. He never moved. Prosper galloped through the wood.

The snapping branches, thunder of hoofs, labouring belly and hard-won breath of his beast, more than all the wind that sang in his ears, prevented him from hearing what Galors and his prey had already heard. He went headlong down the slope of the ground; but before anything more welcome he caught the music of the brook in the bottom.

There was a gap in the trees just there; the moon swam in the midst large and golden. Then at last he saw what he wanted, and knew that the hour had come.

CHAPTER XXXIII

SALOMON IS DRIVEN HOME

Galors, too, knew that the hour had come; but his spirit came up to meet it, and he made a push for it. He was over the brook; if he could top the ridge he would have the advantage he had a year ago, which this time he swore to put to better use. The girl knew his thoughts as she had known the accolade of the thundering hoofs behind them. She would have thrown herself if the steel trap had loosed ever so little; as it was, she fluttered like a rag caught in a bush; the filmy body was what Galors held, the soul shrilled prayers to the man's confusion. He could not stay her lips; they moved, working against him, as he knew well. "Mother of God, send him, send him, send him!" It was ill fighting against a girl's soul, it slacked his rein and drugged his heel. By God, let the boy come and be damned; let him fight! "Mother of God, send, send, send!" breathed Isoult. The horse below them shuddered, failed to come up to the rein, bowed his head to the jerked spur. Galors left off spurring, and slackened his rein. Though he would not look behind him he heard the plash of the ford, heard also Prosper's low, "Steady, mare, hold up!" Prosper was over; Galors halfway up the hill. It would be soon.

The black and white gained hand over hand; the red and green felt him come. The soul of Isoult hovered between them. Black and white drew level; red and green held on. Side by side, spears erect and tapering into the moon, plumes nodding, eyes front, they paced; the soul of Isoult took flight, the body crouched in the steel's hug. The gleam of the white wicket-gates caught their master's eye; they were risen in judgment against him. *Entra per me* was to play him false. This trifling thing unnerved him till it seemed to speak a message of doom. But doom once read and accepted, nerve came back. By God, he would die as he had lived, strenuously, seeking one thing at a time! But to be killed by his chosen arm, overshrilled by his own shout—that sobered him, little of a sentimentalist as he was. As for love-lorn Prosper, he had still less sentiment to waste. True, he had not chosen his arms, his motto had been found for him by his ancestors— they were cut-and-dried affairs, so much clothing to which Galors at this moment served as a temporary peg. Sweet Saviour! the Much-Desired was near him, close by. He could have touched her head. She never moved to look at him; he knew so much without turning his own head. And he knew further that she knew him there. The soul of Isoult, you see, had taken wings. Thus they gained the ridge and halted. Backing their beasts, they were face to face, and each looked shrewdly at the other, waiting who should begin the game.

Then it was that Isoult suddenly sat up and looked at Prosper. He could not read her face, but knew by her stiff-poised head that she was quivering. He said nothing, but made a motion, a swift jerk with his head, to wave her out of the way. Galors responded by first tightening, finally relaxing, his hold upon her waist. She slipt down from the saddle, and stood hesitating what to do. She had waited for this moment so long, that the natural thing had become the most unnatural of all. Prosper never glanced at her, but kept his eyes steadily on Galors. The times—in his mannish view—were too great for lovers. Isoult stept back into the shadows.

The two men at once saluted in knightly fashion, wheeled, and rode apart. The lists were a long alley between the pines, all soft moss and low scrub of whortleberry and heather. Galors had the hill behind him, but no disadvantage in that unless he were pushed down it; the place was dead level. They halted at some thirty yards' interval, waiting. Then Prosper gave a shout—*"Bide the time!" "Entra per me!"*came as a sombre echo; and the two spurred horses flung forward at each other.

Each spear went true. Prosper got his into the centre of Galors' shield, and it splintered at the guard. Galors' hit fair; but Prosper used his trick of dropping at the impact, so that the spear glanced off over his shoulder. Galors recovered it and his seat together. It would seem that Prosper had taught him some civility by this, for he threw his lance away as soon as the horses were free of each other. Both drew their swords. Then followed a bout of wheeling and darting in, at which Prosper had clear advantage as the lighter horseman on the handier horse. Galors' strength was in downright carving; Prosper's in his wrist-play and lightning recovery. He, moreover, was cool, Galors hot. At this work he got home thrice to the other's once, but that once was for a memory, starred the shoulder-piece and bit to the bone. Left arm luckily. Prosper made a feint at a light canter, spurred when he was up with his man, and, as his horse plunged, got down a back-stroke, which sent Galors' weapon flying from his hand. He turned sharply and reined up. Galors dismounted slowly, picked up his sword, and went to mount again. He blundered it twice, shook the blood out of his eyes, tried again, but lurched heavily and dropped. He only saved himself by the saddle. Prosper guessed him more breathed than blooded.

"Galors," said he, "we have done well enough for the turn. Rest, and let me rest."

"As you will," said Galors thickly.

The two men sat facing each other on either side of the way. Galors unlaced his helm and leaned on his elbows, taking long breaths. Prosper unlaced his; and then followed a lesson to Isoult in warfare, as he understood it. The girl had run down the hill-side to the brook, so soon as she saw they must give over. She now came back, bearing between her hands a broad leaf filled with water. This she brought to her lord. Prosper smiled to her.

"Take it to Galors, Isoult, whom we must consider as our guest," he whispered.

She turned at once and went dutifully, with recollected feet and bosom girt in meekness, to give him the cold water cupped in her palms. Galors drank greedily, and grunted his thanks. As for Prosper, he praised men and angels for a fair vision.

She came back after another journey to feed her lover, and afterwards stood as near to him as she dared. Galors, the alien, looked ever at the ground.

"Galors," said Prosper presently, "how do you find my harness?"

"It has served me its turn," he answered.

"That also I can say of yours," replied Prosper, with a little laugh; "for it has taken me into places where, without it, I should have found a strait gate in. For that I can thank you more than for the head-ache and cold bath at Goltres."

"Ha!" said the other, "that was a sheer knock. I thought it had finished you, to be plain. But do not lay it to my door. I fight truer than that."

"Truly enough you have fought me this night," Prosper allowed heartily, "and I ask no better. But will you now tell me one thing about which I have been curious ever since our encounter in this place a year ago?"

"What is it?"

"Your arms—the blazon—do you bear them as of right?"

"I bear them by the right a fighter has. They have carried me far, and done my work."

"They are not of your family?"

"My family? Messire, you should know that a monk carries no arms. My family, moreover, was not knightly, till I made it knightly."

"The arms you assumed with your new profession?"

"I did."

"May I know whence you took them?"

"No, I cannot tell you that. They are the arms of a man now dead, Salomon de Montguichet."

"They are the arms," said Prosper slowly, "of a man now dead. I saw him dead, and helped to bury him. I knew not then how he died, though I have thought to be sure since. But you are wrong in one thing. The bearer of those arms was not Salomon de Montguichet."

"It is you who are wrong, Messire. It is beyond doubt; and the proof is that on the shield are the *guichets*, taken from the name."

"Galors, the name was taken from the *guichets*, and the *guichets* from Coldscaur in the north. The man's name was Salomon de Born."

Galors gave a dry sob, and another, and another. He threw up his arms, twisting with the gesture of a man on the rope. Prosper and Isoult rose also, Prosper pale and hard, the girl wide-eyed. Galors seemed to tear at himself, as if at war with a fiend inside him. Prosper stepped forward; you would not have known his voice.

"Man," he said, "our account is not yet done. But I know what I know. If you have accounts to settle, settle them now. I will bear you company and wait for you where you will."

The words steadied Galors, sobered and quieted him. He began to mutter to himself. "God hath spoken to me. Out of my own deeds cometh His judgment, and out of my own sowing the harvest I shall reap.*Entra per me*, saith God." He turned to Prosper. "Sir, I accept of your allowance. I will not take you far. One more thing I will ask at your hands, that you give me back my own sword— Salomon's sword. After a little you shall have it again."

"I will do it," said Prosper, knowing his thought.

They changed swords. Prosper set Isoult on his horse and himself walked at her stirrup. The three of them moved forward without another word given or exchanged. Galors led the way.

Instead of following the line of the chase, which had been north, they now struck east through the heavy woodland. So they went for some three hours. It must have been near midnight, with a moon clear of all trees, when they halted at a cross-ride which ran north and south. Before them, over the ride, rose a thick wall of pine-stems, so serried that there was no room for a horse to pass in between them. Isoult started, looked keenly up and down the ride, then collected herself and sat quite still. Prosper took no notice of anything.

"Prosper," said Galors quietly, "you will wait here for me. You know that I shall return. It will be within half-an-hour from now."

"Good. I shall be here."

Galors dismounted and plunged into the wall of pines; they seemed to move and fold him in their mazes, and nothing spoke of him thereafter but the sound of his heavy tread on dry twigs. When this was lost an immense stillness sat brooding.

Neither Prosper nor Isoult could speak. Her presence was to him a warm consolation, to be apprehended by flashes in the course of a long battle with black and heavy thoughts; her also the pause (more fateful than the battle it had interrupted) affected strangely, the more strangely because she did not know the whole truth. I may say here that Prosper never told her of it; nor did she ask it of him. It was the one event of their lives, joint and disjoint, upon which they were always as dumb as now when they thought apart. Thoughtful apart though they were, they felt together. Prosper's hand stole upwards from his side; Isoult's drew to it as metal to magnet; the rest of that heavy hour they passed hand-in-hand. So children comfort each other in the dark.

Very faint and far off a solitary cry broke the vast dearth of the night. It rose like an owl's hooting, held, shuddered, and then died down. Prosper's clasp on the girl's hand suddenly straightened; it held convulsively while the call held, relaxed when it relaxed. Then the former hush swam again over the wood, and so endured until, after intolerable suspense, they heard the heavy tread of Galors de Born.

His bulk, his white impassive mask, were before them.

"I have settled my account, Prosper," he said. "Now settle yours."

Prosper shivered.

"I am quite ready," said he.

They changed, then crossed swords, and began their second rally on foot. You would have said that they were sluggish at the work, as if their blood had cooled with the long wait or sense of still more dreadful business in the background, and needed a sting to one or other to set it boiling again. They fenced almost idly at first; it was cut and parry—formalism. Galors was very steady; Prosper, breathing tightly through his nose, very wary. Gradually, however, they warmed to it. Galors got a cut in the upper arm, and began making ugly rushes, blundering, uncalculated bustles, which could only end one way. Prosper had little difficulty in evading most of these; Galors lost his breath and with it his temper. The sight of his own shield and sword, ever at point against him, made him mad. He could never reach his adroit enemy, it seemed. For a supreme effort he feigned, drew back, then made a rush. Prosper parried, recovered, and let in with a staggering head-cut which for the time dizzied his opponent. Galors lowered his head under his shield, made another desperate blind rush, and got to close quarters. The two men struggled together, fighting as much with shields as swords, and more with legs and arms than anything else. They were indistinguishable, a twisting and flashing tangle; they locked, writhed, swayed, tottered—then rent asunder. Galors fell heavily. He got on his feet again, however, for another rush. As he came on Prosper stepped aside, knocked out his guard and slashed at the shoulder—a dreadful thirsty blow. Galors staggered, his shield dropped; but he came on once more. Another side-cut beat his weapon down, and then a back-handed blow crashed into his gorget. He threw up his arms and staggered backwards; a last cut finished him. Galors with a cough that ended in a wet groan fell like lead. He never spoke nor moved again.

Prosper sank on his knees, beaten out. Isoult started from the wood to hold him, but he waved her back. All was not done. He put his sword in his mouth and crept on all fours to his enemy, lifted his visor, looked in his face. Then he got up and stood over him. He swung back the bare sword of Salomon de Born with both hands. It came down, did its last work and broke.

Prosper threw the pommel from him and lifted up the head of Galors. The times were grim times. He tied it to his saddle-bow. Then he turned to Isoult.

"Come," he said, "the fight is done."

They did not stay. He took his own shield and sword from the dead, girt on the first and slung the latter to the spare saddle. He took his wife in his arms, not daring to kiss her in such a place, and put her on Galors' horse; and so they went their way into the misty woods.

Dark Tortsentier took up the watch amid the sighing of its pine-tree host. Its array of shields, its swords and mail kept their counsel. The figures in the singular tapestry of Troilus went through their aping unadmired, and the grey dawn found them at it. Then you might see how idle Cresseide, peering askance at Maulfry with her sly eyes, watched the black pool drown her hair.

CHAPTER XXXIV

LA DESIRÉE

Prosper broke the silence there was between them.

"Whither should we go?" he said.

Isoult took the lead. "Follow me, I will lead you. I know the ways."

A great constraint kept him tongue-tied. The prize was his; the silence, the emptiness, the night, gave him what his sword had earned. He trembled but dared not put out his hand. What was he—good Lord!—to touch so rare a thing? He hardly might look at her. The moon showed him a light muffled figure swaying to the rhythm of the march, the round of her hooded head, the swing of her body, the play of her white hand on the rein. Whenever he dared to look her face was turned to his; he saw the moon-glint in her eyes. He absolutely had nothing to say, and for the first time in his life felt a clumsy fool.

By all which it would seem that love is a virtue going out of a man as much as any that enters in.

Isoult was in very different plight, enjoying her brief moment of triumph, making as it were the most of it. When a woman loves she humbles herself, and every prostration is matter for an ecstasy. Her love returned, she ventured to be proud; but this is against the grain. It is more blessed to give. The freed soul welcomes the prison-gates and hugs the yoke and the chain.

Just now she was on the verge of her freedom. In thus looking at him who had been her lord yesterday and would be her lord to-morrow, she was taking his measure. In her exalted mood she found that she could read him like a book.

There was no doubt about his present docility, but could she dare to mould it? She must woo, she saw; dare she trail this steel-armed lord of battles, this grim executant, this trumpet of God, as a led child by her girdle-ribbons? If hero he had proved in his own walk, to be sure he shambled pitifully on the edge of hers. Her superiority sparkled so hard and frosty-bright that she began to pity him; and so the maid was thawed to be the mother of her man. Isoult knew she must beguile him now for his soul's ease and her own.

When the ride grew broad and ran like a spit into a lake of soft dark she stopped. There was moss here, there were lichened heather-roots, rowan bushes, and a ring of slim birches, silver-shafted, feather-crowned and light; more than all there was a little pool of water which two rills fed.

"We will stay here," said Isoult.

Prosper dismounted and helped her down. She felt him trembling as he held her, whereat her courage rose clear and high.

"I will disarm you"—had she not done it, indeed!—"and dress your hurts. Then you shall rest and I look at you at last."

"I am not much hurt. We could well go on."

"Nay, you must let me do as I will now. I must disarm you. 'Tis my right."

She did it, kneeling at his knees or standing before him. For once he was that delight of a woman in love, her plaything, her toy—her baby, in a word. She girdled him with her arms at need; her fingers busy at neck or cheek-pieces unlaced the helm.

"Now kneel."

He obeyed her, and she grew tenderly deft over his wounds. She washed them clean, bound them up with strips torn from her skirt. She pushed back his hair from eyes and brows, and washed him clean of blood and sweat and rage. Her petticoat was her towel; she would have used her hair, but that she dared not lose command of herself and him. She wished for once to draw him, not to be drawn.

She knelt down on the moss, touching her lap meaningly as she did so.

"Rest here," said the gesture; "rest here, my dear heart," said the smile that flew with it.

He knelt beside her—all went well up to this. The moon was low, the night wearing; but the pure light came flowing through a rent in the trees, and she caught his look upon her. She tried, but she could not meet it. Then it befell her that she would not meet it if she could.

Prosper took something from his breast.

"Look," he said, as he held it up.

She watched it quivering in the moonbeams; her eyes brimmed; she grew blush-red, divinely ashamed.

"Hold your hand out," said Prosper. She had risen to her knees; they were kneeling face to face, very near.

Isoult's hands were crossed at her neck. Prosper remembered the gesture. Now she held out her left hand and let him crown it. He held on—alas! he was growing master every minute.

"Isoult."

"Yes."

"Oh, my dear love, Isoult! Now I shall wed thee, Isoult the Much-Desired."

She began to shake. But she put her hands up till they rested on his shoulders. She laughed in a low thrilled tone.

"I am La Desirée now, and no longer La Desirous. For what I desired was another's desire." Also she said—"Kiss my mouth, and I shall believe that thou speakest the truth of the heart."

He held her with his hands, looking long and steadily; nor did her eyes refuse him now. Love was awake and crying between the pair. He drew her nearer, kissed her on the eyes and on the mouth; and she grew red and loved him dearly.

So in the soft night, under the forest trees, in the hush that falls before dawn, those two kissed and comforted one another. It was as in a field of blood that the rod of love thrust into flower at last. But the forest which had seen the graft held

225

the flower by right. None watched their espousal save the trees and the mild faces of the stars.

CHAPTER XXXV

FOREST LOVE

With the sun rose Isoult, transfigured and glorified, Love's rosy priest. She slipped from her man's arms, hung over him wonderfully, lightly kissed his forehead without disturbing his deep sleep. Then she went to bathe herself in the pool, and to bind up her hair. The woodland was jewelled with dew, it went in misty green and yellow, all vocal of the joy she had. She was loved! she was loved!

Fresh and full of light she came dancing back, without a trace of the haggard beauty upon her which had stolen about the ways of Holy Thorn. Her mouth had the divine childishness, the rippling curves of the naked god's bow; her eyes were glossy-soft and rayed a light from within. Warm arms stole round Prosper, a warm cheek was by his, warm lips kissed him awake. The duet, as of two low-answering doves, began—

"Is this Isoult la Desirous who cometh?"

"You called me Desirée."

"How long sought, how long prayed for!"

"Found now, and close at last."

"Closer yet, closer yet."

"Oh heart, oh desire! Prosper!"

"Yes."

"Tell me one thing."

"Ask."

"When began you to think of me?"

"Will you put me to shame, Isoult?"

"Never, never! There is no shame in you. Look what I am."

"The purest, the loveliest, the bride of all delight!"

"You are a great lord; and I——"

"The great lord's lady—out of his reach."

"Prosper! No, no. If I am out of reach, reach not for me. Tell me instead what I ask you."

"But you know when I began, and what you said."

"Ah, it was then?"

"No, it was not then. It was after that. It was when I knew that you loved me."

"Did you not know from the first? Oh, what men must be! And I called—as I was called."

"La Desirous? Ah, yes. Tell me now why that was?"

"Yes, I will tell you now." She hid her face on his breast and whispered her story. "I was twelve years old—a sheepgirl on Marbery Down. There are many, many herds there, and five of us that kept them that day, huddling together to be warm. For I was cold enough—in rags as you have seen me, but worse; my shoulder and side went bare then. Then there came riding over the brow a company of lords having falcons on their wrists; and I stood up to watch them fly their birds. There was an old man, tall and very noble, with white hair and beard, and a brown keen face; and there were others, young men, and one was a lad, his son. The lad it was who flew his bird at a heron. The falcon shot up into the air; she towered over my head where I stood, and after stooped and fell upon me, and clung to my raiment, pecking at my heart. And I cried out at the sharpness of the pain, and wrestled with the falcon to get her off me, but could not for the battling of her sails. Then the lad, the owner of the hawk, rode up to me and took away the bird and killed her. He was a ruddy lad, with the bright blue eyes of his father; but his hair was long and yellow as gold. To me he gave money, and what was dearer than money and rarer, gentle words. For he said —'Maiden, my haggard hath done thee a wrong, and I through her. But when I am a man I will amend it.' Now the wound over my heart kept fresh and could never be healed; and I was thought shameful for that, because men said I went bleeding for love. And God knows it was a true saying."

"Oh, Isoult, was it true, was it true? For that old man was my father, and the lad was I."

Said Isoult—

"Ah, when thou didst ride into the quarry and foundest me with Galors there, I knew thee again; and when thou didst wed me the wound stayed bleeding, but remained fresh. But now—now it is healed."

They turned their lips to each other and murmured comfort with kisses.

"By the Lord," cried he, "I could eat a meal."

"O greedy one, I will put you to shame. All my desire is to take God's body. For I know that we have had no marriage-mass."

"That is a true saying. But the Host is harder to come by. There is a place in Morgraunt, nevertheless, where you may hear Mass and break good bread after. I have been there, but not from here."

"But I have been there too, Prosper, and from here, or near here. I remember. I know the road."

"Come then, lead me, my bride."

She armed her lord, being now entered into her old self, radiant, softly fair, guarded, and demure. He also was the man of her choosing, invincibly lord. They found their beasts near by and were soon on the way, with their pale trophy hidden in a cloth.

Mass was said by the time they reached the yew-tree close, and saw the shrine and image of Saint Lucy of the Eyes. Alice of the Hermitage came out into the open, shading her face against the sun. Prosper she remembered not, but when she saw Isoult she gave a little cry. The two girls were in each other's arms in no time.

"Oh, you!"

"Yes, yes, I have come back. And you know me like this?"

"I would know you anywhere, by what you can never cut off."

"Now you must know my lord," said Isoult with a great heart.

Prosper came up.

"Ah, damsel," says he, "you sped me into your forest, and so sped me to my happiness in spite of myself. Have you forgotten the white bird? Look again and tell me if I have redeemed the quest."

"Ah, ah," said glowing Alice, "now I remember my dream of the bird. Is this possible?"

She looked at Isoult. Isoult blushed; but she was all for blushing just now.

"If it is true," Alice continued, "you make me very happy. Now let me serve you."

"You shall," said Prosper. "Pray give us something to eat."

"Alice," said Isoult, "it was my lord who taught me how to pray—to Mother Mary and Saint Isidore. We have had no marriage-mass."

"Ah, that is serious. You are not yet wedded then?"

Isoult blushed again.

"Will the father wed us?" she contented herself to ask.

But Prosper would not have it.

"Nay, by God and His Christ, but we are one soul by now!" he cried. "The year of agony for her, the year of schooling for me, is past. God has upheld my arm, and her heart is mine. But I beg of you, Alice, prevail upon the priest to give us his God and ours. For though we have been wedded by a Churchman, we have not been wedded by the Church."

"The father shall do it," said Alice. "Fear nothing."

There were two scruples in the good man's way. If he said Mass twice in the morning he broke the law of the Church; if he put off his breakfast, he broke that of nature, which bids a man fill when he is empty. And the priest was a law-abiding man. In the end, however, the bride and bridegroom had their marriage-mass. Kneeling on the mossy stone they received the Sop. Alice of the Hermitage brought two crowns of briony leaves and scarlet berries; so Morgraunt anointed what Morgraunt had set apart; the postulants were adept. Afterwards, when the priest had gone and all things were accomplished, Alice of the Hermitage kissed a sister and a brother; and then very happily they broke their bread sitting in the sun.

"Whither now, my lord?" asked Isoult when they had done.

"Ah, to High March, pardieu!" Prosper said; "there is a little work left for me there. You shall go in as a queen this time. Clothe her as a queen, Alice, and let us be off."

Alice took her away to be dressed in the red silk robe; she drew on the silk stockings, the red slippers. Then she went to tire her hair.

"Stay," said Isoult, "and tell me something first."

"What is it, dearest?"

"My hair, how far does it reach by now?"

"Oh! it is a mantle to you, a dusky veil, falling to your knees."

"Now bind it up for me, Alice; it has run to its tether."

The glossy tower was roped with sequins, the bride was ready. Alice adored her.

"Come and meet the bridegroom," said she.

Prosper watched them coming over the sunny plat. He was not lettered, yet he should have heard the whisper of the Amorist—*"Behold, thou art fair, my love; behold, thou art fair, thou hast dove's eyes."*

At least he bowed his knee before her. She could have answered him then—*"I am as a wall, and my breasts like towers; then was I in his eyes as one that found favour."*

"Good-bye, my sister Desirée," said Alice of the Hermitage. Tears and kisses met and answered each other.

"Surely now, surely here is love enough!" she cried as they rode away. For my part, I am disposed to agree with her. But Prosper found her glorious.

"Can our lord have enough of incense, or his mother weary of songs? Can La Desirous sicken of desire?"

For two more nights green Morgraunt made their bed.

CHAPTER XXXVI

THE LADY PIETOSA DE BRÉAUTÉ

Evidently they were expected at High March; for no sooner the white plumes had cleared the forest purlieus and came nodding over the heath in view of the solemn towers, than a white flag was run up the keep. It floated out bravely—a snow patch in a pure sky.

"Peace, hey?" quoth Prosper, asking. "Well then, there shall be peace if they will take it. It is for them to settle."

Isoult said nothing. She had no reason to welcome High March, or to attend a welcome. She might have doubted the wisdom of their adventure had she been less newly a wife. As it was, she would have followed her man into the jaws of hell.

When they drew closer still, they could see that the great gates were set open and the drawbridge let down. Soon the guard turned out and presented arms. Then issued in good order a white-robed procession, girls and boys bare-headed, holding branches of palm. A rider in green marshalled them with a long white wand which he had in his right hand. It was all very curious.

"I should know that copper-headed knave," said Prosper.

"It is the seneschal, dear lord," said Isoult, who would know him better, "with his white rod of office."

Prosper gave a mighty shout. "Master Porges, by the Holy Rood! Oh, Master Porges, Master Porges, have you not yet enough of rods white or black? Look how the rascal wags the thing. Why, hark, child, he has set them singing."

The shrill voices, in effect, rose and fell along the devious ways of a litany to

Master Porges' household gods. Mention has already been made of his curiosity in these commodities. The present times he had judged to be times of crisis, big with fate. Who so apt as his newest saint to propitiate the hardy outlaw Galors de Born, and the young Demoiselle de Bréauté?

For the shocked soul of Porges had fled into religion as your only cure for esteem and a back cruelly scored. In such stresses as the present it still took wing to the same courts. "*Sancta Isolda, Sancta Isolda, Genetricis Ancilla,*" went the choir, "*Ora, ora pro nobis.*"

And then—

"*Quoe*	*de*		*coelis*	*volitans,*
Sacras		*manus*		*agitans,*
Foves		*in*		*suppliciis*
Me,	*ne*		*extra*	*gregulo*
Tuo		*unus*		*ferulo*
Pereat in vitiis."…				

and so on. The youngsters sang with a good will, while Master Porges, as poet and man of piety, glowed in his skin. The verse limped, the Latin had suffered, perhaps, more violence than Latin should be asked to suffer even of a Christian: but what of that? It was the pietist's own; and as his pupils sang it, they bore before his eyes the holy image of the saint trampling under her feet the hulking thief Prosper. And gaily they bore it, and gaily sang their unwitting way towards the unwitting couple of lovers, who never let go hands until they were near enough to feel all eyes burn into them to read their secret.

This was vastly well; but Master Porges' present bent was towards policy. Her ladyship had advised with him in her new occasions. "Sir Galors de Born," she had said, "is a late enemy of mine no longer to be feared, since I have won back all my fiefs by the readiness and prudent discretion of the High Bailiff of Wanmeeting."

This good man had indeed made the most of his achievements, and, reflecting that Prosper had gone alone to tackle Galors,—whereof he was indubitably dead,—and that it was a pity no one should be any the better for such a mishap, had told the whole story to his mistress, carefully leaving the hero's name out of account. "For why," said the Bailiff, "cause a woman to shed unavailing tears?"

"Remember, however," the Countess went on, "that this Galors may be the escort of the Lady Pietosa de Bréauté, my daughter and your mistress, to her home. Pay him then the respect due to such an esquire, but no more. Receive from him my Lady Pietosa, and put yourself between her and him—yourself at her right hand and in the middle. She is not his; at the worst of all he is hers."

Master Porges bowed, observing. Here was need of a high stroke of policy. Now policy to him meant mastery, and mastery when it did not mean a drubbing, as it had done with Prosper (the greatest politician he had ever known), meant a snubbing. With a cue from Prosper's handling of the science, Master Porges thought he could show Galors, politically, his place.

The white-robed throng of singers stopped, with wondering simple faces, before the great black knight and his rose-clad lady. Prosper doubtless looked grim—he hardly filled the headpiece of Galors: the white wicket-gates, with many a dint across them, gleamed harshly from the coal-black shield. *Entra per me* had an uncompromising ring about it. His visor was down; he did not wish them to see a too good-humoured face until he had exacted a tribute.

But Master Porges cantered up with many a sweep of hand and cap to the lady.

"My lady, welcome to your halls and smiling goodly lands. We have done what honour we might. Your ladyship will read it for an earnest of our duties and good-will."

Thus Porges. Isoult sat wondering, very much confused. She was coming in as a queen indeed. Master Porges went on to handle the esquire.

"Master Galors, good-day to you," he said. "My lady the Countess of Hauterive hath heard of you. She may possibly send for you anon. In the meantime, in the pendency of her motions to that grace, I am to receive from you the Lady Pietosa, who has suffered your attentions so far, and who thanks you, through me, her inherited minister. At your ladyship's pleasure now. Follow us, good Master Galors."

Unfortunately Prosper saw no need for playing Galors just then. But the seneschal always pleased him.

"Master Porges," he said in his suavest tones, "the gentleman you name is indisposed to wait very long—he must not indeed be delayed—and is wholly incapable of travel unattended. He must therefore ride where I ride. As for the lady upon whom you bestow so decorous a name, I cannot answer. The lady whom I escort will please herself. Step behind us, Master Porges, I entreat of you. You would not ask so much of Sir Galors de Born if you knew him as well as I do."

"Now, who is this? What am I then, Messire?" the seneschal gasped.

"You are the most worshipful Master Porges, if I am right, by the grace of God Seneschal of High March, and so forth."

"Ah! Good! And you, sir?"

"I am not Galors de Born," replied Prosper modestly, "though he is not far removed from me."

"You bear his coat, Messire."

"Ah, Saint Mary! I bear more than that of his."

"Messire, I have it in command——"

"And I have it to command. Behind, sir," said Prosper shortly and finally. Then he rode forward with Isoult and met the minstrels.

"My little singers," cried he, "sing your blithest now, and take us happily to the Castle. Come—

"'Love   is   Lord   of   the   land,
Master   of   maid   and   man;
Goeth   in   green   with   a   ruddy   face,
Heartening whom he can,'" etc., etc.

The thing was a country catch which he had himself caught up from the High March maids. It went to a free breathless measure, ran easily into a gallop, must be jigged to. The fluttering cavalcade came skipping home, all save the boy who carried Sancta Isolda, and he at last tucked her under his arm and tripped with the rest. So it befel that the man of policy came in the rear; so also it befel that, when at the gates Prosper demanded his audience, Master Porges went in chastened with the message, and came back still more chapfallen to report—that her ladyship, his mistress, would receive the messenger of Sir Galors de Born at once, with the lady in his escort. Thus finally Prosper, with Isoult behind him, stood in the great hall, and saw the Countess Isabel trembling on the dais.

She came down the way left her by the assembled household, pale and misty with tears to meet them. Prosper was softened at once, but before he could speak she was holding out her hands to him as a suppliant, striving to steady her voice.

"Oh, Galors," she began, "thou hast been my enemy declared for no fault of mine, and dreadful wrong hast thou done to many harmless folk who had never wronged thee. Yet, if I had never won back what was mine, and still owed thee a living grudge instead of a grudge for the unhappy dead, for the sake of her thou bringest me I must receive thee here. Now give me that which thou didst promise. Let me see her."

Prosper stood melted by the pent passion of the woman, but by her words stricken dumb. He understood that she should think him Galors, and cared little if she did, for discovery must make his case the stronger. But what she wanted with Isoult, what Galors had promised on her score, passed all comprehension. He thought he knew enough of the Countess to be sure she would not lightly forgive; yet here was the Countess asking to see the girl who had made a fool of her! Withal her need was painfully plain. He therefore took Isoult by the hand and led her forward.

The Countess, shaking so that she could hardly stand, caught the girl from him. But she could not look at her, only steadied herself by clutching at her arms.

"Let me see the token," says she in an eager whisper.

So then Isoult unfastened her gown and took it out by its golden chain.

The Countess received it in both hands as a relic. Yet hand and head shook too much that she might see it. The poor lady held her wrist with the other hand, lifted it up near her face; then she blinked her eyes close to it. So for some time she remained, looking upon the jewel, but seeing nothing, seeming to love the feel of it in her hands, and crying all the while freely and noiselessly with streams of tears down her cheeks. Next she dropped the crystal and took Isoult by the shoulders, to peer in the same blind fashion into the girl's wondering eyes. And then at last, with a little smothered cry, she caught her to her bosom, straining her there with desperate hunger of affection, while her tears and passionate weeping shook and shuddered through her. In broken words, with sobs, half-moaning prayers, and half-crazy thanksgivings, she spoiled herself of the tenderness and frantic love a mother has, but no other under heaven.

Commanding herself in time, she raised her marred face high above her

daughter, who lay close in her arms, and turning to Prosper, said steadily enough
—

"Galors, now declare thyself. Thou hast spoken so far the truth. This is my true daughter, Pietosa de Bréauté, the daughter of my murdered lord, Fulk de Bréauté, born in wedlock, and by me suffered to be stolen away by him who first stole my body (but never my soul) from my lord. Now ask of me, and I will give thee all, even to this treasure at my breast. Declare thyself."

Prosper forgot everything but to blurt out his wonder.

"Galors, madam, Galors! But I am not Galors, good Lord! Ah!" (and he pulled up his visor). "Look upon me, madam, and judge if I am Galors."

The Countess gasped, then blushed: all the household grew dumb. Master Porges went out suddenly into the air. The first to recover breath was the lady paramount.

"Ah, my Lord Prosper le Gai," she said, "in your revenge I see your father's son. Should I not have known? I am at your mercy, my lord. You have struck me hard at last, harder than before, but may be not harder than I deserve."

"Madam," said Prosper, "it seems I have struck you harder and nearer than I knew. For your present joy has given me the most wondrous news that ever I had in the world."

"But the letter of Galors, was it not from you?" she cried out.

"I know nothing of letters from Galors, Countess. When I write it is in my own name."

"There is mystery here. He wrote me of my daughter, that he would bring her— ah, and take her again. She has come as he said. But where is Galors?"

Prosper lifted on high the head of his enemy. "Here he is," said he.

A timely diversion was caused here by a certain red-cheeked girl, by name Melot. She had already proved the sharpness of her sloe-black eyes; she proved it now again by seeing, alone of all that company, the hounded page-boy in the Lady Pietosa de Bréauté. After her first gape of re-discovery, being a girl of parts, conscious that generosity was afoot, she edged her way to the front, stooped suddenly and caught at the hem of the red silk robe to kiss it.

"What is this, wench?" said the Countess, glad of the relief.

Then said Melot on her knees, "My lady, I do this because I was the first who sinfully found out your ladyship's lady daughter when she was here before like a boy; and I pray her pardon, and yours, my lady, and yours again, Messire, for the deadly sin I did."

Red-cheeked Melot ran on glibly up to this point on a beaten track. All maidens of her class wallow in contrition. But when her words failed her, she sought a distressed lady's proper shelter, and began to cry. Isoult stooped and caught her up before she could be stayed. She was too newly a Countess, you see.

"This is Roy's answer to thee, Melot," she laughed, and kissed the rogue.

But for Isabel, long a Countess—otherwise. This unhappy lady felt herself whipped. Her abasement was now so deep, so desolately did she stand among her dependents, a naked woman spoiled of all her robes, that Prosper's honest heart smote him.

"Countess," he said, smiling, "will you give me what Galors might have won?"

But Isoult did better still. She came back to her mother's breast, put up her hand timidly and touched the cold cheek. "Mother," was all she said. It was all the woman needed to cover her shame in a cloak of warm tears. The two wept together, and then Prosper knelt to his mother-in-law's hand.

But the Countess was stronger than he had thought. In truth, she never spared herself any of her dignities. Her humility now became her admirably; never was she more certainly the great lady of romance than when she led Prosper and Isoult to the dais, set them each on a throne, and then, turning to her people, opened her hands to them, her heart, and her conscience.

"Lo! you now," she cried out, "heed what I shall speak. This is the Lady Pietosa, called Isoult le Gai, my daughter indeed, Countess after me of Hauterive, Lady of Morgraunt and the purlieus, whom I, unknowing and to my shame, despised and misused—unworthy mother, that in trying to befoul the spotless but stained herself the deeper. And you, people, sheep of a hireling shepherd, followed in my ways and became as I am, most miserable in shame. If now I lead you aright, follow me also that road. You shall kneel therefore with me to the young

Countess and to the Earl (in her right), my Lord Prosper."

Before either could stop her she was on her knees at her daughter's foot. Isoult dropped with a little cry, but the elder had her way. She kissed the foot, and then stood by the throne to watch the homage paid.

One by one they came sidling up. Melot was pushed into the front rank; her shrewdness paid so much penalty. She knelt and laid her forehead on the ground. Isoult lightly set her foot on the bowed head; but he who watched the ceremony with dimmed eyes saw that the treader was the humblest there.

Master Porges, flap-cheeked and stertorous, grovelled like a fat spaniel. Prosper came to the rescue as he swam up to the height of a man again, gasping for the air. "Ah, seneschal," he said, "we each love honour and ensue it after our fashion. We should be better acquainted."

The seneschal kissed his hand, and never doubted for one moment more but that Prosper was the pattern of knighthood. The image-maker at March was thereafter busy with the figure of one in the similitude of an Archangel, under whom ran the legend-"*Properate vias ejus*." It is reported that he had a further commission for a great bronze Saint Isidore, destined to the chapel at High March.

Days of festival followed, with jousting and minstrelsy. Isoult sat in a green silk bower, clothed all in white, her black hair twisted with pearls, a crown of red roses upon all. The hooded falcon showed again on baldrick and girdle, the *fesse dancettée* flickered on a new shield, the red plumes danced; "Bide the Time" was the cry. After this came all the mesne lords to do homage for their lands, and among them was Malise le Gai, Lord of Starning and Parrox. Prosper, when the two met, laughed at him, made him angry, got forgiven, and shook hands. He thus put the man at his ease, and won a tolerable friendship with his brother against the time when the elder would be, in respect of certain fiefs, the vassal of the younger. But from Goltres came none to do fealty, nor from Hauterive, nor from Malbank Saint Thorn. Goltres, in fact, was escheat, and granted out to Prosper's brother Osric and his new wife from Prè. A new abbot was set over Holy Thorn; but the charter of pit and gallows was revoked by the Countess, withal she said—"It was the granting of that charter which won me my child again."

It does not appear that there is anything more to record.

"What am I to call you, lady wife?" said Prosper, when he had her in his arms again.

"Ah, lord, thou shouldst know by now!"

"Pietosa?"

"Prosper!"

"Isoult la Desirée?

"If you must."

"Isoult la Desirous?"

"It would be true.

"What will you have then, child?"

"Ah, ah, I will have that!"

It was, after all, but a rosy child that Prosper kissed.

EXPLICIT

Printed in Great Britain
by Amazon

41646102R00139